# Doing Theology in Context

# DOING THEOLOGY IN CONTEXT
## South African Perspectives

*Edited by*
*John W. de Gruchy and Charles Villa-Vicencio*

THEOLOGY AND PRAXIS: VOLUME ONE

ORBIS BOOKS
Maryknoll, New York

DAVID PHILIP
Cape Town and Johannesburg

The Catholic Foreign Mission Society of America (Maryknoll) recruits and trains people for overseas missionary service. Through Orbis Books, Maryknoll aims to foster the international dialogue that is essential to mission. The books published, however, reflect the opinions of their authors and are not meant to represent the official position of the society.

First published 1994 in southern Africa by David Philip Publishers (Pty) Ltd, 208 Werdmuller Centre, Claremont 7700, South Africa, and in the United States of America by Orbis Books, Maryknoll, NY 10545

ISBN 0-86486-265-2 (David Philip)
ISBN 0-88344-989-7 (Orbis Books)

Printed by The Rustica Press, Old Mill Road, Ndabeni, Cape, South Africa

CIP data are available upon application to the Library of Congress

D2680

# Contents

List of Contributors                                                    vii
Introduction                                                             ix

## PART ONE: INTRODUCTORY ISSUES

1: The Nature, Necessity and Task of Theology
   JOHN W. DE GRUCHY                                                      2
2: The Bible and Theology   GERALD WEST                                  15
3: Theology and Faith: Tradition, Criticism and Popular Religion
   JAMES R. COCHRANE                                                     26

## PART TWO: THE DOCTRINE OF GOD

4: The Self-Disclosure of God   DIRKIE SMIT                              42
5: Jesus the Christ   STEVE DE GRUCHY                                    55
6: The Spirit of Life   MARIE-HENRY KEANE                                68
7: Trinitarian Experience and Doctrine   BRIAN GAYBBA                    77

## PART THREE: CREATION AND REDEMPTION

8: The Wonder, Agony and Promise of Creation
   FELICITY EDWARDS                                                      90
9: The Broken Human Image of God   ADRIO KÖNIG                          102
10: Redemption: Freedom Regained   JOHN SUGGIT                          113
11: Christian Community   JOHN W. DE GRUCHY                             125
12: Towards a New Heaven and a New Earth   KLAUS NÜRNBERGER             139

## PART FOUR: THEOLOGIES IN SOUTH AFRICA

13: African Theologies   LUKE LUNGILE PATO                              152
14: Confessing Theology   JOHN W. DE GRUCHY                             162
15: Black Theology   BARNEY PITYANA                                     173

16:  Liberation Theology   CHARLES VILLA-VICENCIO                    184
17:  Faith and Feminism: Women Doing Theology
         DENISE ACKERMANN                                            197
18:  Kairos Theology   ALBERT NOLAN                                  212
19:  Theological and Religious Pluralism   ROBIN PETERSEN            219

Index                                                               229

# Contributors

JOHN W. DE GRUCHY is Professor of Christian Studies at the University of Cape Town

GERALD WEST is a lecturer in the School of Theology at the University of Natal, Pietermaritzburg.

JAMES COCHRANE is Professor of Theological Studies at the University of Natal, Pietermaritzburg.

DIRKIE SMIT is Professor of Systematic Theology at the Universities of the Western Cape and Stellenbosch.

STEVE DE GRUCHY is a minister of the United Congregational Church and Director of the Moffat Mission in Kuruman.

MARIE-HENRY KEANE was Professor of Systematic Theology at the University of South Africa, and is presently a director of studies for the Dominican Order in England.

BRIAN GAYBBA is Professor of Systematic Theology at Rhodes University.

FELICITY EDWARDS is Associate Professor of Systematic Theology at Rhodes University.

ADRIO KÖNIG is Professsor of Systematic Theology at the University of South Africa.

JOHN SUGGIT is Professor Emeritus of New Testament at Rhodes University.

KLAUS NÜRNBERGER is Professor of Theology at the University of Natal, Pietermaritzburg.

LUKE LUNGILE PATO is Rector of the College of the Transfiguration, Grahams-town.

BARNEY PITYANA is a senior research officer in the Department of Religious Studies at the University of Cape Town.

CHARLES VILLA-VICENCIO is Professsor of Religion and Society at the University of Cape Town.

DENISE ACKERMANN is Professor of Practical Theology at the University of the Western Cape.

ALBERT NOLAN is a Dominican priest and Editor of *Challenge* at the Institute of Contextual Theology, Johannesburg.

ROBIN PETERSEN is a minister of the United Congregational Church and is completing doctoral studies at the University of Chicago.

MALUSI MPUMLWANA is Executive Director of the Institute for Pastoral Education, Grahamstown.

# Introduction

This volume is intended as an introductory text on the study of Christian theology. It has been written by South African theologians primarily for theological students in South Africa today, but also for students abroad. This does not mean that the book is not relevant for others who are interested in the subject. On the contrary, we believe that this volume, like its companion on Christian ethics, will be of interest to a wide circle of people who are concerned to understand what Christianity is all about. This wider circle would obviously include both clergy and lay people within the various Christian denominations of our country and abroad, but it may also include people of other faiths or no religious commitment who are simply interested to find out more about Christianity.

The authors represent a variety of Christian traditions and theological perspectives, and that they teach theology in a number of different universities and theological seminaries. As such, this volume is an ecumenical effort which seeks to interpret the meaning of Christianity in a broad and inclusive way. Some essays may be more traditional than others in approach and focus, but all are written from the perspective of a committed faith which is seeking to express what that faith means today. Although the editorial pen has been wielded with varying degrees of restraint, the intention has not been to provide a set of essays which reflect identical understandings of Christian faith, but rather to portray something of the rich diversity of approach and understanding which is part and parcel of the Christian theological tradition. At the same time, there is a unity and coherence to the volume, without which it could not possibly serve the purpose for which it is intended.

As the table of contents indicates, the book is divided into four parts. The first part deals with introductory questions such as the nature of theology, how it is done, and how it relates to the Bible, human experience and the wider world of culture, experience and discourse. The second part has to do with the Christian understanding of God. This rightly begins with the way in which Christians believe that God is revealed, which leads next to a consideration of that revelation in Jesus of Nazareth whom Christians confess as the Christ, and then to the presence of God as Spirit in human experience and the world as such. It is on the basis of this revelation that the doctrine of the Trinity has been developed, a doctrine which is fundamental to the Christian understanding of God.

The chapters in Part three explore key elements within the doctrine of creation and redemption, mindful that these two should be regarded together rather than in separate compartments.

The doctrine of creation is of paramount importance for us today, not least because of its relevance for questions relating to the environment. Equally important is the need for clarity on what it means to be a human being in a world in which people are often reduced to ciphers, dehumanised and oppressed, and where human life is treated too cheaply far too often. The doctrine of redemption is at the heart of the Christian gospel, for it tells about the way in which human life can be restored in relation to God, how people can become a community of faith, and how we can all journey together towards the promise of a 'new heaven and new earth'.

Although the volume has been written by South Africans especially for South Africans, this does not mean that the chapters in the first three parts are parochial in their scope or interpretation. On the contrary, they are all expositions of key theological themes which are of importance to Christians everywhere. The South African character of many of the illustrations and allusions is indicative of the fact, however, that the chapters have been written from within a specific context, and that this context has undoubtedly had an important influence on the way in which Christianity is understood and expressed. This brings us to the fourth and final part of the book, a section which is specifically South African in orientation.

Those from beyond the borders of South Africa who have been interested in the church's role in the struggle against apartheid will already be familiar with the fact that several distinctly South African approaches to Christian theology have evolved during the past few decades. While most of these approaches have links with similar theologies elsewhere, especially in the third world, they are nonetheless clearly South African in their ethos and focus. Indeed, one of the issues we faced when originally discussing the format of the book was whether or not we should have asked that all the chapters be written from one of the theological perspectives dealt with in Part four. We decided against this because the volume would then have expressed only one approach, however important, to the subject. But we did encourage the authors in the first three parts to write their chapters from the perspective with which they would identify. Some have done this more than others. In this final part we have sought to provide some understanding of these specific perspectives, and to show how Christian faith and practice is perceived in relation to them.

The concluding chapter helps us to bring this plurality of theologies into relation with each other, and also into relation with the insights of religious faiths other than Christianity. This is a fitting conclusion, for it not only reminds us of the pluriformity of Christianity, but also of the religious pluralism of the society in which we live. There can be little doubt that the relationship of Christianity to other religious traditions is one of the major issues facing theologians at the end of the twentieth century, not least in South Africa, which is seeking to create a new and united identity in this period of reconstruction.

There is a bibliography at the end of each chapter which will be of help to those who wish to read further on each topic. This volume is, after all, only intended as an introduction to a subject that is vast in its scope and different dimensions. We hope that what we have offered here will lead to a greater interest in theology, especially in South Africa, and that this in turn will whet the appetite for further study and reflection. But as will become clear in several of the chapters, Christian theology is not an end in itself; it is intended as a critical resource for both faith and action. Thus our hope is not only that our readers may be better informed about the meaning of the Christian faith for today, but that those who seek to follow Jesus as the Christ today may be enabled to do so with greater insight, faithfulness and even a good dose of humility.

The editors wish to thank all those who have so willingly contributed chapters to this volume, and also David Field, Stephen Martin and Nan Oosthuizen of the Department of Religious Studies at the University of Cape Town, who have assisted so ably in the editorial process.

# PART ONE
# Introductory Issues

# 1

# The Nature, Necessity and Task of Theology

## JOHN W. DE GRUCHY

Just a week or two after I was inducted as minister of my first congregation, the young son of a family who were members was run over and killed by a drunken driver. Quite apart from the suffering and pain which this caused, you can imagine the kind of questions which the parents and others in the community asked in trying to understand and make sense of what had happened. You will also appreciate how much I had to try to remember what my study of theology had taught me about God's providence, the problem of evil and suffering, and related issues. Let me say that within a very short time I recognised that while I had indeed learned much about these agonising issues as a theological student, and while much of this helped me to respond to the questions being asked, I really had to work through the issues myself in the light of my understanding of the gospel and the particular needs of the people to whom I was ministering. Theology was essential in order to minister to the needs of my congregation, but a second-hand theology was not of great use. When I simply regurgitated 'textbook' answers I immediately became aware that I was sounding and acting like one of Job's 'comforters' — good, sound, traditional teaching, but bad theology. Somehow I had to learn how to move from the study of theology to doing it within the context in which I found myself.

## Studying or Doing Theology?

Those training for the ordained ministry go to college, so we say, in order to study or, as it is described in some universities, to 'read theology': It all sounds so academic. The advantage of using the phrase 'doing theology' is that it indicates that theology is not simply something one learns about through reading textbooks (such as this one!), or listening to lectures, but through engaging in doing theology in particular contexts and situations. This does not mean that we should not study theology. If that were the case, then this book would be irrelevant. An integral part of 'doing theology' is examining the way in which Christian thought and action have developed and been expressed by others both in our own time and throughout Christian history. But studying theology has significance only in so far as it enables us to do theology today with better insight and greater faithfulness to the gospel. Hence the use of the word 'praxis'[1] in the title of this series (of which this is the first volume) to emphasise the connection between theological reflection and Christian witness or mission in the world.

Consider another illustration of the connection between studying and doing theology. Sipho Dhlamini, Esther du Plessis and Peter Smith are newly ordained ministers. They have studied the Bible, church history, systematic theology, ethics and some practical theology in college. But now they are in parishes and congregations and wondering what on earth to do with all they had studied. They were 'theological students', but what precisely have they learned and of what relevance is it? Hopefully they were given some clues while they were students, though too often this is not the case, hence many ministers see no need to continue 'studying theology' once they have graduated. At any rate, they have now been thrown into the deep end. They have to preach, counsel, baptise, marry, and bury, provide leadership in mission and evangelism, enable their churches to minister in ways which relate to the wider needs of society, help in dealing with violence in the community, and answer questions (both stupid ones and profound ones) from confirmation candidates.

In doing all this, Sipho, Esther and Peter could simply function as ordained technicians – doing what needs to be done without thinking much about what they are doing, or why they are doing it. They could, for example, use sermons from books in order to preach, adopt the latest evangelistic techniques without any critical evaluation, and teach a catechism by rote. But let us say that Sipho, Esther and Peter are really serious about their ministry. They want to relate the gospel to the needs of their people, and they want their congregations to be truly engaged in mission. So they begin to think about what they are saying and doing in the light of the Scriptures; they begin to reflect on the meaning of the gospel for their situation; they begin to analyse what is going on in their community and the way in which their church is responding from the perspective of the reign of God.

Hopefully as they do this, the resources which they gathered through their studies while at seminary will begin to inform their thinking and acting, as well as the thinking and acting of their congregations. What could be more important now than a good understanding of the Scriptures, an insight into the way in which Christians have engaged in mission through the centuries, an understanding of the Christian approach to ethical issues, an ability to understand society and its problems, and the necessary skills to relate all this to their congregations. As Sipho, Esther and Peter do this, their congregations should become part of the process, for 'doing theology' is not simply the task or prerogative of ordained clergy. Theological reflection should be central to the life of the people of God as a whole. So our newly ordained ministers will want to develop their skills as theologians in order to enable their congregations to become more aware of what their mission is all about. Doing theology will become an essential part of their ministry rather than something they once did in college. Instead of being ordained technicians, they will have become practical theologians.

This was the goal of theological education as promoted by Friedrich Schleiermacher, a German Protestant theologian during the first decades of the nineteenth century, who was instrumental in designing the kind of theological curriculum which has been used in many theological seminaries and faculties since then. It was his conviction that all theological study, which he divided into Philosophical (fundamental theology, dogmatics, ethics) and Historical (which included biblical studies, church history, and the history of doctrine), was intended to serve the third division, namely Practical Theology — that is, the task of preaching and pastoral care in the ministry of the church.[2] We may have a wider vision of what Practical Theology means today, but 'praxis' remains the goal.

Since Schleiermacher's day there have been many developments both in theology and in theological education which we need to take into account in theological education. Unfortunately one of the developments, which Schleiermacher would have strongly opposed, was the fragmentation of theology into a number of sub-disciplines, each with its own methodology, guild of scholars, and goals. As a result the study of theology has lost much of the organic wholeness which was envisaged by Schleiermacher. This is one of the main reasons why theological students and ministers have had difficulty in putting what they have studied all together. Too often their teachers were working independently of and sometimes at variance with each other. For this reason there have been recent attempts to rediscover theology as a unified and coherent discipline, and to ensure that this shapes the redesigning of theological education.[3]

We have just used the word 'discipline' to describe theology. This refers to the fact that Christian theology, as we know it today, has developed over the centuries into an academic discipline alongside many others. In stressing the need to 'do theology in context' we are not saying that theology is not such a discipline; we are trying rather to show how such a discipline as theology relates to Christian praxis. In order to do this, let us take a few steps back and briefly consider how Christian theology has developed into the scientific discipline it has become.

## Theology as Spirituality and as Science

The word 'theology' derives from two Greek words, namely *theos*, God, and *logos*, word, meaning 'reason'. Literally speaking, theology has to do with our attempt to speak about God, or to explain what we mean by God. In the same way the word *logos* is used in other academic disciplines such as anthropology (the study of human beings), sociology (the study of society), geology (the study of the earth) and so on. The word 'theology' goes back to the ancient Greek philosophers who used it to describe explanations of the mysteries of the world. Later on it was used by early Christian theologians to refer to the mystery of the being of God, as well as to the proclamation of the truth about God revealed in Jesus as the *logos* of God (John 1:1–14).

Up until the Middle Ages, theology was not understood so much as an academic discipline but as a way (*hodos*, way, and *meta*, with or towards; hence *meta-hodos*, methodology) of knowing God, as God is made known through self-disclosure in Jesus Christ 'according to the Scriptures'. Thus for the theologians of the first centuries of the Christian movement theology was more related to prayerful reflection on the Scriptures, and to the development of spiritual insight and wisdom, than it was to rational discourse. The task of theology was quite literally 'to know God'. This does not imply that these early Christian theologians were not people of intellectual ability; on the contrary, they numbered amongst themselves some of the best intellects of their time. What it meant, rather, was that theology was done within the context of the life of the church as a worshipping community engaged in prayerful reflection on the Scriptures. Theology was, essentially, divine wisdom or insight, and, as such, a gift of the Holy Spirit.

This is an important reminder that long before theology became a scientific discipline and therefore, as we shall see, a human construction based on reason and dialectic, theology was understood as a form of spirituality in and through which the living Word of God was known and communicated. This understanding of theology remains of fundamental importance today in 'doing theology', and nothing we shall say in what follows should detract from it. But it also begs a number of questions which arise from the fact that much has happened in the time which separates us from the first centuries of Christianity. For example, we have become far more aware of the problems relating to the understanding and interpretation of the Bible, or what we now refer to as the problem of hermeneutics, a subject to which we will return later. In any case, while human nature may well be the same as before, the world is a very different place.

With the foundation of the universities in the Middle Ages in Europe, the study of theology as a scientific discipline was established.[4] Indeed, theology was regarded as the 'queen of the sciences' because it provided a hierarchical and holistic framework within which all other forms of knowledge could be located. One of the major theologians of this period, Anselm of Canterbury, provides the bridge for us between theology as spirituality and theology as science. This can be seen from the fact that his theology is cast in the form of a prayer to God, though it is a highly rational discussion. In one of the classic statements on the nature of theology, Anselm prays:

> I do not endeavour, O Lord, to penetrate thy sublimity, for in no wise do I compare my understanding with that; but I long to understand in some degree thy truth, which my heart believes and loves. For I do not seek to understand that I may believe, but I believe in order to understand. For this also I believe, — that unless I believed, I should not understand.[5]

Anselm's understanding of theology has had a profound influence on the development of theology as a science. Theology, in his terms, is not a way of thinking which leads to faith, but a way of believing which leads to understanding. The leading exponent of this approach to theology in the twentieth century was Karl Barth, widely recognised as the greatest Protestant theologian of the twentieth century.[6] Barth, who laid great stress on the scientific character of theology, also stood in continuity with those earlier theologians for whom theology was primarily an engagement with Scripture, its exegesis and interpretation. The difference was that Barth was more fully aware of the hermeneutical problems involved.

A good illustration of this difference is Barth's off-the-cuff response to the question which someone asked him about the essence of all the many volumes of his *Church Dogmatics*. His response was in the words of the children's hymn: 'Jesus loves me, this I know, for the Bible tells me so.' At one level there is something rather naïve about his response; but it actually is an example of what has been called a 'second naïveté' — that is, an ability to get to the heart of the matter fully aware of the problems involved. In a sense, the early Christian theologians were 'naïve' in their reading of the Scriptures. It is very difficult today for anyone who is aware of the critical issues which have faced us since the Middle Ages and especially the Renaissance and the Enlightenment, to be 'naïve' in the same way. But that does not mean that we cannot go to the heart of the matter, and express the gospel in all its wonder and simplicity. If that were not so, nobody could understand the heart of the Christian message without years of theological study. What theology as a science is about is the attempt to give that faith some coherence in relation to the critical questions that are raised about it. It is giving a reason for what Christians believe in and hope for (1 Pet. 3:15).

In speaking about theology as a 'science', we use the word in its proper sense as a rational and systematic way of knowing, hence scientific methodology. Science does not refer only to what are more correctly called the 'natural sciences' but to any discipline which seeks to understand some aspect of reality in a reasoned, systematic and coherent manner. Many critics would object to theology being called a science because, unlike geology or anthropology or the many other sciences, its subject matter (God) is by definition beyond empirical investigation. For this reason some sceptics would relegate theology to the realm of superstition. Its basic presupposition, they would argue, cannot be proved. This is, of course, true. There may be good reasons for believing in God, but no final proof can be provided on the basis of empirical evidence or reason. Belief in God will always remain a matter of faith, even though it may be a conviction which can be reasonably argued and maintained. Yet this is not unlike other sciences which proceed on the basis of certain assumptions, and then seek to understand reality from that perspective. Theology as a science proceeds, likewise, on the reasoned assumption of the reality of God, and then develops logically and rationally on that basis.

But there is another dimension to this problem which is of considerable importance. God is not an object to be studied, like a distant star or a nuclear particle. God is, in fact, not only the 'subject' of theological enquiry, but also *the* Subject in a much more fundamental sense. God is, by definition, the mystery behind creation who can be known only to the extent to which God discloses Godself.[7] Thus it is better to speak about the subject of theology as God in relation to the world and ourselves, rather than God in God's own essence or being. Indeed, the study of God is inseparably linked to the study of ourselves, and we in turn cannot be truly understood apart from our relationship to God and our existence in the world as a whole. This connection was expressed by John Calvin at the beginning of his *Institutes of the Christian Religion*, when he argued that the knowledge of God and that of ourselves belong together.[8] Theology, then, has to do with that knowledge of God which is inseparable from the knowledge of ourselves and the world. The subject matter of theology is not 'God' in splendid isolation, but God as revealed, and therefore God in relation to everything. This understanding of God is essentially trinitarian and, as such, fundamental to Christian faith and theology.

As is the case with any scientific project, the method which is used should not only be rational and systematic but also appropriate for the subject which is being investigated. If it is true that God is only known through self-disclosure or revelation, and therefore in relation to us, then clearly the fundamental task of theology is to seek some understanding of that revelation and relationship. In what way is God revealed, and how do we receive and appropriate that revelation? This question will be examined in detail in Chapters 4 and 5, and therefore need not detain us here except for us to say that for Christians, as already intimated, the Bible plays a fundamental role in this regard as the witness to that revelation. Indeed, it is only through the witness of the Scriptures that we are able to remain in touch with the foundation of Christian faith, especially the narrative of the life, death and resurrection of Jesus Christ.

A word may be appropriate at this point about the role of tradition in doing theology. Tradition can be understood in two ways. Firstly, as something negative, that which comes between us and the liberating message of Scripture. This was the reason why Jesus himself criticised the way in which religious leaders of his day used tradition. But secondly, tradition can be understood as that which is handed down (*paradosis*, handing on teaching; see 1 Corinthians 11:2) in order to help us interpret the meaning of Christian faith. Or, put differently, tradition embodies the way in which Christians through the centuries have understood and expressed their faith, whether in creeds, confessions of faith, liturgies, or in mission. While none of this has the same kind of authority for us as the witness of Scripture itself, it nevertheless enables us to understand better what that witness may, or may not, mean for us today. It is for this reason that most chapters in this book, especially in Parts two and three, include some reference to the history of a particular doctrine without which it would be difficult to understand and express Christian faith today. Tradition should be a guide, not a straitjacket for contemporary theology; a resource for interpreting Scripture, not a substitute.

In so far as theology is an attempt to understand reality from the perspective of faith in God, it not only has to grapple with the sources for such faith in God but also has to seek to understand human nature, as well as the nature of the world in which we live. The Bible has much to say about both, but there is also much to be learned from other forms of knowledge. Thus from earliest times Christian theologians have been in dialogue with the dominant philosophical questions and ideas of their day.

One of the earliest and greatest examples of theology as a science is the *Summa Theologiae* written by Thomas Aquinas in the thirteenth century, in which Thomas built a Christian understanding of God as revealed in Scripture on what has been called 'natural theology', or truth about God and the world which can be arrived at through reason.[9] In doing this, Thomas made use of some recently rediscovered writings of the Greek philosopher Aristotle. The use of philosophy as a handmaiden for doing theology went back at least to the second century when the Christian Apologists attempted to relate the gospel to Hellenistic culture. The main philosophical resource was Neoplatonism, which gave much Christian theology a strongly mystical flavour. Aristotle's metaphysics provided a better resource as well as the categories for understanding reality.

Thomas's synthesis of reason and revelation was a major theological achievement, and one which has greatly influenced theology, especially Roman Catholic, ever since. The greatest twentieth-century Catholic theologian, Karl Rahner, has reinterpreted Thomism for our day in dialogue with contemporary philosophers such as Martin Heidegger.[10] In like manner, the Protestant theologian Paul Tillich based his theological method on what he called the 'method of correlation', in which theology responds to the questions posed by human existence as these are articulated in philosophy, in his case primarily existentialism. His statement of the task of theology has been very influential: 'In using the method of correlation, systematic theology proceeds in the following way: it makes an analysis of the human situation out of which existential questions arise, and it demonstrates that the symbols used in the Christian message are answers to these questions'.[11]

One of the dangers in doing theology in tandem with philosophy has always been that of allowing the prevailing world-views of the day to distort the Christian message.[12] Hence the second-century North African theologian Tertullian asked with considerable scepticism whether 'Jerusalem had anything to do with Athens'. The fact is, however, that Christianity by its very nature is the incarnation of truth in cultural form (God's presence in human history in the person of a first-century Jew), so that there is no escaping the need for the meaning of the gospel to be expressed in the language and therefore the culture of the contexts in which it is found. What is required is a dialogue which is both open to the insights of culture and yet always critical of them in the light of the gospel.

The task of interpreting Christian faith in God in relation to culture and the philosophical questions raised as a result has continued through the centuries as Christianity has expanded into new contexts and cultures, and it remains a very important element in doing theology today. In more recent times, however, with the rapid expansion of knowledge and different ways of understanding reality, theologians have found it essential to enter into a critical discussion with a much broader range of disciplines than philosophy. These include both the natural and the social sciences, indeed any form of inquiry which helps us to understand better the nature of reality, including our own nature as human beings. Some would argue today that theology has to be understood as 'queen of the social sciences' because it provides a way of putting together what has been torn asunder since the Enlightenment.[13] That is at least one reason why it is appropriate to locate the study of theology within a university context, and also in relation more broadly to the scientific study of religion, or religious studies.

From what we have said thus far, then, theology clearly has what David Tracy has called different 'publics'.[14] That is, it addresses issues within different arenas, each of which has its own purpose and particular forms of discourse. Theology as 'spirituality' clearly serves the worship, proclamation and witness of the Christian community in a direct and meaningful way; theology as 'science' is especially appropriate within a university or academic context where theology seeks to engage other disciplines in the search for and articulation of truth. But we should be careful not to separate these out into different compartments. They belong together and should inform each other, even if the discourse of doxology and that of the social sciences is very different.

## Doing Theology in Context

One of the dangers of the notion of theology as a science is the implicit assumption that the theological systems which have evolved in Western European theology are universal, and therefore paradigmatic for all Christian theology. What needs to be recognised is that all theology is contextual, including Western European theology, simply because every theology develops within a particular historical context. What the systems of theology which have developed in Western European theology from Thomas's *Summa* to the modern *Systematic Theology* of a Wolfhart Pannenberg have attempted to do remains important for us today. As Pannenberg himself puts it: 'the underlying interest in the systematic unity of Christian doctrine and its agreement with the principles of reason remains permanently valid.'[15] But this way of doing theology is only one of several, and it is very much the product of the particular way in which scientific thought has developed in the West. We need to recognise its contextual character and therefore its limitations in a post-modern world where a variety of theological paradigms or models arising out of different contexts and using different methodologies may have equal validity. This is a subject addressed specifically in the final chapter of this volume. But let us look more carefully at what is meant by doing theology *in context*.

Christian theology has its beginnings within the New Testament itself. Just as the writings which comprise the Hebrew Bible (or Old Testament) are theological interpretations of the Israelite experience of God over many centuries, so the writings of the New Testament are theological interpretations of the life, death and resurrection of Jesus of Nazareth. However much the canon of the New Testament may reflect a unity derived from faith in Jesus as the Christ, there can be no gainsaying how diverse are its component parts. There are, indeed, different interpretations of Christianity within the New Testament canon that derive from different theological perspectives and historical contexts.[16] It is not for nothing that there are four gospels in the New Testament, and that each one interprets the significance of Jesus in different ways. Their authors, who were essentially theologians, were addressing different audiences, writing in different contexts, and approaching the material with different insights, even though each believed in Jesus as the Messiah.

In like manner, most of the letters in the New Testament, as well as the Apocalypse of John, are addressed to specific contexts. When Paul expounds his teaching in Galatians on 'justification by faith' he is dealing essentially with the relationship between Christianity and first-century Judaism, and especially with the problem of whether or not Gentile Christians had to keep the Jewish law. In doing this, Paul makes use of a text from the Hebrew prophet Habakkuk, 'the just shall live by faith' (2:4). At one level, both Paul and Habakkuk are saying the same thing, namely faith in God is primary in terms of our relationship with God. But the issues being addressed are quite different, and what is therefore meant by the use of the same words has a different sense. Jumping sixteen centuries beyond Paul, we find Martin Luther, the Protestant Reformer, using the same texts in his struggle against the legalism of the Roman Catholic Church in his day. Once again, Luther's use of 'justification by faith' is in continuity with both Habakkuk and Paul at one level, but by no means identical. The context has changed.[17] Perhaps the most striking illustration of all is the way in which Christian theologians had to translate what were essentially Hebraic thought forms and ideas in primitive Christianity into the language and cultural idioms of the Hellenistic world as Christianity moved beyond the confines of Judaism.

What we are confronting here is the *hermeneutical* task of theology; that is, interpreting the gospel in terms of the context in which we find ourselves. 'Hermeneutics' is a word derived from Hermes, the messenger from the gods to humans in ancient Greek mythology. In other words, hermeneutics is the task of relating the message of the Bible to the situation or context in which we live. But it is more than simply interpretation. To use a helpful expression derived from Hans-Georg Gadamer, it is a 'fusing of two horizons', that of the text and that of the context, but with the awareness that the interpreter himself or herself also stands in a given historical context and tradition.[18]

A great deal of theology since the beginning of the nineteenth century has concentrated on this hermeneutical task. For example, the pioneer of modern theological education as well as of liberal theology, Friedrich Schleiermacher, was also one of the major figures in the development of hermeneutics as an academic discipline more generally. Much of the debate about hermeneutics in our own century was sparked off by the work of the New Testament scholar Rudolf Bultmann, whose programme of demythologisation was essentially an attempt to state the gospel in such a way that contemporary persons did not have to accept the world-view of the first century in order to believe in Jesus as the Christ.[19] But all major twentieth-century theologians have, in different ways and from different perspectives, engaged in this fundamental task.

What theology as hermeneutics is about is dealt with in several chapters of this book. But some preliminary comments might be useful. The first is the need to recognise that hermeneutics is a circular task, or more correctly, there is a *hermeneutical spiral* involved in this way of doing theology.[20] This means that doing theology begins with the witness of the church in the world, then proceeds to reflect critically on that witness both through reflection on the Scriptures and through an analysis of what is happening in the world, and finally it seeks to inform Christian witness so that it may be both more faithful to the gospel and more relevant to the needs of the world.[21]

Theology as hermeneutics is clearly dependent upon the careful exegesis of Scripture; that is, understanding the biblical text within its own context. But it is about far more than simply taking such exegetical insights and applying them today. This can be clearly seen in the next two chapters. What is also required is a careful analysis of the context in which the church is called to witness to the gospel, as well as a critical understanding of the role which the church is playing and where those engaged in 'doing theology' are, to use a colloquial phrase, 'coming from'.

The classic expression of contemporary contextual theology is found in Gustavo Gutiérrez's *Theology of Liberation*. Gutiérrez accepts the need for an understanding of theology both as spirituality and as science, but for him the central concern of theology is 'critical reflection on Christian praxis in the light of the Word'.[22] In other words, theology exists primarily to assist in the mission of the church in the world, and only part of that task is to give a reasoned account of why Christians believe what they do. The specific task in serving the church in this way, as Gutiérrez expresses it, is through a critical examination of the way in which the church is engaged in mission within its particular context, in relation to the message of Scripture itself. As several chapters in this volume indicate, the primary context within much theology has to be done today is that of poverty and oppression, and this has far-reaching implications for both its method and its substance.

One reason why theology today has found it very important and useful to engage in dialogue with the social sciences, such as sociology, social psychology, political science and economics, is that they help provide necessary tools and resources for analysing the context within which the church is called to proclaim and live the gospel. That is why Juan Luis Segundo says that the 'fundamental difference between the traditional academic theologian and the liberation theologian is that the latter feels compelled at every step to combine the disciplines that open up the past with the disciplines that help explain the present'.[23]

In proclaiming the gospel of the reign of God in Jesus Christ, and therefore of God's demand for justice, reconciliation and peace, it is of the utmost importance that the church has some understanding of what this means concretely in the life of each situation. Otherwise proclamation and witness would be a very vague set of propositions rather than a clear statement of what the Word of God means in the most concrete terms possible.

Of course, there are many situations in which it is difficult to speak and act as clearly as we might want to, not least because of the ambiguous nature of the many critical issues facing us in the world today, and the difficulty of relating them to the gospel in an unequivocal way. The problems facing Christian ethics are particularly acute, as can be seen in the second volume in this series. There are times when theology has to speak a clear and necessarily definite word, as, for example, when some churches in South Africa declared 'apartheid a heresy'. This is partly what 'confessing theology' is about, a topic dealt with in Part 4. But theology also has to wrestle with situations and issues where such a clarion call is just not possible or appropriate.[24] Nonetheless, theology cannot avoid the need to understand its context, and to address the issues which arise within it.

## A Committed Discipline

All those engaged in doing theology have particular interests, inadequacies and past failures. This applies to both individual theologians and the church as a community engaged in doing theology. The idea that there is a neutral theology which is unaffected by our place in society or by our own material interests must be questioned. This does not mean that theologians and the church should not seek to transcend their own interests in doing theology, especially if theology is in any way attempting to be faithful to the gospel. But it is important to recognise that we who are engaged in doing theology are fallible and sinful, and precisely because we are dealing with matters of such ultimate importance we have to be especially sensitive to the dangers of our task.

In order for the church to be faithful in its witness, then, theologians have to listen carefully to the criticism which comes from both the gospel itself and the world, pointing out the gap between the gospel, what is proclaimed, and what is in fact being done by the church. It is not for nothing that the critiques of religion and of Christianity propounded by Ludwig Feuerbach, Friedrich Nietzsche, Karl Marx and Sigmund Freud have been labelled under the category of the *hermeneutics of suspicion*, for they radically question the motives and the interests which lie behind what we say and do. This raises the whole question of the *ideological* character of theology. To what extent, we have to ask ourselves as theologians, is our theology a mask which is hiding self-interest, either our own or that of the church?

All of this brings us to our final comment. There has long been a debate about whether it is necessary for a theologian to be a person of faith and Christian commitment. This may not be necessary if we are simply going to engage in 'studying theology'. Anyone can examine what Christians believe and why, and may well be able to do this better than many Christians themselves. But if we locate the study of theology within the framework of 'doing theology', as we have done, then we must assume that the theologian is part of the Christian community. From this perspective, 'doing theology' can never be a neutral exercise, nor can it be a substitute for faith and commitment. It assumes faith, and it requires commitment.

In his *Cost of Discipleship*, Dietrich Bonhoeffer brings together the need for faith *and* obedience in knowing God: 'only he who believes is obedient, and only he who is obedient believes.'[25] The God who is revealed in Jesus of Nazareth is known through following him. Christian theology is, in the end, an attempt to understand God *from the perspective of discipleship*. Theology is, then, about more than 'faith seeking understanding' in an academic way; it is also about obedience or faithful praxis. When these are brought together in struggling to witness to the gospel in our context, then our study of theology, with all the critical rigour which that requires, is placed at the service of 'doing theology' and thus is able to make its vital contribution to the task of the church.

---

[1] 'Praxis' is a German word which is usually translated into English as 'practice'. But when used in theology and other disciplines, it means action which arises out of and contributes to critical reflection.

[2] Friedrich Schleiermacher, *Brief Outline of the Study of Theology* (1811) (Westminster: John Knox, 1966).

[3] Edward Farley, *Theologia: The Fragmentation and Unity of Theological Education* (Philadelphia: Fortress, 1983), pp. 29ff.

[4] On the history of theology as a science, see Wolfhart Pannenberg, *Theology and the Philosophy of Science* (Philadelphia: Westminster, 1976), Part Two.

[5] Anselm, *Proslogion*, chapter 1, published in *St. Anselm: Basic Writings*, translated by S.N. Deane (Las Salle, Illinois: Open Court, 1968), p. 7.

[6] Karl Barth, *Anselm: Fides Quaerens Intellectum: Anselm's Proof of the Existence of God in the Context of his Theological Scheme* (London: SCM, 1960).

[7] We use the word 'Godself' throughout this volume rather than 'God himself' in order to remind ourselves that God is neither male nor female, and that all our images of God are in fact metaphors. That is, they are ways of speaking about God which derive from our own experience and are subject to the limitations of language and vocabulary. We must therefore try to avoid ways of speaking about God which can be misleading or even hurtful, thereby 'taking God's name in vain', or, literally, emptying it of meaning.

[8] John Calvin, *The Institutes of the Christian Religion* (Philadelphia: Westminster Press, 1960), I/i/i.

[9] For a good modern and concise translation see St. Thomas Aquinas, *Summa Theologiae*, edited by Timothy McDermott (Westminster, Maryland: Christian Classics, 1989).

[10] See Geoffrey B. Kelly, ed., *Karl Rahner: Theologian of the Graced Search for Meaning* (Minneapolis: Fortress, 1993).

[11] Paul Tillich, *Systematic Theology*, vol. 1 (London: Nisbet & Co., 1953), p. 70.

[12] The classic study of this problem is H. Richard Niebuhr, *Christ and Culture* (New York: Harper and Row, 1951).

[13] John Milbank, *Theology and Social Theory: Beyond Secular Reason* (Oxford: Blackwell, 1992), pp. 380f.

[14] David Tracy, *The Analogical Imagination: Christian Theology and the Culture of Pluralism* (London: SCM, 1981).

[15] Wolfhart Pannenberg, *Systematic Theology*, vol. 1 (Grand Rapids: Eerdmans, 1991), p. 20.

[16] James D.G. Dunn, *Unity and Diversity in the New Testament* (Philadelphia: Westminster, 1977).

[17] Kristar Stendahl, *Paul Among Jews and Gentiles* (Philadelphia: Fortress, 1976), pp. 82f.

[18] Anthony C. Thiselton, *The Two Horizons: New Testament Hermeneutics and Philosophical Description* (Grand Rapids: Eerdmans, 1980), pp. 10ff.

[19] Rudolf Bultmann, *Jesus Christ and Mythology* (London: SCM, 1960).

[20] George Casalis, *Correct Ideas Don't Fall from the Sky* (Maryknoll: Orbis, 1984).

[21] For a more detailed exposition see John W. de Gruchy, *Theology and Ministry in Context and Crisis* (London: Collins, 1987), pp. 87f.

[22] Gustavo Gutiérrez, *Theology of Liberation* (New York: Orbis, 1988), pp. 5–6.

[23] Juan Luis Segundo, *The Liberation of Theology* (New York: Orbis, 1976), p. 8.

[24] See, for example, Charles Villa-Vicencio, *A Theology of Reconstruction* (Cape Town: David Philip, 1992).

[25] Dietrich Bonhoeffer, *The Cost of Discipleship* (London: SCM, 1959), p. 54.

## Select Bibliography

The literature on the task of theology is vast. In addition to the books mentioned in the footnotes, and in the bibliographies which follow each essay, we suggest the following.

Bath, Karl. *Evangelical Theology: An Introduction*. New York: Holt, Rinehart and Winston, 1963

Evans, Gillian R., Alister E. McGrath and Allan D. Galloway. *The Science of Theology*. Grand Rapids: Eerdmans, 1986

Hall, Douglas John. *Thinking the Faith*. Minneapolis: Augsburg, 1989

Hodgson, Peter C. and Robert H. King, *Christian Theology: An Introduction to Its Traditions and Tasks*, revised edition. Philadelphia: Fortress, 1985

Küng, Hans. *On Being a Christian*. London: Collins, 1974

For an introduction to some of the leading theologians of the nineteenth and twentieth centuries, and how they understood the task of theology, see the series entitled *The Making of Modern Theology* (Minneapolis: Fortress). There are volumes on Friedrich Schleiermacher, Adolf von Harnack, Karl Barth, Rudolf Bultmann, Paul Tillich, Karl Rahner, Dietrich Bonhoeffer and Reinhold Niebuhr.

To keep in touch with theological developments in southern Africa, see the *Journal of Theology for Southern Africa (JTSA)*, c/o Department of Religious Studies, University of Cape Town.

# 2

# The Bible and Theology

## GERALD WEST

In recent years there have been repeated attempts to construct a biblical theology. However, this task has proved to be so problematic that it has been abandoned by most biblical scholars and theologians.[1] In recent years there have also been repeated attempts to construct theology without reference to the Bible. This task too has proved to be problematic.

In this chapter I will explain why both these attempts are flawed. I will then go on to suggest how we in South Africa, and those in similar contexts, might begin to explore the relationship between the Bible and theology.

### Constructing a Biblical Theology

Behind attempts to construct a biblical theology is the assumption that the Bible has a theology. This assumption is based on the commonsense view of most Christians that the Bible is about one thing. However, while this may be true to some extent, more careful and critical reflection on the Bible leads us to acknowledge that the Bible is really a collection of theologies.

Attempts to construct a biblical theology usually start with theologians trying to locate the centre or trajectory of the Bible. Various trajectories have been proposed, for example 'law and grace', 'liberation' and 'salvation'. But there has been little consensus among theologians, which is not surprising when we examine the Bible itself.

While there have been biblical scholars who have attempted to construct a biblical theology, most biblical scholars are distinctly uncomfortable with the idea. This is because we recognise the many different theologies that are collected in the Bible. If, therefore, we are to take the Bible seriously, we cannot simply accept that the Bible has a theology. There is no easy path from the Bible to theology. This does not mean that the Bible should not play a significant role in the construction of theology. Before we come to examine the place of the Bible in the construction of theology we must briefly explore some of the problems associated with the attempt to do theology without the Bible.

## Constructing a Theology Without the Bible

Ironically, biblical studies itself has contributed to the omission of the Bible in the doing of theology. The more detailed and diverse biblical studies has become, the more inaccessible the Bible has grown to anyone who is not an expert. Increasing specialisation and the absence of consensus among biblical scholars have removed the Bible from many theologians (and ordinary people). It is difficult for theologians to keep up with the results of biblical studies research, and so many theologians either work with outdated biblical research or no longer even bother to attempt to relate their doing of theology to the Bible.

But there is also another reason why the Bible is omitted in the construction of theology. This reason is more specific to our South African context and other contexts in which the Bible has been oppressive. The dilemma that confronts black South Africans in their relationships with the Bible is captured in the following well-known story: 'When the white man came to our country he had the Bible and we had the land. The white man said to us, "Let us pray." After the prayer, the white man had the land and we had the Bible.' This story clearly points to the central position that the Bible has occupied in the process of oppression and exploitation. The story also reflects the paradox of the oppressor and the oppressed sharing the same Bible and the same faith. In recognising this dilemma some black theologians have argued that it may be better to do theology without the Bible.[2]

For those who find the diversity and detail of biblical studies too inaccessible and who find the Bible socially and politically too ambiguous, there are other resources for doing theology. These include church history, tradition and doctrine, the experience of people, and 'reading the signs of the time' (social analysis). These resources are, of course, an important part of the constructing of theology. But what about the Bible? Should we ignore it, or if not, is there a way in which we can creatively and critically use it in doing theology?

## The Bible and Ordinary People

The cry of many Christians is that the crisis in South Africa 'impels us to return to the Bible and to search the Word of God for a message that is relevant to what we are experiencing in South Africa today'.[3] The Bible is important for ordinary people in South Africa. Two recent studies have clearly demonstrated this.

In discussing the constructing of an indigenous theology of work, James Cochrane makes some penetrating comments on workers reading the Bible. He argues that besides being 'the primary source of the Christian *mythos*', the Bible 'is probably the only source of theology for most members of our churches. It is, as some have said, the people's book *par excellence*.'[4]

Cochrane's argument is supported by the Institute for Contextual Theology's Church and Labour Project Research Group. The report of this group notes that perhaps 'the most interesting question of all, given the response to it, was whether or not the Bible had any significance for workers, and if so, what kind of a meaning it could have'. 'The answers are astonishing,' the report continues, 'at least to anyone who might have thought that the general picture of a relatively high level of alienation from the Church would be echoed in this question', and 'we would not intuitively have expected that an effective 80% of our respondents would regard the Bible as significant.'

This is a very high positive evaluation in the light of all the other generally more negative data concerning, for example, the relevance of the church. 'Overall', the report concludes, 'the most important conclusion to be drawn from this question is that the Bible is a rich source of interpretation for the worker's life, certainly of much greater significance than the liturgical and pastoral operations of the Church.'[5]

In his research with the informal peri-urban shack community of Amaoti in the Natal Midlands, Graham Philpott examines 'how members of that community use and reinterpret the symbol of the kingdom of God to make meaning of and communicate their reality of poverty and oppression, of suffering and hope'. He notes that 'The reinterpretation of this symbol has emerged from a particular Bible study group which has met regularly over a four year period to reflect on their involvement in the struggles of their community *in the light of the God who is revealed in the Bible* and in their community life.'[6] Philpott goes on to argue that 'This reflection has equipped them better to dialogue with and engage the oppressive reality of their community, so that they can work against the forces of death and be involved in engendering life.'[7]

Once again we notice the important role the Bible plays in the theological reflection of ordinary people in South Africa. And this we must take seriously if doing theology in our context is to be rooted in the lives of ordinary Christians. By 'we', I mean both those who read the Bible (including biblical scholars) and those who do theology (theologians). In the next section I will explore how biblical scholars and theologians can work together with ordinary people in doing theology in our South African context. My aim will be to provide a framework in which we can read the Bible with ordinary people in a way that takes seriously both its ambiguous nature and the results of biblical studies research.

## Reading the Bible and Doing Theology with Ordinary People

There are two guiding assumptions in this section. The first is that theologians and biblical scholars have something significant to offer to hearing God in the South African context. The second is that ordinary people who read the Bible and do theology have something significant to offer to hearing God in the South African context. The central concern of the chapter is to explore how trained and ordinary people can work together to read the Bible and do theology in an individually and socially transformative way in South Africa. These two assumptions form the framework for what follows.

What I am arguing is that the relationship between the Bible and theology should be explored at the interface between trained Bible readers and theologians and ordinary Bible readers and theologians. In what follows I will outline a process in which the Bible is central and which involves both trained and ordinary people working with each other in reading the Bible. My argument is that this process, which I call contextual Bible study, is a vital component in the doing of theology in our context; and my argument is not just theory, but is based on ongoing work in the church and community.[8]

The contextual Bible study process includes at least four central concerns or commitments. They are, first, a commitment to read the Bible from the perspective of the South African context, particularly from the perspective of the poor and oppressed; second, a commitment to read the Bible in community with others, particularly with those from contexts different from our own; third, a commitment to read the Bible critically; and fourth, a commitment to individual and social transformation through contextual Bible study.[9]

## Reading the Bible in the South African Context

We all bring our contexts with us to our readings of the Bible. This has always been the case, but it has not always been acknowledged. My context includes, for example, at least the following factors: I am a white, middle-class, Western–African, male Christian. Contextual Bible study recognises that we are all to some extent shaped by our contexts, and that our contexts influence our readings of the Bible. Again, this has always been the case, but it has not always been acknowledged.

However, contextual Bible study is also more specific about context. We read the Bible in South Africa, and this must be acknowledged and recognised. Like any context, the South African context has affected us and our readings of the Bible.

Acknowledging and recognising the influence our South African context has on our readings of the Bible is important because not only do we read the Bible in this context, but we should also want to read the Bible explicitly from and for the South African context. The Bible itself shows that particular people interact with God in particular contexts and that God speaks specifically to specific people in specific life situations. How are we to hear God speaking to us in South Africa unless we explicitly acknowledge and recognise this context in our readings of the Bible?

Yet there are many different realities within the South African context, and many readings of the Bible from these differing realities. For example, the Bible has been read to support apartheid by some and to support the struggle for liberation by others, and the Bible continues to be used by some to maintain wealth and power and by others to struggle for justice and democracy. So we have to be even more specific about what we mean by 'reading the Bible from and for the South African context'.

Those who are committed to the contextual Bible study process have decided to read the Bible from a particular perspective within the South African context, the perspective of the poor and oppressed (including women). The poor and oppressed are those who are socially, politically, economically or culturally marginalised and exploited. We have made this choice because we believe God is particularly concerned for the poor and oppressed. Our readings of the Bible and our concern for justice and righteousness in South Africa clearly indicate that God is particularly concerned for the marginalised and vulnerable. Throughout the Bible we read that God hears the cry of widows, orphans, women, strangers, the handicapped, the poor and the oppressed. God sees the suffering and hears the cry of the slaves in Egypt (Exod. 3:7), and the prophets constantly speak and act against injustice to the poor (Isa. 58:6–12; Amos 5:11–12). From the gospels it is clear that Jesus himself was born among the poor and oppressed in Palestine, that he chose to remain with and work among the poor and marginalised, and that he died the death of the poor and oppressed on a cross. We also believe that justice and righteousness will only come in South Africa when the needs of the poor and oppressed are addressed. So when we choose to read the Bible from the perspective of the poor and oppressed in the South African context we choose to hear the concerns of the vulnerable and marginalised, and God's concern for them.

Clearly such a commitment requires not only an acknowledgement and recognition of the effect of the South African context on ourselves and our readings of the Bible; it also requires an understanding and analysis of our South African context. We cannot hear either the concerns of the poor and oppressed or God's concern for them unless we are prepared to analyse our context. Initial questions like 'Who are the poor and oppressed in South Africa?' and 'Why are they poor and oppressed?' lead us to deeper and more complex questions. While these questions may be difficult both to ask and to answer, we must be willing to probe and analyse every aspect of our South African context: the religious, the political, the economic, the social and the cultural.

For those of us who are not from among the poor and marginalised, this may seem a difficult commitment. However, if we are willing to acknowledge and recognise our own situation in South Africa and to analyse South African reality from the perspective of the poor and oppressed, and if we are willing to take the next commitment of the contextual Bible study process seriously, then we have already begun to share in the process of doing theology with ordinary people in our context.

## Reading the Bible in Community

For those of us who have participated in group Bible study this commitment needs little justification. But it is important to reflect on this commitment more carefully. The Western industrialised world's emphasis on the individual shapes us all, and so it is easy to lose a sense of community consciousness. In addition, those of us who have been theologically and biblically trained usually find it hard to genuinely hear and learn from ordinary people. We have to honestly believe that we can learn from the readings and theology of ordinary people. So for us, reading the Bible with ordinary readers requires the need to be converted to a sense of community consciousness.

In this chapter I have repeatedly used the phrase 'reading the Bible *with* ordinary readers'. I use this important word 'with' deliberately because there are two temptations that trained readers of the Bible face. The first is that we interpret for ordinary readers, and the second is that we simply accept the interpretations of ordinary readers. Let me explain.

Because of our training in theology and biblical studies we tend to read the Bible *for* ordinary people. We may give the impression that we are hearing the contributions of ordinary readers, but we are really concerned to tell them how they should read the Bible and what they should learn from it. The danger here is that we minimise and rationalise the contributions and experiences of ordinary people.

Simply accepting the readings of ordinary people is also a temptation. Because we are sometimes aware of our privileged and powerful position (on account of our skills and training) in the group, and because we are committed to reading the Bible in community, we sometimes tend to accept uncritically the readings of ordinary people. The danger here is that we idealise and romanticise the contributions of ordinary readers.

The contextual Bible study process, however, attempts to avoid these two dangers by reading the Bible *with* ordinary readers. What this means is that we as trained readers acknowledge the privilege and power our training gives us in the group. It also means that we must empower ordinary readers in the group to discover and then to acknowledge their own identity and the value and significance of their own contributions and experiences. This is particularly important when we are reading the Bible with people from poor and oppressed communities. Readers of the Bible from these communities have usually had their interpretations silenced and suppressed by the dominant interpretations. Some readers from these communities have even come to accept the dominant interpretations as their own. So if we are really going to read the Bible with ordinary readers we must work together to break the 'culture of silence' and to recover the identity and experiences of the poor and oppressed. The poor and marginalised are not really silent, but they are often not heard and what they say is often the product of centuries of colonisation. It is only by talking with and to each other, recognising the unequal power relations between us, that we can begin to construct transforming discourse.

It is only when both trained and ordinary readers are active 'subjects' in the reading process that we really have a process of *reading with*. In other words, for the contextual Bible study process to be a *reading with,* both trained and ordinary readers must be active participants who are aware of who they are. For trained readers, being active subjects means that we need not feel guilty about our theological and biblical training. We must feel free to share sensitively and creatively what we have learned from and about the Bible through our training. For ordinary readers, being active subjects means that they must be able to speak with their own voice, no matter how different this voice is from the dominant voices.

Reading the Bible with ordinary people is a challenge for us trained readers, but if we are willing to make this commitment we will never be the same again. Reading the Bible with poor and oppressed readers is a challenge both to trained readers and to ordinary readers who come from communities which are not poor or oppressed. But it is a challenge which clearly makes a claim upon us if we are to take seriously these first two commitments. Once again, if we are willing to take up this challenge to read the Bible with poor and marginalised ordinary readers we will be profoundly changed. We will also learn a great deal from the Bible. Let me illustrate.

In the Lord's Prayer, what is the first request concerning their needs that the disciples are taught by Jesus to make of God when they pray? Why does Jesus teach his disciples to make this their first request? The answer you give to these questions will indicate something about who you are and the context from which you come. If you look at the scholarly commentaries you will, usually, not even find these questions asked. Other questions are asked about the Lord's Prayer, but normally not these. The questions at the beginning of this paragraph were asked by a black person from a poor community because he noticed that the first request Jesus teaches his disciples to ask of God is for daily bread. Because he comes from a poor community, this reader understands how important basic food like bread is each day to someone who is poor. Jesus knows this too; that is why he teaches his disciples to make this their first request when they pray. God is concerned about many things, but God is particularly concerned about the basic needs of the poor. Now you will not find this interpretation in any of the scholarly commentaries, but you and I will hear penetrating and profound interpretations like this when we read the Bible with ordinary readers from poor communities.

As I have already acknowledged, this is not an easy commitment for those of us who live in communities which have almost no contact with the poor and oppressed. But we must heed the call of the Scriptures and we must heed the cry of our country for justice and reconciliation. So we must commit ourselves to finding and forming Bible study groups in which we can become the community of God's people.

## Reading the Bible Critically

Just as community consciousness is a crucial commitment of the contextual Bible study process, critical consciousness means asking questions, especially the question 'Why?' It means probing beneath the surface, being suspicious of the *status quo*, and thus includes systematic and structured analysis.

An example might help clarify what I mean. Dom Helder Camara, now retired archbishop of Recife in Brazil, said, 'When I give food to the poor, they call me a saint; when I ask why the poor have no food, they call me a communist.' Giving the poor food is good, but we need to do more. We must also be critical. So we must not simply accept that the poor have no food; we must probe beneath the surface of this reality; we must be suspicious of the *status quo*. Like Dom Helder Camara we must ask the question 'Why?' Why do the poor have no food? Here we are beginning to be critical, particularly when this and other related questions are part of a systematic and structured analysis.

Many people in South Africa, particularly those from poor and marginalised communities, are critically conscious in socio-political matters. They do think and act critically in the social, economic and political areas of life, though they may not be very systematic or structured in their analysis. However, very few of those people have a critical consciousness in the area of their faith. Most Christians in South Africa do not ask questions about their theologies and their readings of the Bible. Few of us probe beneath the surface or are suspicious of *status quo* Christianity. We do not usually analyse in a systematic way the Christian tradition and its effects on our context. And yet the Christian faith has had both a profound oppressive and liberatory effect on our context.

So one of the commitments of the contextual Bible study process is to facilitate the development of critical consciousness by beginning with critical Bible reading. This is a small beginning, but through critical Bible reading we participate in the important process of building a critical church and community which can play a role in analysing the past and present, and thus in shaping the future. Readers of the Bible are not the only ones who are contributing towards constructing a more critical society, but we can make a small (and significant) contribution, particularly in the church.

We should be committed to reading the Bible critically for two reasons: because we are concerned that all readers recognise the ideological nature of the Bible and its interpretations, and because we are concerned that all readers develop critical skills and tools so that they are empowered to do their own critical analysis of the Bible and its interpretations.

While most of us can accept that interpretations of the Bible are shaped by the interests and experiences of those who read it, we find it hard to accept that the Bible itself is shaped by the interests and experiences of those who produced it. However, in the same way that various interpretations of the Bible represent differing (and sometimes conflicting) perspectives, so too the various texts of the Bible represent differing (and sometimes conflicting) perspectives. This is implicit in the very construction of the Bible. We have four gospels, not one, and each presents a different perspective on Jesus. A careful comparison of Kings and Chronicles provides two different perspectives on the period of David's kingship. So the Bible itself contains different perspectives, or what some people refer to as 'ideologies'.

Commitment to reading the Bible from the perspective of the poor and oppressed and to reading the Bible in community with others requires that the ideological (or perspectival) nature of the Bible and its interpretations be investigated. This must be done because the Bible and its interpretations have often been used both to oppress ordinary people and to legitimate oppression of ordinary people. We in South Africa have many examples of this, with apartheid theology being the most obvious.

These two commitments also require that trained readers continue to read and appropriate the Bible. Some trained readers, when they realise how the Bible has been used to oppress black people and women, for example, decide to reject or abandon the Bible. But I would argue against such a decision. We must continue to read the Bible because the Bible is a significant resource and symbol for ordinary people and because it is important to stand in continuity with and to bear witness to the suppressed voices within the Bible and its neglected interpretations.

The Bible is and will continue to be a significant resource for ordinary people in the church and community. If we do not find ways of reading the Bible which are transformative and liberating in our context, then we are abandoning the Bible to those who use it to legitimate domination and oppression. We also must not abandon the memory of our foremothers and forefathers in the Bible who have struggled for the values of the community of God. Our struggle for justice and peace in South Africa is a part of their struggle. Their faithfulness to God's calling provides us with a 'dangerous memory' which reminds, challenges and empowers us. Instead of separating ourselves from the Bible and its interpretations, we should continue to find critical and creative ways of reading it in and for our context.

Once we admit that the Bible is ideological there is the danger that we may become selective in our reading. In other words, we pick and choose what fits our perspective and ignore what does not. But this is not a critical reading of the Bible. If we read the Bible critically, we can and should read any and every part of the Bible. But how do we do this?

I would suggest that there are at least three different ways or 'modes' of reading the Bible critically.[10] One way is to read the Bible in its historical and sociological context. This 'mode of reading' focuses on the historical and sociological context from which the text comes. It concentrates, for example, on the historical and sociological situation lying behind the gospels in order to understand the gospels and Jesus more fully.

Another way of reading the Bible critically is to read it carefully and closely in its literary context. This mode focuses on the different types of literature or writings in the Bible and the various relationships within the text. It focuses, for example, on what a 'gospel' is and how and why Mark structures his gospel in the way that he does.

The third way of reading the Bible critically is to read it in its thematic and symbolic context as a whole. This mode focuses on the major themes and symbols in the Bible as a whole. It emphasises, for example, the central themes that run like a thread throughout the Bible.

These three critical modes overlap and can be used together in the contextual Bible study process. But it is useful to differentiate between them because we then become aware of a range of critical skills and concepts which are useful both in reading the Bible and in 'reading' our context. Trained readers have been introduced to critical skills and concepts in their theological and biblical training. But while ordinary readers do have critical resources, they do not usually have a systematic understanding of the skills and concepts which constitute a critical reading of the Bible.

At this point it might be useful to state once again that what I mean by a critical approach to the Bible is that we ask questions in a systematic and structured way; it does not mean that we have a negative attitude towards the Bible. In fact, a critical reading attempts to minimise manipulation of the Bible by allowing the Bible to speak from its own contexts. So whereas 'critical' is often used to mean 'find fault with', I am not using it in this sense. I am using it in a positive sense to describe a person's careful and systematic reading. To be critical readers of the Bible means that we question and study the Bible rather than just accept and repeat what others have told us about it. We must be willing to work with others in a positive critical way so that we can discover and recover the true meaning of God's message for us today. A critical approach to the Bible is not in opposition to the life of faith. Faith is, in fact, nourished and deepened as we seek to understand the relationship between our faith and our context.

So one of the commitments of the contextual Bible study process is that trained readers share their critical resources with ordinary readers, drawing wherever possible on the critical resources they already have.

*Reading the Bible for Personal and Social Transformation*

While a critical approach to the Bible and our South African context is something we must learn, there is already a remarkable willingness and ability on the part of ordinary readers to appropriate and apply the Bible to reality — that is, to do theology. The Bible is already a resource for transformation for many readers. So this fourth commitment is usually an integral part of Bible study.

However, within this readiness to read the Bible for transformation there are two areas of concern. In South Africa, and elsewhere, the Bible tends to be appropriated and applied uncritically, and this can be dishonest and dangerous. Apartheid theology is an example of a process of appropriation and application of the Bible which is both dishonest and dangerous. It is dangerous because it has led to oppression and death, and it is dishonest because it uses the Bible selectively for narrow interests. So while the contextual Bible study process embraces the readiness of ordinary readers to appropriate and apply the Bible to the South African context, it emphasises that this must be done critically.

Doing theology within the contextual Bible study process requires two steps. Reading the Bible critically is the first step in a critical appropriation, and 'reading' our context critically is the second step. These two steps enable us to appropriate the Bible more carefully because we are able to identify both the similarities and differences between the Bible and its contexts, on the one hand, and between ourselves and our contexts, on the other hand. Appropriation is perhaps the most important part of the process, but it is a complex exercise which requires critical reflection.

The second area of concern is that our readiness to read the Bible for transformation should include both the personal and the social. In some contexts in South Africa, for example in white churches and communities, Christians have concentrated on individual transformation, while in other contexts, for example in black trade unions, Christians have concentrated on socio-political transformation. The contextual Bible study process is committed to both personal and social transformation, and includes the existential, the political, the economic, the cultural and the religious spheres of life. The contextual Bible study process is committed to reading the Bible for the transformation of all aspects of social reality.

*Facilitating the Process*

Contextual Bible study, as a process, will not just happen; it needs to be facilitated. In a recent workshop on contextual Bible study, participants agreed that the five most important characteristics of a facilitator were the following: the facilitator should use a method that encourages the whole group to participate; should manage conflict and make the group a safe place for members' contributions; should train others to become facilitators; should clarify what is not clear and summarise the discussion; and should enable the group to become aware of and involved in the needs of the community. A facilitator, then, is one who helps the progress and empowerment of others, who makes it easier for others to act, contribute and to acquire skills.

Anyone can be a facilitator, provided he or she is willing to learn to be an enabler and not a dominator. Community consciousness and critical consciousness cannot develop in authoritarian forms of Bible study. Democratic processes can only develop where there is mutual respect and trust and a deep sense of community. Only in such a context do self-confidence, responsibility and accountability grow.

## Conclusion

The focus of this chapter has been on how to read the Bible in such a way that it becomes useful for doing theology in our context. Contextual Bible study is an important component of doing theology in our South Africa today. It provides a process in which ordinary people are important agents in the reading of the Bible and the doing of theology, in which critical biblical research and the ambiguity of the Bible are taken seriously, and in which the Bible is an integral part of the doing of theology. While there are other components which are necessary if we are to do theology in our context (see the other chapters in this volume), doing theology must include the contextual Bible study process.

[1] Elisabeth Schüssler Fiorenza, *In Memory of Her: A Feminist Theological Reconstruction of Christian Origins* (London: SCM, 1983).

[2] Itumeleng J. Mosala, *Biblical Hermeneutics and Black Theology in South Africa* (Grand Rapids: Eerdmans, 1989).

[3] *The Kairos Document: Challenge to the Church* (Grand Rapids: Eerdmans, 1986).

[4] James Cochrane and Gerald West (eds.), *The Three-fold Cord: Theology, Work and Labour* (Pietermaritzburg: Cluster Publications, 1991).

[5] Ibid.

[6] Graham J. Philpott, 'A Contextual Investigation of the Symbol of the Kingdom of God' (Unpublished MA thesis, University of Natal, Pietermaritzburg, 1993), my emphasis.

[7] Ibid.

[8] Gerald West, *Contextual Bible Study* (Pietermaritzburg: Cluster Publications, 1993).

[9] Ibid.

[10] Ibid. See also my *Biblical Hermeneutics of Liberation: Modes of Reading the Bible in the South African Context* (Pietermaritzburg: Cluster Publications, 1991).

## Select Bibliography

Childs, Brevard S. *Biblical Theology in Crisis*. Philadelphia: Westminster Press, 1970

Cochrane, James R., and Gerald O. West (eds.) *The Three-fold Cord: Theology, Work and Labour*. Pietermaritzburg: Cluster Publications, 1991

Fiorenza, Elisabeth Schüssler. *In Memory of Her: A Feminist Theological Reconstruction of Christian Origins*. London: SCM, 1983

Mosala, Itumeleng J. *Biblical Hermeneutics and Black Theology in South Africa*. Grand Rapids: Eerdmans, 1989

Philpott, Graham J. 'A Contextual Theological Investigation of the Symbol of the Kingdom of God'. Unpublished MA Thesis, University of Natal, Pietermaritzburg, 1993

West, Gerald O. *Contextual Bible Study*. Pietermaritzburg: Cluster Publications, 1993

West, Gerald O. *Biblical Hermeneutics of Liberation: Modes of Reading the Bible in the South African Context*. Pietermaritzburg: Cluster Publications, 1991

# 3

# Theology and Faith:
# Tradition, Criticism and Popular Religion

## JAMES R. COCHRANE

... we need to balance the hope for certainty and clarity in theory with
the impossibility of avoiding uncertainty and ambiguity in practice.
— Stephen Toulmin[1]

### Questioning Emancipatory Theologies

Praxis-oriented theologies have been with us for a long time now. People like
Paul Tillich were already exploring the relationship between faith and praxis in
the 1930s, as part of a dialogue with friends and confidants in the neo-marxist
Frankfurt School of Critical Theory. But it is only since the rise of liberation
theology (Gutiérrez), Black theology (Cone), political theology (Moltmann),
feminist theology (Ruether), Minjung theology (Kim Chi-Ha) and Kairos
theology that the issue of praxis in faith has become a dominant feature of the
dialogue of the global Christian community.

This 'spiritual movement', as I would describe it, has during the thirty years or
so of its life led to a belief among many that we are witnessing a paradigm shift in
the way theology is understood and done, a shift occasioned by the increasingly
important place of Christians of the third world in the life of the church. Their
perspectives and experiences have become significant in Christian reflection on
faith.

The movement, whatever the differences between the various theological
expressions of it, has its focus in the idea and practices of emancipation. This
focus has given important new meaning for millions of Christians to the
doctrines of redemption and salvation. But the movement has also generated
theological, pastoral and ecclesial problems of its own. I want to focus on three
of them.

First, Christians who have recognised themselves, their lives and their faith in
the statements of these emancipatory theologies have often found themselves
questioning the Christian tradition they have inherited. Too frequently, for them
tradition has been oppressive and repressive.

26

Moreover, Christians who, on the basis of their faith, have concretely engaged in struggles for liberation have discovered that they have no monopoly of those practical values they regard as centrally Christian, and they sometimes come across those of other religions or beliefs whose spiritual strength and resources seem at least as great as any Christian they know. They wonder, then, about the uniqueness of Christianity and the specific contribution of their Christian faith.

Secondly, emancipatory theologies arise out of the pastoral realities of oppression and repression, where people are hurt, stripped of their dignity, broken by deadly economic and political forces, left resigned or crushed and weak. In such circumstances, people discover that a responsible use of their God-given reason provides them with many critical tools to understand their situation. These same critical tools also help them find appropriate routes to recovering their dignity, their wholeness and their God-given right to participate with others in deciding about their lives. As children of God, they realise that they are not meant to be at the mercy of others, nor are they meant simply to accept the evils that others practise upon them.

Yet the use of critical reason to understand one's life context always spills over into faith. Critical questions about the faith one inherits and proclaims cannot be avoided either, especially when the critical tools one uses, for example from sociology, economics, political science and history, have themselves often been turned precisely against the hypocrisies, prejudices and illusions of faith.

Thirdly, theologies of emancipation are critical of the dominant powers and structures in their context: political and economic elites, patriarchies, racist overlords and colonisers, centralised bureaucracies, defenders of ill-founded privileges. By implication or by proclamation, they also state their 'preferential option' for those who are poor, oppressed, marginalised or outcast.

Yet very often they are confronted with religious experiences and beliefs among the poor and the marginalised which appear conservative, reactionary, illusory or delusory. They encounter what many now call popular religion. Popular religion often does not fit with the formal categories of emancipatory theologies, while activist and avant-garde Christian groups often find that those people whose reality they believe they are addressing do not understand them or may even be hostile to their criticisms of the Bible or of their tradition.

The relationship between tradition, criticism and popular religion is my concern here. I shall argue that doing theology in context must pay proper attention to all three categories in such a way that the importance of each is taken seriously and included in the whole. Any attempt to 'do theology' without finding a way to include tradition, criticism and popular religion is bound either to fail in the long run or, equally sadly, to leave theology in the hands and under the control of a highly trained elite.

Once this is clear, I shall suggest a way of going about the 'doing of theology' which makes space for all three elements while respecting the life and faith of ordinary Christians above all. For this purpose I will build on the idea of what some have called 'local theologies'[2] and on an important understanding of the role and significance of popular religion.[3]

## Faith and Doubt

Doing theology in context brings us into confrontation with ideas, experiences and practices which challenge us uncomfortably. Whether one considers the role of tradition, of criticism or of popular religion, in all these areas Christians have been faced with deep-seated doubts about their faith.

Doubt is not to be feared but may be embraced. Doubt will expose where we are shallow and what we hide behind because, for good or bad reasons, we lack 'the courage to be' (Tillich) or the strength to take risks. For this reason, emancipatory theologies accept a 'hermeneutic of suspicion' (Ricoeur), a use of contemporary intellectual tools of criticism, a willingness to question and to accept questioning.

The deeper questions we must face and respond to with our faith always push us beyond what we already know or understand. They require a transcendent theology, one which goes beyond pat answers and rigid dogmas, one which accepts that our faith will be tested and that the tests we face are sometimes greater than ourselves and our current answers.

One of this century's most significant theologians, Paul Tillich, went as far as to build his entire understanding of the theological task around the idea that life provides the questions which theology seeks to answer. He called this the 'method of correlation'. If we are to take his approach seriously, then the kinds of questions raised by life in the context of apartheid and post-apartheid South Africa must become an essential part of any attempt to do theology: to say who God is, why and how this God is present in Jesus Christ, and what this demands of the community of Christians we call the church.

The South African struggle has put the Christian faith to severe test. Evil policies which deeply hurt millions of people were formulated and carried out in the name of Christianity. In struggling against these policies Christians have discovered that other challenges to their faith are also present. They have found themselves alongside many others who worship through different belief systems — Islam, Judaism, Hinduism — or who have no belief in God at all. They have discovered women who find the Christian faith to be so strongly patriarchal that they feel at best alienated from it, at worst forced to reject it.

But as many as there are who have serious doubts about Christianity and the Christian faith, there are more who find in Christian faith a source of life. Particularly among the vast numbers of Christians who are members, by day (openly) or by night (secretly), of African-initiated or independent churches, there is a sense of vitality which is lacking elsewhere. Political philosophies in support of the struggle for liberation have often denigrated this grassroots vitality, often seeing it as reactionary or as 'opium' of the poor and oppressed.

Yet the vitalities remain despite such views, and this represents a challenge to our understanding of a contextual faith as well. Latin American liberation theologians have begun to accept this challenge in criticising themselves. Many now speak less of 'liberation' and more of 'the God of Life who confronts the forces of Death'.[4] As Costa Rican theologian and economist Hinkelammert puts it, 'any image of God that is incompatible with real life will be a fetish; the true

God cannot be anything but a God that is compatible with real human life. . . That is the God of the Bible.'[5]

Our context demands of us new theological responses to the questions posed by life. Yet, as I have indicated, some questions posed by life in our context are directed at Christian faith itself. This forces us to rethink what theology is and how we 'do theology'. We need to look for approaches to constructing an indigenous theology which link popular faith, the inherited tradition and critical reason. In order to explore what such an approach might look like, I turn to the story of a particular group of women.

## Mary and the Women of Mpophomeni

Megan Walker has carried out a small but admirable study of the meaning that Mary, mother of Jesus, has for the lives of a group of women from Mpophomeni, a black township near Howick, north of Pietermaritzburg, Natal.[6] She shows how the doctrinal traditions of the church are altered, affirmed, contradicted or added to as this group of Mpophomeni women theologically reflect on their lives, in this case through the memory and image of Mary. I want to point to certain aspects of her story and findings which are of importance for our theme.[7]

Many of these women participate in two different annual Marian pilgrimages, each now part of a strong tradition. The one pilgrimage, to Kevelaer, includes a solemn mass, a candle-light procession, sermons, adorations, a penitential service and many songs. Its focus is on Mary as the 'mother of the afflicted', the one who consoles those who suffer. For many women, Mary can identify with their suffering because she too suffered as a mother who saw her son leaving her, being vilified, outcast and ultimately tortured.

The other pilgrimage to Nshongweni is similar, but it includes a strong emphasis on confessions and it lasts through the night. One is expected to stay awake; rain is not uncommon, cold not abnormal. This is a penance in veneration of Mary, who here is seen as the 'mediator of all graces', the one who assists people in their various needs.

Walker found in both these pilgrimages that the influence of ordinary people on the character of the event was great, even though priests and catechists took the lead in most activities. The public prayers and sermons of the religious leaders are often not connected to what is going on in the personal prayers and devotions of the pilgrims as they move around the shrines and other places associated with the venue. The people themselves have also played a powerful role historically in determining which shrines are appropriate for their devotions, in each case against the ideas and desires of the priests who originally initiated these pilgrimages many years ago.

What do these women think of Mary when they are back home, away from the special focus of the pilgrimage? The township of Mpophomeni has been a particular centre of struggle in the last decade, strongly affected by widespread strikes against local industry, an ensuing consumer boycott, unfair dismissals, the arrival of refugees from violence in other areas, vigilante attacks, security police crackdowns and political factionalism. Oppression and violence have been the stuff of their daily life, and even their local church building was burnt down on one occasion because of the involvement of clergy and lay religious in their struggles.

## Liberating or Oppressive Faith?

Modern Catholic thought on Mary can be divided into two tendencies. The first sets Mary apart from ordinary human beings, linking her in a subordinate role with Christ, facing humanity from a removed, divine realm (Christotypical Mariology). The second tendency places Mary with the church, 'down below with us' so to speak, facing God on our behalf and concerned with our humanity (ecclesiotypical Mariology). Vatican II, by the closest of all votes taken at any of its meetings, placed Mariology in *Lumen Gentium*, the dogmatic constitution on the church. It backed the second of the two tendencies.

Feminist theologian Rosemary Radford Ruether takes a different line, seeing both the church and Mary as identified above all in the Magnificat of Luke's gospel: a symbol of revolutionary transformation and co-creatorship between God and humanity. For many women and others, Catholic or otherwise, this is a way forward in thinking constructively about the place of Mary in Christian belief, but it is out of line with the main traditions of the church. It requires that we rethink our ideas of God as male, and our ideas of the relationship between God and humanity.

Such rethinking has already begun to happen in Latin America, where the experience of the poor and the marginalised has allowed a different, liberating view of Mary to emerge. There Mary has long been an important figure in religious and even national life, though by no means always in a liberating way (conquerors and dominant elites have also used the figure of Mary to their own ends). But she has also inspired many peasant and other resistance movements. She is often pictured as a poor person with the features of the local people, speaking their language and siding with them against the powerful figures in the church and political life. She is the faithful one who is with the poor, who — as in the Magnificat — foresees the mighty falling from their thrones under the judgement of God.

What about the ordinary, semi-literate, theologically untrained women of Mpophomeni? Where among all these options do their understandings of Mary fit? What Walker's study shows is that Mary in the popular religion of the women of Mpophomeni plays an ambiguous role. On the one hand, the women have learned traditions about Mary from the orthodoxies of the church, mediated primarily through stories, including the Bible, sermons and songs. Mary is important personally as the Divine Mother, but she is not necessarily linked to any judgement on social or national life. Many of the women also belong to the Legion of Mary, a conservative international sodality ('comradely fellowship') which sees itself waging war 'against the world and its evil powers'.

On the other hand, the women of Mpophomeni do not simply repeat the orthodoxies of the church, but 'invent' their own interpretations of Mary in relation to the daily realities and struggles of their lives in their context. They do their own theology, in other words. They draw on powerful oral traditions which may not be scripturally located. They compare Mary to an African ancestor through whom one normally approaches God in petition and intercession.

Other elements of Marian devotion in Mpophomeni include a belief that speaking to Mary, telling her everything, helps face the fear which is so often part of life in that context. Mary protects in times of danger, which are not infrequent. She helps people obtain jobs, pass school, find the right spouse, settle domestic quarrels. Prayer to Mary on the pilgrimages is important in part because it is direct communion with Mary, unmediated through priests and liturgical formulae.

Walker suggests that while such views of Mary may function as a source of support and a tool for survival, it may also enforce patriarchal stereotypes and diminish people's responsibility for taking control of their own lives. However, there is another stream of consciousness around Mary which is more directly liberating. For many of the women in Mpophomeni, Mary's suffering is crucial, especially in her being forced to give birth in a stable and to live in a situation of poverty, and in seeing her son condemned to death and crucified. They derive strength from this Mary, because she had the strength in faith to go through all of this. Mary did not run away from the Cross.

Similarly, many identify with Mary as a woman who understands what they go through as women, though there are ambiguous feelings about what this means. Yet Mary as a woman also legitimises strong women's participation in the life of the church. In the face of violence, Mary stands against the killers, wanting the killing to stop. She also stands against poverty and oppression, having experienced this herself. She challenges and confronts the rich and the poor (here the impact of the Magnificat is clear). The fact that it is Mary who takes these positions indicates that Jesus does too, that God takes sides. Not surprisingly, the women of Mpophomeni, despite visibly 'white' statues in local churches and pictures in printed works, have no trouble seeing Mary as a black woman.

Here then are the elements of an inherited tradition (about Mary in this case) and a contextual reflection of faith, intertwined with each other, neither destroying the other, each element adding something to the religious understanding of these women about their faith. The result is not necessarily orthodox theology, but it is real theology.

A third element is introduced by Walker's study: her own critical questioning, using her training and her knowledge of the tradition. Her concerns are based on her commitment as a woman to find interpretative strategies for reading Scripture and tradition in context which will be liberating for women as such. To the popular religion of the women, partly shaped already by the received tradition, partly shaped by their own critical thought arising from their life experiences, is now added the critical reasoning of a trained intellectual.

What she discovers overall is the primary importance of Mary as an object of devotion, the great mother who answers prayers, protects, heals and mediates between people and God. From the point of view of orthodoxy, this raises questions about the status of Mary in relation to Christ and God, and the implication that God is remote and inaccessible. There is a clear need for a direct relationship to the feminine aspect of the divine reality, though the tendency here is to accept a patriarchal structuring of this divine reality and a passive relationship to the world.

Yet alongside this dominant role of Mary is another stream of consciousness, one which sees Mary as taking sides for the poor and oppressed as one of them, standing alongside those who suffer, not running away in the face of danger and death, exemplifying the defiance of life against the forces of death: Mary the fellow-struggler.

Thus both the passive and the liberating understandings of Mary are present in the same women. The struggle to interpret Mary and the contradictions of those interpretations in the attempt to link the images of the tradition with their daily lives of poverty and oppression are present together. Walker takes one side of this duality about Mary, the liberating strand of consciousness, and seeks to build the foundations for a new contextual Mariology on this basis, while not ignoring the importance of 'mere' survival and comfort for the poor and oppressed.

What Walker represents in relation to the women of Mpophomeni is the trained interpreter of the Christian faith who has been exposed to the wider tradition and to the tools of critical reason. She represents the community of intellectuals whose role is to utilise the knowledge that the human and natural sciences provide, in dialogue with the tradition and experiences of faith. The method her study presents is the important point for the purposes of this chapter.

## Tradition, Criticism and Popular Religion

I have chosen to focus in detail on the significance of Walker's study on the meaning of Mary for a group of women in Mpophomeni because it brings into focus all of the issues I wish to address, and simultaneously it provides some important clues for the way in which I believe we must go about 'doing theology' in the South African context, if we are to renew more than our social institutions alone.

The tension between tradition, criticism and popular religion is clear. Equally clear is the need to keep the tension alive, not to collapse the tension so that all we have in 'doing theology' is a mere repetition of doctrine and dogma from tradition unconnected to the real experiences and contexts of the life of ordinary Christians; or the work of an intellectual elite and the belittling of the reflection on faith that happens in local contexts; or an unquestioned mirror-image of popular religious ideas which themselves may be flawed or oppressive.

Interpretation depends upon who is doing the interpreting, from what position in society, and from what condition of life. The kind of context which determines our interpretation — ecclesial, local, poor, etc. — has also to be defined and publicly declared so that others may make their judgements on what we say without being misled by hidden agendas or unstated commitments and interests. For these reasons, we cannot avoid the task of using our critical faculties of reason and the tools which the efforts of reason have provided us in disciplines such as sociology, psychology, political science and economics.

But theological meanings take on life and acquire substance primarily among ordinary, theologically untrained Christians, those for whom the Christian faith is part of their daily struggle to find wholeness, part of their vital celebrations of even tiny victories and inspiring hopes. Not only does popular religion here overcome high theological and ecclesial doctrine, but here too there are well-springs of theological renewal which we too often neglect because what might be communicated to us is not clearly articulated or because we do not understand its significance.

As the story of the women in Mpophomeni and their understanding of Mary shows, 'ordinary' Christians draw on the Christian tradition: its symbols, images, narratives and so on. This puts them in dialogue with those Christians of the past, through the centuries, whose struggles are expressed in the traditions passed on to us. This element of 'doing theology' requires a dialogue with a community that is dead in the flesh, but whose struggles and resolutions of those struggles may live again in the way they assist us.

But the next step is to interpret the past in ways which unlock important, 'dangerous' memories (Metz) capable of infusing our struggles with wisdom and insight. Then tradition as Scripture, doctrine, confession and so forth cannot be taught or passed on dogmatically, or as if there is only one acceptable use of tradition. The authority of tradition will lie in its accord with life as we actually experience it, and not merely in 'right teaching'.

What controls an arbitrary use of the tradition is the requirement that the dialogue with tradition does not stop. Respect for the ancestors of our faith means more than just taking from them what we like and discarding anything that challenges our prejudices, limitations and errors. What further controls an arbitrary use of the tradition is the necessary dialogue with others in our time, by which we may edify them and be edified by them, correct them and be corrected by them.

In short, I am suggesting that we must recognise in tradition the dialogue we carry on with our brothers and sisters of the past (the diachronic community), whose sufferings have produced a legacy we should respect, even as we critically explore why a particular view emerged contextually for them. The dialogue is also with our sisters and brothers in the present (the synchronic community), whose sufferings are a necessary expansion of our understanding of the scope and the meaning of faith in the world. In one of his last letters from prison before he was executed for his resistance to the Nazi tyranny, Dietrich Bonhoeffer pointed to this understanding of our relationship to God as the 'Body of Christ' in the world:

> I discovered later, and I'm still discovering right up to this moment, that it is only by living completely in this world that one learns to have faith... In so doing we throw ourselves completely into the arms of God, taking seriously, not our own sufferings, but those of God in the world — watching with Christ in Gethsemane. That, I think, is faith; that is *metanoia*.[8]

## A Specific Commitment

Throughout this chapter one assumption has been at work: that a contextual theology which takes seriously the praxis of ordinary Christians implies an acceptance of what has been widely referred to as the 'preferential option for the poor'. This commitment to a particular reality in life or, more accurately, to human beings whose reality is fundamentally shaped by poverty, oppression and marginalisation has been extensively argued elsewhere.[9]

I accept this commitment as definitive for any transformative contextual theology, even as I know that it has to be worked out in personal, spiritual and communal terms and not just in political terms. In what follows, on the basis of this commitment, I want to argue for the importance of the production of theology out of local base ecclesial communities, and to suggest a model by which they may find a recognisable, systematically integrated place in the construction of theologies for the wider ecumenical community.

## Incipient Theologies

Elsewhere, in a different context, I have argued that a contextual theology will be related overtly to our place in the social hierarchy, and that we need to uncover the effect of our social location on our current perceptions and practices. I have also said that our perspective, in part inevitably shaped by our social location, will condition the kind of theology we will produce.[10]

I am a trained, highly educated theologian whose faith could never again be that of an 'ordinary, untrained' Christian. Everything I am part of and heir to drives me to 'do theology' in a way which reproduces the intellectual and practical domination of the ecclesial elite over those whose faith works at the level of popular religion, at the grassroots, in base Christian communities.

What do my challenges mean for me or, indeed, for anyone charged with leadership in the church, especially where leadership is exercised with more respect for the thoughts and views of privileged and educated members than for the earthy faith and simple but often profound wisdom of illiterate Christians in an informal settlement?

One implication is this: I can use my skills and training to assist in articulating and systematising whatever persuasive theology arising from 'the people' may emerge in South Africa; but I cannot produce this theology without beginning with 'the people' and their local context. I could try by simply relying on what had been written by others elsewhere and through time, by drawing on the books and documents of scholars and theologians who have shaped the historical tradition and the present academic debate.

But then any theology 'for the people, of the people' I would produce would be artificial, imposed upon the real conditions and experiences of the life of ordinary people in South Africa. This is essentially anti-theological: first, because my dialogue would be limited to those I regard as having 'acceptable' theological credentials; and second, because I would be giving a privileged status to my world of experience and reflection upon faith above that of those who suffer more profoundly than I.

Theology only becomes real to those who actually suffer poverty, oppression and marginalisation in any society if it also connects with the quite specific material and historical conditions which shape their local contexts of life. It is from this 'base' that the living force of any adequate contextual theology will have to come.

Indeed, theology is not absent from this base, in so far as ordinary Christians reflect upon their faith in the light of their daily experiences and struggle for existence. Their reflection may be, and usually is, that of the theologically untrained mind. It may be naïve and pre-critical; it may be unsystematic and scattered; it may draw incongruently on a range of symbols, rituals, narratives and ideas which express the encounter with the sacred. In these senses, the theology present in communities of ordinary Christians may be seen as incipient rather than overtly articulated. But it remains nevertheless theology.

It is this incipient theology which I claim to be the necessary starting point for an authentic contextual theology. But, as I have tried to show in the kind of story represented by the women of Mpophomeni in their understanding of Mary, this incipient theology is formed by the tradition and also alters the tradition. In addition, it is left weak and marginalised if the wisdom and insight it contains remain locked into one local context. It must, for the edification of the church in the first place and for correction in the second place, enter into the wider dialogue (synchronic and diachronic) by which the community of faith knows the meaning of God present in Jesus Christ. In order for this to happen, I suggest that theology would have to be constructed at different levels, each level building upon the others. I consider this the appropriate way to reach a method for constructing a contextual theology.

I choose to call this method a 'gestalt of theological construction'. Its essential feature is the integration of different levels of theological reflection into a whole which is greater than its parts (the meaning of gestalt). Its starting point remains the local community. Its commitment is shaped by the 'epistemological privilege of the poor'.[11]

## A Gestalt of Theological Construction

The 'whole of theology which is greater than its parts' begins with the faith of ordinary, untrained Christians who struggle in life against all those forces of death that threaten life, spiritual and bodily life. Their faith experiences and the way they think about them must be taken seriously as data for the wider theological reflection of the church.

This is not to suggest we will find among ordinary, untrained Christians some full-blown or even conscious theology which we now simply accept. But it does mean that theology takes into its intellectual heart, as seriously as the reflection of scholars and ecclesial leaders, the life context of the ordinary people of God: their struggles, their wisdom, their insight into the darkness and the lightness of faith. Where faith touches the practical realities of the daily lives of the suffering, celebrating people of God, there theology begins in order to find its intellectual source of life and the corrections it needs to the deadliness of forcing the formulations of the past on the needs of the present.

Central to the task of constructing a contextual theology, therefore, is local theology: the scattered reflections by local base communities, which are the way they think about the meaning and significance of their faith in relation to the struggles and hopes of their daily lives, and the practices which communicate these reflections (including ritual and symbolic practices). But this local theology is only a beginning point. A 'local theology' will be cut off from the larger Body of Christ unless it enters into conversation with others by which it may edify the church and be edified by its relation to the wider community.

This is the mark of any enduring theology, that it is communal and has universal intent. So a local theology requires what I will call a communal theology, a larger framework of dialogue and of explanation into which it fits, and within which it might become edifying or prophetic for the church.

Beyond this, however, local theologies, mediated communally to the wider church, will challenge and alter the tradition. At a theological level, this implies that reflection upon faith at the local level, enriched and corrected by dialogue with the wider Christian community, should be able to enter into our very understanding of who Jesus Christ is for us today, what kind of God is revealed in this Christ, what kind of church is adequate to the mission which this revelation will call forth, and so on. In other words, it should be able to affect the foundations of our faith claims. This is what I call a foundational theology, a meta-level of explanation and formulation in which the fundamentals of our faith are questioned and clarified again.

Now it should be noted that a great many people experience the impact of theology through the assertion of fundamentals in the first place. An example: 'This is what the faith proclaims, that you must be twice born in the Spirit truly to receive the gifts and grace of God.' Beginning with this fundamental claim, the theologian (educator or cleric or lay leader) then proceeds to test whether or not any local Christian meets the claim. If so, then they are confirmed as believers. If not, then they are scolded, alienated or regarded as heretical. This is the direct opposite of the method I am seeking, which seeks to give maximum weight to the actual faith experiences and reflections of the ordinary believer.

The fourth level, therefore, I describe as a missiological theology. It is the proclamation of what has been learned about the present significance of the Christian faith through the process I have described. It is the proclamation of a foundational theology which is capable of helping people grasp the full significance and extent of their faith, but which remains methodologically (and not just in principle) open to continuous correction from the ongoing life and practice of 'the people'. Then it has the capacity to communicate good news, because it has the capacity to affirm the reality of those to whom it is addressed, even as it offers ways of correcting error, clearing up misunderstanding and challenging commitment.

What this approach or gestalt implies is that the task of constructing an indigenous contextual theology requires an integration of popular religion, tradition and criticism. Trained scholars and clerics or lay leaders will have a different role from prescribing or dictating which 'truths' others should know or accept.

They will have the task, in the first place, of listening to the voices of the ordinary, untrained people on the margins of society, whose lives and experiences profoundly challenge and question the easy assumptions of lives of privilege and power, and who prevent us from sitting on comfortable pews.

They will have the task, in the second place, of encouraging those with skills to do the phenomenological work necessary to capturing the faith-in-relation-to-life of base Christian communities, and to use their skills and training at the meta-level — that is, the level of secondary reflection and analysis of what had been discovered in collaboration with the local community.

The empirical data they collect (in various forms) from local base communities of an oppressed people are the source of the local theology which I am seeking. The work they do in reflecting on their data and in discussing these data with others — including the local base communities concerned — using their own training and skills, is the beginning of communal theology. Not only does this empower local communities through a growing sense of the significance of their own experiences and reflections,[12] but it relates what is happening in one part of the Body of Christ to what is happening in other parts.

The next step is into the realm of foundational theology, where the implications of the theology produced in context are developed to correct, alter and, if necessary, discard fundamental, doctrinal claims about who God is, who Jesus Christ is, what the church is, what the nature and destiny of human life are, and so on.

If anything worthwhile at this level is to be achieved, it will be shown by the extent to which those who have produced the local theology upon which it depends recognise their own life and experience, are confirmed by it, and are challenged by it. Only then will the results show themselves to be a missiological theology of these and other similar base communities, with missionary significance for the church at large.

## Conclusion

To repeat what Tillich claimed, theology seeks to answer the questions which life poses. But this 'method of correlation', widely accepted and used by many others in one form or another, is deficient. It allows one to present theology as a relatively fixed set of answers, an orthodoxy ('right teaching'), derived from Scripture and tradition, which we need to learn and which we then apply in response to the questions we face. Much formal theological education assumes this approach.

Scripture and tradition are essential elements of any Christian theology. Without the stories, symbols, images and sayings linked to the origin of Christian understandings of the world, and without the subsequent history of those who have sought to demonstrate in word and deed what difference these understandings make in life, there is no Christian identity at all and thus no need for Christian theology.

But to leave Scripture or tradition alone as normative while treating the actual life of believers as nothing more than the occasion for an application of truths others have decided on elsewhere, perhaps in another time, is to restrict theology to the monologue of the guardians of tradition, directed at the believer who is presumed to having nothing substantial to add. I do not believe any profound theology in any period of Christian history emerged in that way, and I do not believe we need to train people today as if it did.

I am convinced that profound theological reflection emerges out of contexts of struggle and suffering by opening a dialogue between life and faith, by making theology properly dialectic. Life gives rise to questions which faith must answer, but the faith's answers are also affected quite directly by life, in the struggle of life for life, against the forces of death. They are not simply taken from the past, from the handed-down tradition, from the orthodoxies of others. On the contrary, the realities of life and death where people — even the earth itself — are broken and hurt may force us to confront and alter our worn orthodoxies, to reconstruct the tradition anew, to risk doubt for the sake of faith.

[1] S. Toulmin, *Cosmopolis: The Hidden Agenda of Modernity* (N.Y.: The Free Press: Macmillan, 1990), p. 175.

[2] R. Schreiter, *Constructing Local Theologies* (Maryknoll: Orbis, 1985).

[3] L. Maldonado, 'Popular Religion: Its Dimensions, Levels and Types', *Concilium*, 186 (1986), pp. 3–11.

[4] P. Richard (ed.), *The Idols of Death and the God of Life* (Maryknoll: Orbis, 1986).

[5] F. J. Hinkelammert, *The Ideological Weapons of Death: A Theological Critique of Capitalism* (Maryknoll: Orbis, 1986), p. 272.

[6] Megan Walker, 'Tradition, Criticism and Popular Religion: A Hermeneutical Investigation of Marian Theology' (Unpublished MA dissertation, University of Natal, Pietermaritzburg, 1992).

[7] Walker's work was done under my supervision; the categories she utilises (tradition, criticism and popular religion), reflected in the title of her dissertation, have been part of my work as well. For this reason I feel free to use the categories which define her dissertation. At the same time, I wish to note with special gratitude the value of her work for the particular topic with which this chapter deals.

[8] Dietrich Bonhoeffer, letter to Eberhard Bethge, 21 July 1944, reprinted in *Letters and Papers from Prison* (London: SCM, 1971), p. 369.

[9] A. Boesak, *Farewell to Innocence* (Kampen: Kok, 1976); C. Davis, *Theology and Political Society* (Cambridge: Cambridge University Press, 1980); A. Fierro, *The Militant Gospel* (Maryknoll: Orbis, 1977); P. Frostin, *Liberation Theology in Tanzania and South Africa: A First World Interpretation* (Sweden: Lund University Press, 1988); M. Lamb, *Solidarity with Victims: Toward a Theology of Social Transformation* (N.Y.: Crossroad, 1982); T. A. Mofokeng, *The Crucified Among the Crossbearers: Towards a Black Christology* (Kampen: Kok, 1983); S. Thistlethwaite and M. Potter Engel (eds.), *Constructing Christian Theologies from the Underside* (N.Y.: Harper and Row, 1990); M. Kline Taylor, *Remembering Esperanza: A Cultural–Political Theology for North American Praxis* (Maryknoll, N.Y.: Orbis, 1990).

[10] J. R. Cochrane, 'Already . . . But Not Yet: Parameters for a Theology of Work', in J. R. Cochrane and G. O. West (eds.), *The Three-fold Cord: Theology, Work and Labour* (Pietermaritzburg: Cluster Publications, 1991).

[11] Frostin, *Liberation Theology in Tanzania and South Africa*.

[12] M. de P. Mandew, 'Power and Empowerment: Religious Imagination and the Life of a Local Base Ecclesial Community' (Unpublished MTh thesis, University of Natal, 1993).

## Select Bibliography

Boesak, A. *Farewell to Innocence*. Kampen: Kok, 1976

Cochrane, J. R. 'Already . . . But Not Yet: Parameters for a Theology of Work'. In J. R. Cochrane and West, G.O. (eds.), *The Three-fold Cord: Theology, Work and Labour*. Pietermaritzburg: Cluster Publications, 1991

Davis, C. *Theology and Political Society*. Cambridge: Cambridge University Press, 1980

Fierro, A. *The Militant Gospel*. Maryknoll, N.Y.: Orbis, 1977

Frostin, P. *Liberation Theology in Tanzania and South Africa: A First World Interpretation*. Sweden: Lund University Press, 1988.

Hinkelammert, F. J. *The Ideological Weapons of Death: A Theological Critique of Capitalism*. Maryknoll, N.Y.: Orbis, 1986

Lamb, M. *Solidarity with Victims: Toward a Theology of Social Transformation*. N.Y.: Crossroad, 1982

Maldonado, L. 'Popular Religion: Its Dimensions, Levels and Types', *Concilium*, 186, 1986

Mandew, M. de P. 'Power and Empowerment: Religious Imagination and the Life of a Local Base Ecclesial Community'. Unpublished MTh thesis, University of Natal, 1983

Mofokeng, T. A. *The Crucified Among the Crossbearers: Towards a Black Christology*. Kampen: Kok, 1983

Richard, P. (ed.) *The Idols of Death and the God of Life*. Maryknoll, N.Y.: Orbis, 1986

Schreiter, R. *Constructing Local Theologies*. Maryknoll, N.Y.: Orbis, 1985

Taylor, M Kline. *Remembering Esperanza: A Cultural–Political Theology for North American Praxis*. Maryknoll, N.Y.: Orbis, 1990

Thistlethwaite, S. and M. Potter Engel (eds.) *Constructing Christian Theologies from the Underside*. N.Y.: Harper and Row, 1990

Toulmin, S. *Cosmopolis: The Hidden Agenda of Modernity*. N.Y.: The Free Press, Macmillan, 1990

Walker, Megan. 'Tradition, Criticism and Popular Religion: A Hermeneutical Investigation of Marian Theology'. Unpublished MA dissertation, University of Natal, Pietermaritzburg, 1992

# PART TWO
## The Doctrine of God

# 4

# The Self-Disclosure of God

## DIRKIE SMIT

In systematic theology, understanding a question is often as important as giving an answer. What do Christians say about the self-disclosure of God? Simply by phrasing our question in this way, we have already restricted ourselves in several ways. Firstly, we do not pretend to say who God is, in essence. We restrict ourselves to the self-disclosure of God. Secondly, we do not pretend to explain what this self-disclosure of God is in itself. We restrict ourselves to what Christians say, claim or think about the self-disclosure of God. Thirdly, we acknowledge that other people, from other religious traditions and communities, or people with other convictions, may have totally different ideas about God and the self-disclosure of God. We only ask what Christians say. Fourthly, we restrict ourselves to a question which calls for a descriptive answer and not a prescriptive one. We do not attempt to argue what Christians should say or ought to believe about the self-disclosure of God. We simply ask: What *do* they in fact say? Fifthly, that obviously implies that we restrict ourselves to a very general answer.

In our attempt to answer this very general question briefly, we shall focus on three aspects. In the first part, we shall consider what most Christians say about the *nature* of God's self-disclosure. In the second part, we shall remind ourselves of what most Christians claim about the *content* of God's self-disclosure. In the third part, we shall reflect on what most Christians say about present-day *experience* of God's self-disclosure.

### The Nature of God's Self-Disclosure According to Christians

What do most Christians say about the nature of God's self-disclosure? In thinking about this aspect of our question, we should remind ourselves of three convictions that are fairly widely accepted amongst Christians. The three are closely related to one another. The first is the conviction that God has been revealed in Jesus Christ. The second conviction, closely related to the first one, is that God's self-revelation is therefore 'story-shaped'. The third is the conviction that this story-shaped revelation has not been fully completed.

Let us first consider each of these convictions and some of their crucially important implications briefly, before we attempt to continue and answer the question about what Christians actually say about the content of this incomplete, story-shaped self-revelation of God in Jesus Christ.

## God Has Been Revealed in Jesus Christ

In the first place, most Christians claim that God is revealed in Jesus Christ. That is why we are called Christians. It may even seem unnecessary to argue this point. Indeed, in his authoritative study *Models of Revelation*, Avery Dulles concludes, with reference to the Catholic Church:

> The special identification of revelation with Christ is almost a common-place among modern theologians. Vatican II articulated a widespread consensus when it declared, in its Constitution on Revelation, 'Jesus Christ is the mediator and at the same time the fullness of all revelation. . . Many theologians . . . agree that the revelation is supremely, or even exclusively, given in Christ. . .'[1]

At first sight, the claim may seem obvious. It simply says that Christians have come to know God in Jesus Christ, so that when Christians say anything about God, they must be able to show, in the light of Jesus Christ, *why* they make such a claim.

This claim is, however, not so obvious and generally accepted within Christianity as it may seem. The questions concern what people actually mean when they say that God is disclosed in Jesus Christ, and (perhaps even more important) what they want to deny, to oppose, when they make that claim.

Firstly, what Christians mean when they make this claim has often in history been influenced by other sources, whether philosophical, cultural, religious or something else. This process started in the New Testament times and is already reflected in the New Testament documents. The reason is easy to see. Through the centuries, Christianity continually came into contact with new groups, cultures, philosophies, religions, ideologies or whatever. Time and again, the Christians, in their attempts to try to explain the Christian message to people in terms, ideas, concepts and experiences which the people could understand and relate to, took over some of these influences and ideas. Sometimes these influences have had a very strong impact on Christians' thinking about God, on the way they portray God, speak about God, the names they prefer for God, what they expect from God, how they celebrate God's presence in the liturgy, and so forth.

Perhaps the best example is the enormous influence which classical Greek philosophical thought has exercised on Christian thinking and talk about God. This influence is still actively present and powerful in Christian circles. Many of the things Christians say and believe about God do not originate in God's revelation in Jesus Christ, but come directly from Greek thought. And many Christians are unaware that this result, which is of major importance for the question we are thinking about, is obvious. We often say that God is disclosed in Jesus Christ, but in actual fact much or most of what we actually say and believe about God may come from totally different sources, from other cultures, from other philosophies, from other ideologies, of which we may be utterly and honestly unaware.

In recent decades, so-called contextual theologies have helped us to understand this better, to become more aware of this. They have underlined the fact that *all* theology, all thinking and speaking about God, is contextual, is influenced by the contexts in which the believers live, including the so-called traditional theology of Western Christianity in all its forms. Feminist theologies have also drawn attention to the ways in which the patriarchal culture, thought, speech and lifestyles of male-dominated societies have influenced Christian thinking and talk about God.

Even when we claim that God's self-disclosure is in Jesus Christ, we may actually be looking at the Christ-event with our own strongly coloured glasses, without knowing it, and therefore making claims about God that in reality come from different sources.

Secondly, this claim has often been used polemically, to contradict and deny other claims about God. Christians have then said that God is revealed in Jesus Christ and not in other ways. In fact, during the time of the Reformation the Reformers used this claim in such a polemical way, against both the Catholic Church and the so-called *Schwärmer.*[2] According to the Reformers, the one group saw the authoritative tradition of the church as revelatory, while the other saw the indwelling of the Holy Spirit in individual believers as revelatory.

One well-known, more recent example of such a polemical use of this claim has been the struggle of the Confessing Church in Nazi Germany. The so-called German Christians claimed that God was revealed in history, through God's providential care, in the fate of the German people. The Confessing Church rejected this as 'natural theology', as opposed to theology on the basis of 'revelation' (in Jesus Christ). In the Barmen Declaration, which rejected the teachings of the German Christians as false and heretical, the argument rests time and again on the claim that God has been revealed in Jesus Christ and *not* in history, or in the people, or in nature, or in human reason, or in human experience.

Today we face the same questions, for example in the so-called inter-faith dialogue, where Christians meet other believers from other religious traditions and communities with different claims about God's revelation, and particularly in our African context, when Christianity meets traditional African religions.

Keeping in mind, therefore, that it is indeed a widespread, almost generally accepted conviction amongst Christians that God is disclosed in Jesus Christ, but that much will depend on both the *content* (what do we mean?) and the particular *thrust* (what do we want to oppose and deny?) of this claim, we move to the first important implication.

*Revelation Is Story-Shaped*

Since God has been revealed in Jesus Christ, Christians have access to this revelation in the form of a story. God's self-disclosure is, in the first place, story-shaped, narrative in nature. This is the first important implication that we should keep in mind.

When Christians want to answer the question who God is, they tell the story of God-in-Jesus-Christ. Obviously, this story must be taken in a very broad sense. At its heart is the resurrection of Jesus Christ, with which Christianity started.

Without Christ's resurrection, there would have been no Christian faith or Christian church. Many New Testament documents bear witness to the fact that the first 'definition' that Christians used to describe and proclaim their God before the world was the One who had raised Jesus from the dead. The resurrection of Jesus was not only a disclosure of God's approval and a demonstration of God's power, but also of God's heart, will, character and nature.

The resurrection of Christ, however, was so meaningful to them precisely because the *Crucified* One had been raised. In the resurrection, the Christians claimed, God vindicated the crucified Jesus. The resurrection made the Cross important. And so the passion stories came to be written and told. The Cross, in its turn, made the stories about Jesus' life important. What made the resurrection of the Crucified One so important was precisely that it was *this* One whom they knew, whom they followed, whom they loved, that was raised by God. And so the gospels came eventually to be compiled and written. They were telling, already in different ways and with differing emphases, the story of God's self-disclosure in Jesus Christ.

Jesus Christ's story, however, could only be understood as an integral part, as a direct continuation, of the story of God's earlier history of self-revelation, told in the books which Christians used from the beginning and which they later called the Old Testament. Hence in order to understand God, Christians said, one should understand the resurrection; in order to understand the resurrection, one should understand the Cross; in order to understand the Cross, one should understand the life, words and works of Jesus; in order to understand the life, words and works of Jesus, one should understand the traditions of the Christian Old Testament.

Very soon, however, in different places, under changing circumstances and to diverse audiences, the Christians tried to tell this story of their God's self-disclosure in Jesus Christ in different ways, by making use of different notions, traditions, thought categories, expressions and images, and by ever anew addressing new questions and challenges. Very soon, these attempts themselves became part of the story. In the Acts of the Apostles, which one can just as well call the Acts of the Holy Spirit, or the Acts of the Risen Christ, or the Acts of the Early Church, this story is deliberately continued by Luke. In the rest of the documents of the New Testament we find further examples of the continuation of this story, themselves becoming major, integral, foundational, normative parts of the story of God's self-disclosure in Jesus Christ for future generations of Christians.

For this reason, mainline Christianity almost always regarded the whole biblical drama not only as fundamental but also as normative for its own thinking and speaking about God. According to these Christians, the self-disclosure of God in Jesus Christ is somehow at the heart of the authoritative Holy Scriptures. About the way in which this authority must be understood, Christians have had major differences of opinion.

In the history of Christianity, the story was told in many other ways and forms: in liturgies and short credal statements; in other 'gospels', 'letters' and 'testaments'; in prayers and hymns; in confessions and oral traditions; in symbols and signs; in official decisions and doctrines; in the rejection of heresies; in the lives of martyrs, saints and other Christians; and later in books, confessional documents and in theologies.

None of these can ever replace the original self-disclosure of God in Jesus Christ. Of course, people can develop other ideas about God. Millions of people do. But they will not be specifically *Christian* ideas. Any claim that the Christian God is such-and-such must be able, in some way or other, to appeal to the story of God's self-disclosure in Jesus Christ. There, Christians claim to have seen God's character, nature and heart.

It is therefore important that we add the words 'in the first place' when we say that God's self-disclosure is story-shaped, or narrative in form. That simply means that all these other forms in which we today also encounter God's self-disclosure — such as doctrines, symbols, rituals, creeds and confessions — all *presuppose* the narrative, 'the story of God in Jesus Christ'. For example, even the most abstract, theoretical, doctrinal or philosophical statement calls for some kind of narrative explanation. Even when Christians say that God is triune, what that means can only be answered by referring back, in some or other way, to the story of Jesus Christ.

Perhaps we could say that this aspect of the nature of God's self-disclosure in Jesus Christ makes our God-talk pluriform. In itself that does not pose a problem for Christians. In fact, exactly the same is true when we try to answer the question about the identity of any human person as well. If we should ask ten people about someone else, whom they all knew well, 'Who was that person?', we shall receive many different answers. Some will remember this, some may remember that. Some may emphasise this, others may emphasise that. Sometimes they may even disagree. What they say and what they remember may all be true, but still it will not give us a complete picture of the person and, more important, in many ways their true accounts may be different from one another. That different Christian groups, traditions and communities, and also individual Christians, speak in different ways about the same God, revealed in Jesus Christ, is no problem in itself. In fact, it simply reminds us of the personal and story-shaped nature of this self-disclosure.

Obviously, in our example, there are limits to what can legitimately be said about the person. One cannot claim that the person was something or did something which she or he obviously never was or did not do. In the same way, whatever Christians say about the God who has been revealed in Jesus Christ must be in accordance with this self-disclosure. Within that story, however, a rich pluriformity of emphases must be accepted as possible and legitimate.

*Revelation Is Not Yet Complete*

A second extremely important implication of the fact that Christians say that God has been revealed in Jesus Christ is that God has not been fully revealed to us finally, completely. We still look in a glass darkly. We are saved in hope. Hope does not see. We trust in the things we hope for, unseen things. The kingdom must still come. Jesus Christ must still return. We live in the 'in-between' times, in the 'not yet'. The story has not reached its conclusion. God, although revealed, remains hidden. God remains a mystery to us. 'If you can understand it, it's not God,' said the famous North African theologian Augustine of Hippo.

All these expressions are well known to Christians. The implications for our question are, however, enormous, and we do not always take them seriously enough. It means that this story can always also be told in different ways, explained in different ways, understood in different ways. In the gospel of Matthew (27:62–66; 28:11–15) he deliberately warns the readers that there are also other 'stories', alongside his own account in the gospel, giving other explanations of what happened with the body of Jesus, thereby contradicting or denying his own account of the resurrection. And that is the point: whatever Christians say about God, on the basis of the revelation in the story of Jesus Christ, can always be contradicted, denied, questioned. People may always also find good reason to question, doubt or reject it.

The nature of God's self-disclosure in the story of Jesus Christ, according to Christians, is such that it can be questioned and contradicted. It is not self-evident, overwhelming, verified, in the sense that no other interpretation of what happened and is still happening can be offered. We do not see God face to face. We do not know God directly. When we speak about God, we therefore search for words, for images, for metaphors. We are at a loss for words. Our language is inadequate. Our talk about God is always ambiguous. What we say is often, at the same time, true *and* false.

In the history of Christianity, Christians have used many expressions to emphasise this aspect of the nature of God's self-disclosure. Many theologians have underlined the inadequacy of our knowledge and our talk of God. Some went so far as to say that we should rather remain silent. Martin Luther, the Reformer, said that God has been revealed *sub contrario*, under God's opposite, anonymous, masked, in an alien form. We do not yet see God in glory, as God is, but on the Cross, as God is present in our world. The result, said Luther, is that our knowledge of God remains a *theologia crucis*, a knowledge of and talk about God from the perspective of the Cross. We cannot, yet, practise a *theologia gloriae*, a theology in which we know God and speak about God in glory, the way God really and fully is.

What we see or experience therefore often contradicts what we say about God. It is for this reason that Luther said Christian faith means 'not to see the things we see and to see the things we do not see'. What Christians claim about their God, they claim on account of what has been told, what has been proclaimed to them in the story of God's self-disclosure in Jesus Christ and not on account of what they or others see or experience. In fact, they often confess these convictions and cling to them as promises *in spite of* what they or others see and experience. Perhaps we should say that this *theologia crucis* aspect of the nature of God's self-disclosure in Jesus Christ makes all our God-talk extremely ambiguous.

## The Content of God's Self-Disclosure According to Christians

What do Christians say in their pluriform and ambiguous God-talk about this God, who has been revealed in this still incomplete and unfulfilled story of Jesus Christ?

*Ecumenical Creeds*

In the ecumenical movement the 'Faith and Order' section of the World Council of Churches has spent the past few decades talking about 'confessing the apostolic faith today'. This search has had many stages and directions, and many documents have been produced. This is not the proper place to talk about them. What does concern us, however, is the fact that one of the tasks undertaken by the ecumenical movement has been to try to find a common, ecumenically accepted Christian confession of faith. Eventually it was decided to use the text of the old ecumenical creed, the Nicene–Constantinopolitan Creed (AD 381), the only creed accepted by almost all Christian churches, including the Orthodox churches. Several attempts have been made to explain this ancient creed in a present-day way, in the hope that most Christian churches will agree with this explanation or interpretation. During 1993, at the first full meeting of Faith and Order in more than thirty years, representatives from all member churches met to discuss this creed and its interpretation.

What does the Nicene–Constantinopolitan Creed say about God? Like the Apostles' Creed, it is structured according to a trinitarian framework. Perhaps the most basic and the most traditional answer to the question is therefore that the Nicene Creed (as it is popularly known) speaks of God as the triune God. In fact, the Nicene Creed was formulated in a direct attempt to solve the trinitarian controversy in the early church and to answer the question, Who is God?[3] According to the structure of this book, a later chapter will deal specifically with the answer to this question, following two other chapters dealing with Christ and the Holy Spirit. We therefore limit ourselves here to the Christian doctrine of God in a more specific or limited sense, dealing primarily with the first person of the Trinity. What does the Nicene Creed say about this first divine person?[4]

The answer can be brief. The Nicene Creed calls God 'Father'. The Creed, short as it is, uses the expression 'Father' no less than six times. In doing so, the Creed is using the title or name for God most commonly found in the New Testament writings and used in the gospels by Jesus himself. In the gospels, God is called 'Father' on no less than 245 occasions, and of these Jesus himself used the expression 170 times. What is particularly striking is that Jesus used this expression as a form of direct address to God, in prayer. This kind of praying to the Father, to *Abba*, at once became generally current in early Christianity. Small wonder that many theologians, like the influential Dutch Catholic scholar Schillebeeckx, have argued that Jesus' own experience of God as Father, his *Abba* experience, was 'the source and secret of his being, of his message and his manner of life'.

So, we have ourselves given a story-shaped answer to our question. We have reminded ourselves of what ecumenical Christianity says about the content of God's self-disclosure in Jesus Christ, and noted that the ecumenical movement appeals to the early apostolic, catholic tradition, which in turn followed Jesus himself, the Jesus of the gospels. For Christians, God has always been *Abba*, Father.

In saying this, however, we are immediately confronted with the ambiguity of our God-talk. For many present-day Christians, who have grown up in a 'fatherless' society, where the father does not play the key role that fathers played in the time of Jesus, it is no longer meaningful to call God 'Father'. The term 'father' is pluriform, ambivalent; it means different things to different people, and to many it does not mean much at all. The expression has lost its revelatory power for many people, and has become obsolete for them.

In fact, many people, especially women, have had such negative experiences with a male- and father-dominated society that they totally reject the notion that God is a 'Father'. This notion is patriarchal and oppressive, they argue. Feminist theology urges the Christian tradition and community of faith to find a new language, to find new models, metaphors and expressions, that can more adequately express what they believe about God, the God who has been revealed in Jesus Christ.

### The Early Christians and 'God the Father'

So, what did the early Christians mean when they called God 'Father'? Why did they find the expression meaningful? It is rather difficult to answer this question. Obviously, there were many different reasons. The expression 'father' is rich in meaning, and different Christians and Christian groups probably adopted it as designation for the God disclosed in Jesus Christ for different reasons.

Let us consider briefly five possible meanings that early Christians recognised in this name for God. Each time it will be clear that there were many elements in the story of Jesus Christ that made this a meaningful, yet ambiguous name for God — ambiguous because the full truth is still hidden from us.

A first possibility is that the early Christians heard in the name 'Father' overtones of power, strength, ability. To them, a father was powerful, able, capable, one who could help and who did help. There were many important reasons for understanding the Christ-event in this way. We have already said that the Christian faith started with the resurrection of Jesus Christ — God's triumphant victory over the powers of sin, law, Satan and death. To Jesus Christ has been given all power in heaven and on earth. He now sits at the right hand of God, God the Father. 'Right hand' means power or ability. This is a basic idea in the whole of the gospel. God is able. For God, nothing is impossible. God is the One who calls life from death, who creates something from nothing. A variety of Old Testament traditions about God's power come together in this notion. In the rest of the New Testament writings, the power of the God of Jesus Christ plays a crucial role.

Therefore, when Christians confess that God is the Father they can mean that God is powerful, God is able, God is capable of doing things, God rules, God is in command, God is the Lord of all and everything, the *pantokrator*, the Almighty, as the Nicene Creed says.

A second possibility is that the early Christians used the name Father in order to express God's love. Again, there is ample evidence in the Christ-story to lead to this conclusion. Many theologians have even argued that the expression *Abba* itself was used by small children, and points to intimacy and affection, but others disagree. Still, in the incarnation itself New Testament documents have already recognised the love of God for humanity. In his words Jesus proclaimed this love, and through his actions, his miracles and also his meals with the outcast he demonstrated this love. Ultimately, in his death on the Cross he defined love, says

John. Again, the early Christians understood this to be in line with the revelation of God in the Old Testament history and documents.[5] In the writings of the New Testament and the early church this love of God is confessed and proclaimed in a wide variety of ways.

Therefore, when Christians confess that God is the Father they can also mean that in Jesus Christ God is disclosed as love and grace, as the God of widows, orphans and strangers, as the One who cares for the poor, the suffering and downtrodden, as the One who forgives and saves.

A third possibility is that the name Father carries the meaning of giver of life, origin of life, creator and re-creator. It is not surprising that the Nicene Creed immediately after 'Father' adds the words 'the creator of heaven and earth'.

In the story of Jesus Christ, God is indeed disclosed as the God of life, as the giver of life and the protector of life. Jesus came so that we can have life in abundance. Major images used to depict the salvation in Christ demonstrate this, for example eternal life, or the new heaven and earth. God's struggle in Christ is against the powers of death and destruction. His final victory is the resurrection, whereby the ultimate enemy, death, is slain. Once again, these notions originate in the Old Testament traditions. The law, the prophets, the Wisdom literature, all Old Testament traditions emphasise, in a wide variety of ways, that God is a God of life. Therefore, when Christians confess that God is the Father they definitely include this aspect as well.

A fourth possibility is that the God disclosed in Jesus Christ was called Father because of God's care, protection, assistance and help.

In the story of Jesus Christ the early Christians found many grounds for this fundamental trust in God's care and protection. In fact, very often when he is speaking about God's care, Jesus calls God 'Father'. The disciples should not be worried, anxious or afraid because the Father cares. The disciples can pray with confidence and faith because the Father hears and answers. The disciples should not fear other people because the Father knows every hair on their heads. Once again, these convictions are deeply rooted in the Old Testament traditions about the God who was disclosed as 'the One who will be there for them' (Exodus), the One who saved, protected and cared. Moving pictures of this caring God are given by the prophets. In the Psalms, pleas from the depths of suffering and need are expressed to this God. In the New Testament documents these convictions come to the fore in many different ways: James, Hebrews, 1 Peter and Revelation all tell the story of the God in Jesus Christ who protects and cares and saves, amidst suffering and hardships. Therefore, when Christians confess that God is the Father they often mean that God cares, protects and saves like a father.

A fifth possibility is that the early Christians wanted to underscore God's holiness. In a patriarchal society 'father' can also imply authority, distance, respect. The term 'father' can be associated with law, order, justice, obedience, and authoritarian structures. The designation that God the Father 'is in heaven' may carry precisely these overtones. In the Lord's Prayer, called the 'Our Father' and very highly valued by early Christians, we are taught to pray that the Father's name may be 'hallowed'. On the lips of Jesus, we often hear about the Father's will, the justice of God, and the final day of reckoning. According to early

Christian understanding, the suffering and the death of Jesus on the Cross all have to do with God's holiness and justice. The very important political metaphor of the kingdom of God also points in this direction. Clearly, this is in continuity with Old Testament portrayals of God, the One and Only God, the Holy One of Israel, the Law-giver, the jealous One, the Judge, the One to be 'feared'. In the New Testament writings, we encounter similar ideas on many occasions. The final fulfilment of the Jesus-story is often portrayed in exactly these terms.

When Christians confess that God is the Father they can indeed also mean that God is the Holy One, the Law-giver and Judge of the world, the Lord over all history, the King of kings, the One to be respected, feared and obeyed.

### God and the Cross

Christians always confess all of this, however, through a glass darkly. They often see and experience the opposite. They know, believe and claim this in a *theologia crucis*, from the perspective of the Cross. The story of Jesus Christ is not yet complete. We know God *sub contrario*. We so often live, in the well-known words of Dietrich Bonhoeffer, *etsi Deus non daretur*, as if God is not there.

Christians confess that God the Father is disclosed as powerful, but they often experience the opposite. They confess that God the Father is disclosed as loving-kindness, but they live in a world where they do not see this love at work. They confess that God the Father is disclosed as the Giver of life, but they suffer continually under the power of the idols of death and destruction. They confess that God the Father cares and protects, but they daily see only the misery and need of millions of human beings in the world, and the destruction of creation itself. They confess that God the Father is just and holy, and punishes evil-doers and the injustices perpetrated against God's will, but they see the evil-doers, the oppressors and the violent people of this world unconstrained in doing whatever they want to. Small wonder that to many people this is just another story, in addition to so many others, another myth and another perspective, in addition to so many others.

Indeed Christians have often taken over from other stories, societies, cultures, philosophies, religions and ideologies different notions of power, love, abundant life, happiness, trust, spirituality, holiness and justice from those revealed in Jesus Christ. Many people reject these particular constructions of God the Father as unacceptable images of salvation, liberation and good news.

Hence many of the most important discussions taking place in Christian theology today have to do with these issues, with the language, images and metaphors Christians use to re-tell the story of God's self-disclosure in Jesus Christ.

## The Experience of God's Self-Disclosure According to Christians

How can present-day Christians still participate in this story? How can we hear this story and share in it, become part of this story of God's self-disclosure in Jesus Christ? How can we know this God in Jesus Christ? The answer is obvious. Because it is a story, remembering plays a crucial role; and because the story is unfulfilled, hope becomes critical. Christians become part of this story through remembrance and hope.

*Hearing the Story in Community*

Where do we hear this story and become part of it? The answer is: primarily in the worship of the Christian community of faith. In the preaching of the Word and the sacraments, in the celebrations and rituals, in the prayers and songs of the Christian worship, in their praise and in their laments, Christians remember and hope, and in so doing encounter God in Christ. It is therefore not surprising that many ecumenically minded theologians have emphasised the central place of worship in the knowledge of God. A few illustrations can suffice.

In an epoch–making sociological study of the church 'as a human community', *Treasure in Earthen Vessels,* James Gustafson pointed to the fundamental role of worship in the church's life as 'a community of understanding':

> Common memory makes possible common life... The community keeps
> its common memory alive by continually rehearsing the important events
> of its history. The reading of the Bible is one means by which Christians
> understand and relive the past. The Christian Year in the worship life
> of the community is a dramatic presentation of the history of the most
> significant events surrounding Jesus Christ.[6]

In his equally important work, *The Logic of Theology*, Dietrich Ritschl reminds us that it is in genuine worship that Christians celebrate 'the over-arching story in which what is of lasting importance is contained and from which what is of momentary urgency can be seen again. Here theology discovers its tasks and problems, and here it must also prove itself in preparatory clarification and in subsequent criticism and self-reflection.' He goes on to say, 'The "subject matter" about which Jews and Christians speak in their services is ultimately understood by them to be the living God.'[7]

Geoffrey Wainwright likewise develops the whole of Christian doctrine and life, a complete systematic theology, from the perspective of worship and liturgy, in his well-known *Doxology*:

> Worship is ... the point of concentration at which the whole of the
> Christian life comes to ritual focus... If the word liturgy is allowed to retain
> from its etymology the sense of 'the work of the people', it hints at the focal
> place and function which I ascribe to worship in the Christian life as a
> whole. Into the liturgy the people bring their entire existence so that it may
> be gathered up in praise. From the liturgy the people depart with a renewed
> vision of the value-patterns of God's kingdom, by the more effective
> practice of which they intend to glorify God in their whole life.'[8]

*Knowing God and Prayer*

If worship is so central to our participation in the Christian story and therefore our knowledge of God, the crucial role of prayer, at the heart of our worship, must be particularly emphasised. As Ritschl suggests, talk to God is more important than talk about God. The real experience of the story of God in Jesus Christ takes place in prayer, when the Christian community addresses God, remembering God by past deeds and appealing, in hope, for new salvation.

Christian theology and Christian thought about God have their roots in Christian worship and prayer, in liturgy and spirituality, where the story is narrated and celebrated ever anew and where Christians respond in addressing God. Small wonder that the most important Hebrew word describing the true knowledge of God has to do with 'love', 'intimacy', 'relationship', 'community', 'intercourse'.

## Knowing God and Obedience

Knowing God in Christ in this way, remembering, celebrating and hoping, or praying, praising and pleading, involves the worshippers themselves. It requires commitment, dedication, discipleship. Knowing the God who has been disclosed in Jesus Christ is not a theoretical, abstract, academic exercise. It does not occur in the first place by way of study and reflection about God. It calls for faith and commitment. Faith and commitment, however, are two sides of the same coin. Becoming part of the story of God in Jesus Christ requires both. Knowing this God implies saying 'our Father' *and* living accordingly.

[1] A. Dulles, *Models of Revelation* (Garden City: Doubleday and Co., 1983), p. 155.

[2] That is, Anabaptists and other radical groups.

[3] See, for a brief, introductory discussion. D. K. McKim, *Theological Turning Points. Major Issues in Christian Thought* (Atlanta: John Knox Press, 1988), pp. 4–21.

[4] The expression 'person' is in itself an excellent example of the problems we are speaking about. What the Greek-thinking Council meant when they used the expression and what we understand when we use the expression are worlds apart. In fact, one can even say that what we understand when we hear the expression 'three persons' is exactly what they wanted to reject as heretical! Our language is simply not adequate. Our God-talk remains pluriform and ambiguous.

[5] In fact, a major controversy took place around the figure of Marcion, who claimed that the God of the Old Testament was different from the God of love of Jesus Christ (and of some New Testament documents), so that the early church consciously and deliberately affirmed this identity and rejected Marcion's teachings.

[6] J. Gustafson, *Treasure in Earthen Vessels* (Chicago: University of Chicago Press, 1976), pp. 73–74.

[7] D. Ritschl, *The Logic of Theology* (Philadelphia: Fortress Press, 1984), p. 98.

[8] G. Wainwright, *Doxology. The Praise of God in Worship, Doctrine, and Life* (New York: Oxford University Press, 1980), p. 8.

## Select Bibliography

Berkhof, H. *Christian Faith.* Grand Rapids: Eerdmans, 1979

Boff, L. *Trinity and Society.* Maryknoll: Orbis Press, 1988

Braaten, C. E. (ed.) *Our Naming of God. Problems and Prospects of God-Talk Today.* Minneapolis: Fortress Press, 1989

Case-Winter, A. *God's Power. Traditional Understandings and Contemporary Challenges.* Louisville: Westminster/John Knox Press, 1990

Cone, J. *God of the Oppressed.* New York: Seabury Press, 1975

De Margerie, B. *The Christian Trinity in History.* Petersham, Mass., 1981

Duck, R. C. *Gender and the Name of God. The Trinitarian Baptismal Formula.* New York: Pilgrim Press, 1991

Dulles, A. *Models of Revelation.* Garden City, N.Y.: Doubleday, 1983

Durand, J. J. F. *Die Lewende God.* Pretoria: NGKB, 1985

Green, G. *Imagining God. Theology and the Religious Imagination*. San Francisco: Harper and Row, 1989

Jones, M. J. *The Color of God. The Concept of God in Afro-American Thought*. Macon: Mercer University Press, 1987

Kasper, W. *The God of Jesus Christ*. New York: Crossroad, 1984

König, A. *Hier Is Ek!* Pretoria: NGKB, 1975.

Küng, H. *Does God Exist? An Answer for Today*. Garden City: Doubleday, 1980

McFague, S. *Models of God. Theology for an Ecological, Nuclear Age*. Philadelphia: Fortress Press, 1987

McFague, S. *Metaphorical Theology. Models of God in Religious Language*. Philadelphia, Fortress Press, 1982

McGrath, A. *Understanding the Trinity*. Eastbourne: Kingsway Publications, 1987

Migliore, D. L. *The Power of God*. Philadelphia: Westminster Press, 1983.

Miller, J. W. *Biblical Faith and Fathering. Why We Call God 'Father'*. New York: Paulist Press, 1989

Moltmann, J. *The Trinity and the Kingdom of God*. London: SCM Press, 1981

Niebuhr, H. Richard. *The Meaning of Revelation*. New York: Macmillan Publishing, 1941

Richard, P. *The Idols of Death and the God of Life*. Maryknoll: Orbis Press, 1983

Steuer, A. D. and W. J. McClendon Jr (eds.) *Is God God?* Nashville: Abingdon, 1981

Study Commission of the British Council of Churches on Trinitarian Doctrine Today. *The Forgotten Trinity*. London: BCC, 1989

The World Council of Churches: Faith and Order Commission. *Confessing the One Faith. An ecumenical Explication of the Apostolic Faith As It Is Confessed in the Nicene–Constantinopolitan Creed (381)*. Geneva: WCC, 1991

# 5

# Jesus the Christ

## STEVE DE GRUCHY

Christology, or the doctrine of Jesus Christ, is the central doctrine of the Christian faith, and therefore the position we take here will have a decisive influence upon our theology and Christian life as a whole, and vice versa.

For example, in 1992 the Church of the Province of Southern Africa (Anglican) debated the question of the ordination of women to the priesthood. One of the central arguments against such ordination was that a woman could not represent Jesus Christ at the altar because the maleness of Jesus was critical. Opponents of the ordination of women spoke about the 'scandal of particularity', meaning that Jesus was a particular person at a particular time in history. If one starts to strip away the concrete details of who Jesus was, such as his maleness, then in the end, so it was argued, the historical Jesus and the incarnation are denied.

Relying on the 'scandal of particularity' themselves, others asked the question why the maleness of Christ had been chosen as the key issue in representing him today. Was not Jesus also an unmarried, Aramaic-speaking, thirty-year-old circumcised Jew? Rather, it was asserted, by sharing and representing the humanity we have in common with Jesus Christ, we in our own many particularities can represent him.

### The Jesus We Preach

This debate about the ordination of women makes clear that Christology plays a decisive role in many areas of the life of the church. But at the same time it illustrates that there is a great divergence about who Jesus Christ was, and about his significance in the present. Indeed, while all Christians would agree that Jesus Christ is the 'author and perfecter of our faith' (Heb. 12:2), consider the variety of images that people have of Jesus.

There is Jesus the spiritualist, Jesus the political activist, Jesus the lover of children, Jesus the worker, Jesus the exorcist of demons, Jesus the free spirit, Jesus the healer, and so on. Furthermore, Jesus is a world character and marxists, Muslims, New Age sects and others also have their images of him. It has often been noted that people tend to see a reflection of their own face when they go in search of the face of Jesus Christ.[1]

On account of this bewildering variety of images, the church has had to draw some boundaries and set some limits. The reason for this is that Christians believe that 'salvation is found in no-one else' (Acts 4:12), and the question of salvation has serious implications. Concern for salvation is a concern for the work or activity of Jesus Christ, and this is directly related to the identity or person of Jesus Christ. In other words, who Jesus is is closely related to what Jesus does.

We can see a direct and reciprocal relationship between our image of Jesus Christ, our understanding of salvation (soteriology), and our ethical concerns. For example, in answer to our search for salvation, 'Jesus the spiritualist' calls us to forsake the world, 'Jesus the free spirit' calls us to enjoy the world, and 'Jesus the activist' calls us to change the world. And it is because of the implications of Christology for soteriology and thus for our relationship to the world that the church was and is forced to take a clear stand on the identity of Jesus.

As early as his second letter to the Corinthians, Paul expresses this when he refers to 'a Jesus other than the Jesus we preached' (2 Cor. 11:4). This same concern to define the 'Jesus we preach' against the many attempts to create 'another Jesus' continued with the writers of the gospels and the other New Testament documents, and did not end even with the closing of the canon.

Given the centrality of Christology, this conflict to define 'the Jesus we preach' will always be a dominant concern of Christian theology. Yet in the first six centuries of the church the process of Christological reflection enabled the Christian church to reach a basic consensus on those views of Jesus Christ that undermined the Christian view of salvation and the ethical life (which it called heresy), and to place limits on what could be believed by Christians (which it called orthodoxy). It is to this process of limitation that we must now turn.

## From Calvary to Chalcedon

The church's Christological debate from the earliest writings of the New Testament to the Council of Chalcedon in AD 451 was a long and tortuous process characterised by the dialectic involved in overcoming a constant tension between two powerful Christological tendencies. On occasion this debate invoked the authority of the Holy Roman Emperors, made and unmade bishops, led to serious splits in the Christian church, and caused blood to be shed. Nevertheless, by the time the Fourth Ecumenical Council at Chalcedon had made its decision, a basic consensus had been reached.

While conflict did remain, and while it took the church a few more centuries and another three ecumenical councils to establish a certain degree of unanimity, the Eastern Orthodox, Roman Catholic and Protestant churches have never seriously attempted to change this Christological position enshrined at Chalcedon in the Definition of Faith. To understand the issues at stake it is helpful to read this definition in full.

> In agreement, therefore, with the holy Fathers, we all unanimously teach that we should confess that our Lord Jesus Christ is one and the same Son, the same perfect in Godhead and the same perfect in manhood, truly God and truly man, the same [consisting] of a rational soul and body,

consubstantial (*homoousios*) with the Father in Godhead, and the same consubstantial (*homoousios*) with us in manhood, like us in all things except sin; begotten from the Father before the ages as regards His Godhead, and in the last days, the same, because of us and because of our salvation begotten from the Virgin Mary, the *Theotokos*, as regards His manhood.

One and the same Christ, Son, Lord only-begotten, made known in two natures without confusion, without change, without division, without separation, the difference of the natures being by no means removed because of the union, but the property of each nature being preserved and coalescing in one Person (*prosopon*) and one *hypostasis* — not parted or divided into two persons (*prosopa*), but one and the same Son, only-begotten, divine Word, the Lord Jesus Christ, as the prophets of old and Jesus Christ Himself have taught us about Him and the creed of our fathers has handed down.[2]

There would be very few Christians in South Africa today who would explain their faith in this way, and even fewer who would recognise this definition of faith as being the orthodox definition. Yet, it is a conscious and serious attempt by the church to set limits to what may and may not be accepted by Christians if they wish to profess the true and orthodox faith.

When we remember that the context in which these limits were debated, set, tested and challenged was the Roman and Greek world of the Mediterranean in the second to fifth centuries AD, we should not be surprised by the strange and complex language in which it is written. As heirs of the Chalcedonian settlement, therefore, we need to unpack this language and understand just what was being affirmed and rejected by this definition of faith.

## Denial of the Divinity of Christ

The *definition* of Chalcedon makes four affirmations of the divinity of Jesus Christ: 'the same perfect in Godhead'; 'truly God'; 'consubstantial (*homoousios*) with the Father in Godhead'; and 'begotten from the Father before the ages as regards His Godhead'. Thus the first view of Christ that is screened out by this statement is the denial of his divinity in the Ebionite heresy and the Arian heresy.

The denial of the Ebionite heresy makes clear that a heresy is not something that is completely false, but is something that holds only to an aspect of the truth, at the cost of the full truth. For Ebionitism arises from two legitimate concerns: monotheism and the experience of the humanity of Jesus Christ. The concern of monotheism to uphold one God, the creator, who is separate from the creation, made it difficult for certain Christians, particularly those of Jewish background, to conceive how this one God had been born of human flesh.

Furthermore, because Jesus was experienced as someone who lived and died in Palestine at a certain point in time we can understand the Ebionite concern: this man was endowed by God with tremendous powers and extraordinary abilities, but was still a human being after the pattern of Moses or David. This is sometimes called adoptionism because of the idea that Jesus was a human being who was 'adopted' by God to become the 'Son of God'.

It was Hellenistic philosophy, with the concept of the *logos*, or the Word of God, that enabled the church to affirm both monotheism and the divinity of Christ. In Platonic thought, God is totally transcendent, perfect and unchanging, and can have no dealings with the created world, which suffers, changes and decays. Therefore God relates to the world through an emanation — the *logos* — which comes from God as an intermediate revealer or mediator.

The connections with the Hebrew understanding of *sophia* (the Wisdom of God), and the place of the *logos* in the prologue to John's gospel, made this a fruitful area of reflection. Church leaders such as the Apologist, Justin Martyr (who died *c.* 165), and the theologians Clement (d. *c.* 215), Tertullian (d. *c.* 220) and Origen (d. *c.* 254),[3] took this idea of the *logos* and used it to develop Christologies which affirmed the divinity of Christ while not undermining monotheistic faith.

The Arian heresy developed from this, for Arius, a priest in Alexandria (who died *c.* 336), also developed a *logos* understanding of Christ. However, he took an extreme position on the transcendence of God and the radical divide between this God and the created order. The *logos* could not be of the same substance as God because anything which was not God, including the *logos*, was a 'creature'.

Athanasius, a bishop of Alexandria (d. 373), adopted a different position. He was influenced by the biblical image of God in which God remains divine and yet has direct contact with creation. Athanasius wanted to defend the full divinity of Christ, and so was also unhappy with the proposal of Eusebius, bishop of Caesarea (d. *c.* 340), who had argued that the *logos* was of a similar substance (*homoiousios*) to God.

Athanasius made use of a soteriological argument in which he pointed out that only God can create, and therefore only God can redeem. If Christ was not fully God, he argued, then the salvation he offers cannot be fundamentally secure. This soteriological argument won the approval of the Third Ecumenical Council at Nicea in AD 325,[4] where the church made clear that Jesus was not *homoiousios* with God — of similar substance (note the *i* between the *o*'s) — but rather *homoousios* — of the same substance as God.

The Nicene Creed enabled the church to identify as heretical and screen out those views which denied the divinity of Christ. The theology of Athanasius and the Nicene Creed left a number of key issues unresolved, particularly those relating to the Trinity and the humanity of Christ, but their basic defence of the divinity of Christ was affirmed at Chalcedon in AD 451, and remains a key statement that should guide any Christological reflection today.

### Denial of the Humanity of Christ

Parallel with the defence of the divinity of Jesus Christ, the Chalcedonian definition defended his humanity: 'the same perfect in manhood'; 'truly man, consisting of a rational soul and body'; 'consubstantial (*homoousios*) with us in manhood'; 'because of us and because of our salvation begotten from the Virgin Mary, the *Theotokos*, as regards his manhood'. The church also set about declaring heretical and screening out those perspectives on Jesus Christ which denied his true humanity: Docetism and Apollinarianism.

The Docetic heresy grew out of the same Hellenistic philosophy we examined above, but with the exact opposite result, reminding us of the dialectical process at work. While affirming a radical divide between God and the created order, the Docetics put Jesus clearly on the side of divinity. It was therefore impossible for them to conceive of his having mixed with the decaying created order and really become human. He only *seemed* to be human, and the Greek verb *dokein* ('to seem') gives the name to this heresy.

The Docetic heresy was combated early on in the history of the church. The writing of the gospels was undertaken to make clear that Jesus was *really* a human being, who wept, laughed, touched, ate and drank, and got angry. A very clear example of this is John's gospel. The poetic prologue about the *logos* (the Word) clearly seeks to proclaim the divinity of Christ, and yet at the same time it states very boldly that 'the Word *became flesh*, and dwelt with us' (John 1:14).

Right from the start, therefore, the church simply accepted the fact that Jesus was a real human being through the testimony of the first witnesses. Yet by the Council of Nicea, the church had also accepted the full divinity of Christ with the aid of the *logos* concept, and so it faced the task of trying to make use of the *logos* in such a way that the basic witness to the humanity of Christ was not undermined.

The cul de sac that the church first travelled down is called the *logos–sarx* doctrine, where the Greek word *sarx* means flesh or body. It was argued that just as the *logos* is the life-giving force in the world, and the human soul is the life-giving force in a human being, so in the incarnation the *logos* takes the place of the soul in the human person of Jesus Christ. Jesus Christ has a human body (*sarx*), but the human soul is replaced by the *logos*.

It was Apollinaris, a follower of Athanasius and a bishop of Laodicea (d. *c.* 390), who saw the strength of this doctrine as its ability to ensure the unity of purpose and will in Jesus Christ. He argued that if Jesus had both a human soul *and* the divine *logos,* there is always the possibility that there is no *real* connection between the divinity and the humanity of Christ, and therefore no true incarnation of *God.* This would lead to an adoptionist Christology, for Jesus would remain a human being like any other with only an accidental relationship to God.

In seeking to defend the truth of the Nicene Creed, however, Apollinaris illustrates again that heresy is not a denial of the truth but the promotion of only one aspect of the truth to the detriment of the truth as a whole.[5] By replacing the human soul with the divine *logos,* the *logos–sarx* doctrine did not fully account for the true humanity of Jesus Christ, for to be human means to have a human soul as well as body.

Again, it was a soteriological concern which clarified the debate. Scholars such as Gregory Nazianzus (d. 389) pointed out that the soul was the seat of sin, and that in order for humanity to be redeemed, Christ would have to have a human soul. In a famous phrase Gregory argued that 'what has not been assumed cannot be restored; it is what is united with God that is saved'.[6] Against the *logos–sarx* formula, therefore, the church in the Chalcedon definition supports a *logos–anthropos* doctrine in which the *logos* is united not just to the body but to the full humanity of Christ. This basic defence of the humanity of Christ remains a key statement for contemporary Christological reflection.

## Denial of the Unity of Christ

After the first section of the Chalcedonian definition, there is a second section which talks about 'two natures': '[Christ] made known in two natures without confusion, without change, without division, without separation'; and 'the difference of the natures being by no means removed because of the union'. And at the same time it speaks about 'one person': 'the property of each nature being preserved and coalescing in one Person (*prosopon*) and one *hypostasis*'; and 'not parted or divided into two persons (*prosopa*), but one and the same Son'.

What this section of the definition does, therefore, is to set limits as to how the divinity and humanity of Jesus Christ are to be related, screening out the Monophysite heresy which undermined the two natures, and the Nestorian heresy which undermined the unity of person.

The Monophysite position grew out of the concerns of the *logos–sarx* formula of Apollinaris to preserve the real incarnation of God into flesh, and the unity of will in Jesus Christ. Out of a soteriological concern to maintain the possibility of unity between God and humanity in redemption, the oneness of humanity and divinity in Christ was promoted.

It was stressed that Christ could not have two active substances or natures existing side by side, because this would mean that ultimately we as human beings could only exist alongside God, and never in God. Rather, in the incarnation, Christ's human nature was absorbed by his divine nature, so that the church must speak of Christ as having only one nature (in Greek, *monos physis*, from which we derive monophysite). The Monophysites spoke of the divinity not becoming human, but putting on humanity like a cloak.

The metaphysical logic of this argument gave it considerable power, and it certainly had a great following before and even long after Chalcedon, continuing to bear an influence within some streams of the Eastern Orthodox Church even today. The opposition to it did not concentrate on a logical flaw in the argument, but restated the church's simple confession that Jesus was a real human being, and in order to be that human being, he must have taken human nature fully, both body and soul.

The church at Chalcedon therefore rejected the Monophysite position and declared that if both the full divinity and the full humanity of Christ were to be confessed, then regardless of the logical difficulties, he must be understood as having two natures, and these natures are 'without confusion and without change'.

The Nestorian position reminds us of the dialectical process at work, for it is really the assertion of the opposite tendency to that of the Monophysites, and like this doctrine it continued to have long life in certain areas of the church in the East. Following the line of defence against Apollinaris and the Monophysites, the *logos–anthropos* formula was defended, and the fully humanity of Jesus Christ affirmed alongside the full divinity as two natures.

However, the two nature doctrine was also promoted to defend a Greek notion of a God who is wholly transcendent and impassible. For while it enabled the Nestorians to give full recognition to the limitations and suffering of Christ, these were argued to pertain only to his human nature, the divinity remaining unaffected. Critics were quick to point out that this meant that within Jesus Christ there are really two people, one human and one divine, and on key issues — such as suffering — they have a life of their own.

The issue that sparked off this controversy was the ruling of Nestorius, bishop of Constantinople (d. *c.* 451), against the use of the term *Theotokos* (Mother of God) for Mary. Nestorius's position was condemned by the church at the Council of Ephesus (431), because while he sought to defend the humanity of Christ against the Monophysites, he ended up denying his divinity. If Christ really is fully divine, declared Ephesus, then it is permissible to call Mary *Theotokos*. For everything that is said about Jesus Christ is true of him as both human and divine, for he remains *one* person.

After Ephesus the argument was further developed by the philosophical distinction between nature (*physia*) and person (*prosopon*), and what was finally established at Chalcedon was that Jesus Christ has two natures, human and divine, which are 'without division and without separation' for he is *one* person, 'not parted or divided into two persons (*prosopa*), but one and the same Son'.

## From Negative to Positive Christology

### The Content of Positive Christology

What, then, is the relevance of this definition for the church today? Some scholars suggest that we have no further need for it, because it does not speak to the issues of the twentieth century or because they feel it was an illegitimate interpretation of Jesus Christ in terms of Greek philosophy. Some argue that modern biblical studies have undermined many of the assumptions with which the early church worked. The claim, then, is that Christology needs to start again, ignoring the Chalcedonian definition.

Yet by understanding Chalcedon as a 'limit statement' which screens out those views which undermine the truth about Jesus Christ, we can affirm that the guidelines laid down by Chalcedon are just as relevant today as they were when they were first adopted, namely that Jesus Christ is *one* person with *two* natures, both fully human and fully divine. But these guidelines remain as a limit statement, making clear the boundaries of Christology — they do not fill in the content.

Let us illustrate what we mean. The vows that husband and wife take on their wedding day declare that marriage is 'for better, for worse, for richer, for poorer, in sickness and in health ... till death do us part'. This statement defines the boundaries and the limits of the relationship, making clear that it is not a convenience, a casual friendship or a commercial transaction. However, no one asked to describe the meaning of their marriage would simply repeat these vows, however true they are and fundamental as the basis of married experience. A married person would probably tell stories and show photographs using a language of description and emotion to fill in the content of the boundaries.

The same is true with the Christology of the Chalcedonian definition of faith. Like the marriage vows, it sets the boundaries by making the truth about Christ clear (orthodoxy) in the face of false claims (heresy). But it does not fill in the content. The content is far richer and beyond simple description — especially a description in the language of Greek philosophy. Chalcedon, like all earlier and later statements of faith and doctrine about Christ, is thus a form of negative or critical Christology. The church must go beyond this and engage in positive Christology, filling in the content by exploring the meaning of Jesus Christ for us today.

### The Style of Positive Christology

The failing of all the great heresies rejected by Chalcedon — Arian, Apollinarian, Monophysite and Nestorian — is that they started with an abstract notion of divinity or humanity and tried to reflect upon Christ through philosophical speculation. In response the church made clear that once one has started with an abstract view of humanity or divinity it is impossible to work backwards to provide a true understanding of the identity of Christ. What one ends up with is one aspect of the truth, but not the truth itself. And this, as we have seen, is heresy.

What Chalcedon defined is that the *prosopon* — the Person of Jesus Christ — is the key element in Christology because it is the unifying and experienced factor. When we meet Jesus Christ we do not first meet abstract natures (neither divinity nor humanity), but a person in whom these two natures coalesce. Accepting this, positive Christology therefore turns to the concrete story of Jesus Christ. It turns from the question 'How can this be?' to the question 'Who is this?' Dietrich Bonhoeffer writes:

> When one has put the question, 'How?', to one side, one comes to the Chalcedonian Definition, in which the question, 'How?', has been eliminated. What remains is a pointer to the question, 'Who are you?' The Chalcedonian Definition is itself ultimately the question, 'Who?'[7]

So Chalcedon sets limits not only to the content of Christology but also to the style. The centuries of seeking the truth through a dialectical process led the church to use paradox and negation to state its convictions. It put a limit on philosophical speculation and directed people to the concrete person of Jesus Christ, and thus to the story about him. The church is therefore called again and again to read the gospels and there to meet the *prosopon* of Jesus Christ. Philosophical categories fall away in new contexts but the narrative form of the gospels continues to live in each new generation. Positive Christology must therefore 'tell the story', and allow it to answer the question, 'Who is Jesus Christ for us today?'

### Reading the Story of Jesus Christ

The details of the story about Jesus Christ have been under great suspicion in the last hundred years. Albert Schweitzer declared the 'Quest of the Historical

Jesus' to be closed,[8] and the work of biblical scholars such as Rudolf Bultmann, using form and redaction criticism, called into question the factuality of both the words and actions of Jesus in the gospels.

Nevertheless, in recent years there has been a groundswell of opinion that the broad outlines and themes concerning Jesus Christ are clear for everyone to see and grasp.[9] Rather than starting with categories and philosophical schemes, therefore, a contemporary Christology must be forged out of the very material in which the first witnesses expressed the richness of their faith — the narrative of the gospel story.

## The Incarnation: God's Love in Freedom in Jesus Christ

The story of Jesus Christ begins with the incarnation. As we have indicated, a positive Christology does not ask, 'How does divinity manage to be incarnated?' It simply states that in Jesus Christ God *is* incarnate, and goes on to ask, 'What does this mean?'

Rather than the image of a distant and uninvolved God, who cannot relate to this world because it would mean mixing with decaying, suffering matter, the encounter with God in the story of the incarnation of Jesus Christ declares to us a God of love. For here we learn that God is a God who gives, indeed who gives even of Godself by creating a relationship with humanity. God is open to rejection and acceptance, and thus meets us as a God who feels and who loves.

At the same time, in the incarnation God remains fully God, and retains the awesomeness and the holiness of the divine, experienced not as distance and silence but as freedom. God is the one who is perfectly free to be God. Not needing us, yet out of freedom choosing to love, God sends Jesus Christ who reveals the divine — not through being overpowering, omniscient or dictatorial — but through being perfectly free. Free before the law, free before death, free to relate, and ultimately free to love.

## The Life: God's Option for the Poor and Weak in Jesus Christ

Classical Christological formulations have made a fundamental mistake in jumping from the incarnation to the crucifixion, without exploring the nature of the life that was lived by Jesus Christ. Perhaps blinded by their own assumptions and prejudices, theologians and church leaders have not taken seriously that that life was one lived in solidarity with the marginalised and the oppressed.

One of the most incontrovertible facts about Jesus Christ is the kind of people that he chose to befriend and care for. Almost without exception they were those who were poor and weak. Starting with the birth stories, through the themes of the temptation in the wilderness, the choice of disciples, relationships with women, the healing of the sick, the community of outcasts, the love for children, and the point of his many parables, Jesus lived his life in constant relationship to those who were excluded from the mainstream of society.

His journey to the Cross, and the reasons for his arrest and crucifixion, are also full of the prophetic themes of resistance to and rebellion against the arrogance and power of those in authority. In the life of the person of Jesus Christ we have, therefore, a clear indication of God's option for the poor and the weak, and no contemporary Christology can be attempted without this perspective.

### The Crucifixion: God's Suffering with Humanity in Jesus Christ

Suffering constitutes perhaps the primary datum of life, and many people find in suffering the reason for disbelief and the rejection of God. Once again, however, it is easy to start with an image of 'God', rather than with the person of Jesus Christ. For the story of the gospels is that God is not an unmoved mover or uncaused cause, but rather one who makes Godself vulnerable even to the point of death.

The life of Jesus reached the point where both his love in freedom and his option for the poor were such a challenge to the authorities that 'he suffered under Pontius Pilate, was crucified, died and was buried', as the Apostles' Creed has it. In Jesus Christ, God suffers as a victim in solidarity with the suffering of humanity, and thus the meaning of suffering can be explored with God rather than against God.

In and through the crucifixion of Jesus Christ we learn that God does not 'solve' the problem of suffering in this world by divine decree or intervention, but rather through participation and solidarity. For suffering is and remains part of the human experience, but the possibilities of life within the midst of suffering grow from the knowledge that in the crucifixion of Jesus Christ, God too has suffered unto death.

### The Resurrection: God's Victory over Sin and Evil in Jesus Christ

All the gospels are clear that the story of Jesus Christ reaches its climax in the resurrection. Regardless of how we understand the exact events of the resurrection, the point of the story is clear: through the power exhibited in the resurrection of Jesus Christ, God reverses the judgement upon him, vindicates his life and message, and proclaims a victory over the forces of human sin and evil which conspired to consign him to the grave.

We have noted that suffering is the primary datum of life, and indeed the journey of all people ends at the grave. With death at the end, all human effort and achievement have no meaning for us, and we must ultimately face the future in despair. Now, what the resurrection proclaims is that in Jesus Christ God has faced this meaningless future which awaits us all, and has broken its power. Our future lies no longer in the grave but in the resurrected life, and we can therefore face life with hope.

A contemporary positive Christology must therefore not only talk about hope and proclaim hope, but it must give people real hope in the midst of despair, anxiety and uncertainty.

### The Ascension: God's Rule over the World in Jesus Christ

We proclaim Christ who came to earth and who is now 'seated at the right hand of the Father', as the Apostles' Creed has it, which is to say that he plays an active part in God's rule of the world. The rule of God is therefore not that of some distant and coldly objective divine force, but is a 'humanised' rule which has experienced the very depths of human alienation, and has done so alongside the weak and the poor. God rules therefore with a certain bias and advocacy.

Another way of speaking about the rule of God is 'the kingdom of God', which is at the heart of Jesus' proclamation. This rule and this kingdom call into question all other rulers and kingdoms of the world and our allegiance to them. It invites obedience and commitment to Jesus beyond those of nation, volk, class, race, culture or language, even to the point of civil disobedience when the rule of human kingdoms stands against the character and the bias of God's rule.

A contemporary positive Christology must therefore always be a challenge to the forces of death and injustice, because the Christ is a present reality in the power of the Spirit.

### The Parousia: God's Promise for the Future in Jesus Christ

Jesus Christ, we are told in the Apostles' Creed, will 'come again to judge the living and the dead'. Popular notions of the Second Coming tend to sever the connection between the Jesus who lived his life here on earth and the Jesus who will come again. This is unacceptable for a positive Christology that takes the whole story of Jesus Christ seriously. The fact that it is Jesus Christ who will come again gives to our future a human face, a character, a perspective, a bias. And the fact that this Jesus Christ will come again, means that God promises that the future belongs to that specific human face and character. This gives to Christian faith the attitude of expectation, openness, hope and a willingness to dream and envision a reality beyond the present realities, a kingdom beyond the present kingdoms.

That Jesus Christ shall come 'to judge the living and the dead' reminds us that ultimately truth and justice will have their sway in the universe. Before this judgement there is no-one who can claim innocence, so we await his coming with faith in the mercy and grace of God alone, while at the same time living our lives in response to the call to discipleship.

### The Spirit, Participation and Salvation

Jesus Christ, risen and ascended, is yet not absent from us. The church confesses and practises that in and through the power of the Holy Spirit, Jesus Christ is present where the Word is read and preached and where the sacraments are celebrated, where 'two or three gather in my name', and where the one who is hungry is fed and the one who is sick is healed. Without Jesus Christ, who is present and experienced as a reality in the Spirit, Christology would be a form of ancient history or a branch of speculative philosophy.

Another way to talk about experiencing Christ present in the Spirit is to talk about discipleship. For to know Christ is to follow him, and the Spirit leads us and strengthens us to live a discipleship true to the story of Jesus Christ in the face of the selfsame evil and injustice that he faced. Without that discipleship, even the most sophisticated Christology remains an empty caricature of the one who says not 'analyse me', but 'follow me'.

To live in Christ, to experience Christ in the power of the Spirit, to be a disciple — this is salvation. For as we noted right at the beginning, the identity and the activity — or, in traditional language, the person and the work — of Jesus Christ are closely bound together. If we are right that the identity of Jesus Christ is disclosed in the reading of the story about him, then the salvation that is offered in him is also part of the reading of that same story.

It is for this reason that the church has never affirmed an 'orthodox' doctrine of salvation. While it could and did adopt a limit statement about the identity of Christ at Chalcedon, the logic of the activity of Christ or of a doctrine of salvation flows not from this kind of critical or negative Christology, but from a positive Christology. As we have made clear, positive Christology is a telling of the story; thus most doctrines of salvation are in the form of a story which is made relevant to the time and place in which it is told.

At times in the history of the church, various aspects of the story of Jesus Christ have been used almost exclusively in the telling of the story of salvation. A contemporary doctrine of salvation, grounded in the story of the person of Jesus Christ, would, we suggest, need to draw fully on all the moments of that story: incarnation, life, crucifixion, resurrection, ascension and parousia. For it is nowhere else but in the story that we meet and are confronted by the *prosopon* of Jesus the Christ, fully human and fully divine, 'as the prophets of old and Jesus Christ Himself have taught us about him and the creed of our fathers has handed down'.[10]

---

[1] Albert Schweitzer's book *The Quest for the Historical Jesus* (London: SCM, 1954), first published in German in 1906, was an in-depth study of the attempts over two centuries to write a 'history of Jesus'. Schweitzer showed how these attempts had failed miserably.

[2] For this definition and further discussion around Chalcedon see A. Grillmeier S.J., *Christ in Christian Tradition,* Vol. 1 (Atlanta: John Knox, 1975) pp. 540ff.; and J. N. D. Kelly, *Early Christian Doctrines* (London: A. and C. Black, 1977), pp. 310ff. Both are very helpful for tracing the full story of the early Christological debates.

[3] For these approximate dates of death of the ancient theologians, see Jaroslav Pelikan, *The Emergence of the Catholic Tradition (100–600)* (Chicago: Chicago University Press, 1971).

[4] See the text of the Nicene Creed, and the discussion in Grillmeier, *Christ in Christian Tradition,* pp. 249ff. The Council at Nicea was under the leadership of the Emperor Constantine, who was so concerned to have a unified faith throughout the empire that he interfered in the debate at important moments!

[5] For the full story of the anti-Apollinarian controversy see, for example, Grillmeier, *Christ in Christian Tradition,* pp. 329ff; and Kelly, *Early Christian Doctrines,* pp. 289ff.

[6] See the full argument in Kelly, *Early Christian Doctrines,* 296ff.

[7] See Dietrich Bonhoeffer, *Christ the Centre* (San Francisco: Harper and Row, 1978), p. 102.

[8] This was the 'result' of analysing the work of German New Testament scholars.

[9] The ground-breaking book was by the pupil of Rudolf Bultmann, Günther Bornkamm, *Jesus of Nazareth* (London: Hodder and Stoughton, 1973). Edward Schillebeeckx has called it 'a post-critical narrative history'; see *Jesus: An Experiment in Christology* (New York: Crossroad, 1979), pp. 77–80. Scholars who focus on the biblical texts from a sociological perspective have also provided new insights. Third world scholars have also given much attention to the story of the historical Jesus of the gospels. See, for example, Albert Nolan, *Jesus Before Christianity: The Gospel of Liberation* (London: Darton, Longman and Todd, 1977), and Juan Luis Segundo, *The Historical Jesus of the Synoptics* (Maryknoll: Orbis, 1985).

[10] The Chalcedonian definition of faith.

## Bibliography

Boff, Leonardo. *Jesus Christ Liberator.* Maryknoll: Orbis, 1978

Bonhoeffer, Dietrich. *Christ the Centre*. San Francisco: Harper and Row, 1978

Chikane, Frank. 'The Incarnation in the Life of the People in Southern Africa', *Journal of Theology of Southern Africa*, 51

Cone, James. 'Jesus Christ in Black Theology' in *A Black Theology of Liberation*. Maryknoll: Orbis, 1986

Hick, John. 'Jesus and the World Religions' in J. Hick (ed.), *The Myth of God Incarnate*. London: SCM, 1977

Mofokeng, Takatso. *The Crucified Among the Crossbearers*. Kampen: J. H. Kok, 1983

Moltmann, Jürgen. *The Crucified God*. London: SCM, 1974

Nolan, Albert. *Jesus Before Christianity: The Gospel of Liberation*. London: Darton, Longman and Todd, 1977

Pobee, John. 'Toward Christology in an African Theology' in *Toward an African Theology*. Nashville: Abingdon, 1979

Ruether, Rosemary. 'Christology: Can a Male Saviour Save Women?' in *Sexism and God-Talk*. London: SCM, 1982.

Schillebeeckx, Edward. *Jesus: An Experiment in Christology*. New York: Crossroad, 1979

Schillebeeckx, Edward. *Christ: The Experience of Jesus as Lord*. New York: Crossroad, 1980

Schweitzer, Albert. *The Quest for the Historical Jesus*. London: SCM, 1954

Sobrino, John. *Christology at the Crossroads: A Latin American Approach*. Maryknoll: Orbis, 1978

# 6

## The Spirit of Life

### MARIE-HENRY KEANE

The expression 'the new South Africa' is becoming hackneyed from overuse but it is difficult to think of a better expression to describe what is happening in our country: chaotic forces spawned by injustice have seared our land and damaged our people. We long for a fresh beginning, for a new and better life for everyone. Many people look to the politicians and to the economists for 'salvation'. The efforts of the politicians may, no doubt, contribute to the establishment of new and more humane social structures. A healthy economy should provide a better standard of living for the materially deprived. If, however, our society is to achieve *wholeness*, if the hurts of the past are to be healed, then attitudes also need to change. This is where the psychologists and sociologists enter the discussion. They ask questions about good order and about overcoming chaos, about reconciliation and healing, about the dynamics of freedom and about putting an end to alienation, for new life has to take place from within as well as from without. Clearly, emotions and psyches have been severely damaged. On a scale of one to ten, some have suffered more severely than others but none have escaped.

In brief, then, 'salvation' and 'new life', rightly understood, touch on every aspect of the human condition, and since ultimately all of life, birth and rebirth alike fall within the reign of God, theologians also have a significant contribution to make to new beginnings. The Spirit of life, which broods over the deep, is capable of renewing not merely the earth's face but also the deepest recesses of its mind, heart and soul. This may sound overly pious to some people but one either acknowledges the Spirit's capacity for re-creation or one does not.

As you read this chapter on the Spirit of life, I would invite you to bear in mind that theology, faith and our human condition ought not to be kept in watertight compartments. In-depth theological reflection and the insights gained from it should enrich our faith and affect how we conduct our lives. Conversely, poor theology can impoverish our faith and adversely affect the quality of our Christian living. Theologians and 'faithful Christians' in South Africa have only recently woken up to the fact that we have been part of the problem, too, and must acknowledge our guilt. Maybe the fact that we appear to have neglected the Spirit had something to do with our national blindness. Oddly enough, that neglect has not been limited to our country or even to our times. It is a widespread phenomenon.

## The Neglect of the Spirit of Life

Until this century, pneumatology (the doctrine of the Holy Spirit) was neglected by theologians particularly in the Western church. The role which the Spirit ought to play in our lives was, as a consequence, also neglected. On the other hand it should not surprise us that throughout Christianity's long history, theology and Christian piety never overlooked the centrality of Christ as Saviour. Discipleship generally meant taking up the cross, dying to self in order to live in God. Christian art and the writing of the mystics did justice to the suffering of Jesus. Every church had its *pietà*!

Paul preached Christ and him crucified but he also saw beyond the person of Christ to the Body of Christ. His extraordinary Damascus experience compelled him to examine the fundamental truth which lay behind the question: 'Saul, Saul, why do you persecute me?' He discovered that he had to accept not only Christ but also the suffering Body of Christ down to its least and last member.

Christ was clearly not neglected either by theologians or by the faithful, neither was the God who in compassion and love sent him. Less in evidence, however, was the notion of the pathos of God, the One who acts in history, the One who hears the cries of the poor and of the oppressed.

Let me repeat: Christ was never forgotten, the God who sent him was never overlooked, but what is surprising is that we who believe in a triune God should have grossly neglected the life-giving Spirit, especially since we know that we cannot say 'Jesus is Lord', or call God 'God', unless this grace is given to us through the Spirit. As early as the fourth century, Gregory of Nazianzus referred to the Holy Spirit as the *Theos agraptos*, the God about whom nobody writes. The notion of *Geistvergessenheit* (forgetting of the Spirit) has really been seriously addressed only in more recent times. In fact it is only now, for the first time in the long history of the church, that the Spirit is taking centre-stage world-wide. Little wonder then that Christian theology and Christian piety should appear uninspired and jaded at times. We lacked the creative energy which only the Spirit of life could give. Furthermore, we had forgotten how to pray 'Come, Holy Spirit, renew the face of the earth.' As individuals and as communities we were often lack-lustre.

## Why the Neglect of the Spirit of Life?

A number of explanations have been given to account for the neglect of the Spirit of life. One explanation states quite simply that the Spirit chose to take a back seat. Frederick Dale Brunner in his interesting book *The Holy Spirit: Shy Member of the Trinity* develops the notion of the Spirit as a 'backbencher' and pursues the idea that the retiring Spirit is 'shy'! Shyness, however, is not to be equated with timidity (cf. 2 Tim. 1:7). It is, Brunner writes, 'the shyness of a concentrated centring of attention on another'.[1] The Spirit simply puts the 'spotlight' on Jesus, and on the One who sent the Spirit.

Let us look at two examples from John's gospel which well show the shy Spirit of life at work. First: 'But the Advocate, the Holy Spirit, whom the Father will send in my name, will teach you everything and remind you of all I have said to you' (John 14:16). The Spirit keeps Jesus' memory alive and the Spirit alerts the minds and hearts of believers so that they retain what Jesus taught them. That was the Spirit's special mission and that was why the Spirit was sent by God in the first place: to keep Christians 'tuned into' Jesus. In retrospect, the church in South Africa must strike its breast. We could not possibly have been 'tuned in' and not have spoken out more boldly about injustice in the land. Where were all the spirit-driven prophets, and who was listening to them? That is a sobering thought.

A second example: 'But when the Spirit of truth comes, She will lead you to complete truth since She will not be speaking from Herself but will only say what She has learnt' (John 16:13). Let me restate what I said already, for the notion is important and bears repetition. The message which the Spirit carries can never be different from Jesus' life-giving message, for there cannot be two divine but opposing truths. But having said that, we should remember that the Spirit is more than just Jesus' mouthpiece. The Spirit is also, and above all, Jesus' interpreter. The Saviour's words would, and sometimes did, fall on deaf ears: 'They have eyes but they do not see. They have ears and they do not hear', Jesus lamented (Matt. 13:14). What is even more mysterious is that Jesus did not seem to have the capacity to break through to their consciousness. The disciples had to wait until Pentecost to 'come alive', to be enabled by the life-giving Spirit of Jesus to grasp in an instant things which previously had baffled them; only then did they know the extraordinary joy of enlightenment and the surprise of the 'ah' experience. Suddenly their eyes were opened and they were granted glimpses of truths which up till then had been hidden from them and which had evaded them. The 'new life' which the Spirit gave was, by far, more intense, more creative and energetic than they had ever known before.

In looking at the two passages from John's gospel, we are faced with a temptation to speak of the truth which *Jesus* came to bring, or to speak of *God* sending Jesus. It is more sound theologically to acknowledge the mutuality and the interconnectedness which exists within the Trinity. God, Jesus and the Spirit constitute one God, all three persons are life-bringers and life-sustainers. It would seem that the Spirit does not focus on herself, however, but only on honouring and witnessing to the person of Jesus, yet the Spirit remains the key which unlocks the door, granting access to life with God. In that sense the Spirit is truly life-giver. Note, too, that when the disciples, having been transformed, energised and filled with new life at Pentecost, went out on their mission of spreading the gospel, they bore witness not to the Spirit primarily, but to Jesus Christ and to the One who had sent Jesus.

It is perhaps something of a paradox to say that the 'shy' and often neglected and overlooked Spirit of life is most present when Jesus is central. To quote Brunner again: '[The Spirit] does not mind being neglected as long as Jesus is not.'[2] That may be true as far as it goes but to neglect the action of the life-giving Spirit is to expose ourselves to the possibility of spiritual deafness and to the consequences of that condition. On the one hand, the Spirit of life should not be seen as the panacea for all lack-lustre people or as a sort of divine vitamin supplement for jaded spirits. On the other hand, what serious Christians are looking for is, I believe, fullness of life and not mere existence in situations which are often anti-life, not to mention anti-fullness of life. Since the human condition is characterised by vulnerability and by an inability to cope with life very often, Paul's words should be taken seriously: 'the Spirit comes to us in our weakness' (Rom. 8:26). We ignore that coming at our peril.

## The Spirit as Life-giver and as Life-sustainer

It is not only children who are afraid of darkness, of formless voids and chaos. This is the stuff that horror stories are made of. Ancient myths associated with creation told not only of humans but of deities struggling to the death to gain mastery over chaos and darkness. The Genesis myth begins along similar lines: 'In the beginning the earth was a formless void, there was darkness over the deep and God's Spirit hovered over the water' (Gen. 1:2). But unlike other ancient creation myths, the Genesis story tells not of conflict and struggle but about the progressive construction of good order by a good God who can produce light and all kinds of splendid forms out of nothing. Hovering over this now idyllic scene is the Creator–Spirit, a great brooding bird, the vivifier. The Spirit of life broods over the earth as if waiting for it to hatch out.

Clearly one is not expected to treat this story as 'history' in the literal sense. But the myth, like the parables of the New Testament, contains profound truths. The brooding Spirit, the *Creator–Spiritus*, and the *logos* (the eternal Word of God)[3] were there from the beginning as life-bringers, and the triune God was clearly in control. If the *Creator–Spiritus* could overcome chaos and darkness once, then that same Spirit can overcome chaos and darkness again in whatever shape or form it appears. 'Come, Holy Spirit, renew the face of the earth.'

The Hebrew word *toledot* used to describe the 'origins' of the earth (Gen. 2:4) can be translated as 'birth'. 'Such were the origins [birth] of heaven and earth when they were made.' In ancient cosmologies it was common to refer to creation in terms of birth.[4] Traces of the birth motif are also found in the Genesis story. The Spirit becomes mother, the nurturing feminine Spirit of life guarding and protecting the earth. Furthermore, that mother-bird image is seen more than once. Note, for example, how the weak and vulnerable Israel is protected by her against the threats of Egypt: 'You yourself have seen what I did with the Egyptians. How I carried you on eagle's wings and brought you to myself.' (Exod. 19:14)

The *Creator–Spiritus* was not only present at the birth of the world, the nurturing Spirit life-giver was also at hand in times of national disaster. The parenting bird appears again to 'protect', 'rear' and 'guard' Jacob. 'Like an eagle watching her nest hovering over her young She spreads out Her wings to hold Her young. She supports him on her pinions.' (Deut. 32:11) The benign God-spirit feeds Jacob with honey, curds, milk, wheat, wine as well as providing meat and soothing oil (Deut. 32:10–18).

The repetition of the image of the bird as life-giver and provider, as the dispeller of chaos and darkness, raises a number of important questions. In the first instance, how seriously have we taken the notion of the Providence of God? To what extent can we regard the Spirit of life as the caretaker of the world? Does the

Spirit really have a profound role to play in our personal and societal lives? Or is the Spirit still being neglected today?

## The Spirit as Mother

Elizabeth Johnson has some startling things to say about our meagre Western pneumatological tradition.[5] She quotes several leading theologians in support of her contention that pneumatology has been seriously neglected. Walter Kasper, for example, speaks of the Spirit as having become 'faceless'; John Macquarrie as 'shadowy'; Georgia Harkness as 'ghostly — a vague something or other'; and Norman Pittenger as 'the poor relation' of the Trinity. Similarly, Yves Congar describes the Spirit as the 'half-known God'; Joseph Ratzinger, as having become 'homeless' in the West; and Wolfhart Pannenberg, as "watered down" from its biblical fullness'. To counter that, Johnson quotes Paula Gunn Allen as saying: 'There is a spirit that pervades everything that is capable of powerful song and radiant movement and that moves in and out of the mind.'[6]

Amongst others, feminist theologians have sought to redress the problem. Alwyn Marriage in her book *Life-giving Spirit: Responding to the Feminine in God* believes that the Spirit of life, as it is imaged in the Scriptures, has helped us to understand God's capacity for being mother. She begets us not once, but again and again. The brooding Mother was present as life-giver at the beginning, hatching the 'egg' of the world. She was present at the annunciation when the promise of a second creation was made and when, through her creative power, the Saviour is conceived. Finally, at Pentecost she energetically gives birth to the infant church.[7] Since birthing is a feminine activity and a 'biologically related metaphor', one which is repeated throughout Scripture, Alwyn Marriage finds it reasonable to ascribe femininity and fecund motherhood to the Spirit of life. Some may find this emphasis on the feminine surprising or startling. Do not write it off too quickly, however, because that tradition has been around a long time. It goes back as far as the Hebraic tradition which identifies the Spirit as *sophia* (female wisdom): 'For She [*sophia*] is the breath of the power of God and pure emanation of his almighty glory. For She is a reflection of everlasting light and a spotless mirror of the activity of God and a likeness of His goodness.' (Wisd. 7:25–26) *Sophia* as the breath of the power of God, as an emanation of divine glory and of everlasting light, stands directly opposed to chaos, darkness and barrenness, for She is lightsome and a life-giver.

Women in general and third world women in particular have traditionally been relegated to the bottom rung of the socio-economic ladder; they have been exploited and made vulnerable. This practice goes back a long way: 'In antiquity widows and orphans were the prime paradigms of the poor and the exploited', wrote the feminist theologian Elisabeth Schüssler Fiorenza.[8] Women were obliged to maintain links with unjust patriarchal systems, regardless of how oppressive they might have been, because the alternative could have meant destitution. Within the church women were also obliged to conform; to accept the roles assigned to them by the Fathers; to hear themselves being addressed as 'Sons of God', to be designated the 'male' offspring of a 'male' God! If, however, women are made in the image of the living God, then they must have received their femininity from God who is the Source of femininity! Is this not true?

But now the moment of truth has come. Now women are daring to become more independent socially and economically. They are breaking loose from those situations which kept them in thrall. They are challenging unjust church structures, and with new-found confidence join in Mary's Magnificat. They, 'the lowly', are conscious of being 'raised up'. Mary filled with the Holy Spirit provides them with a worthy model. She begot Life. She conceived Jesus not only in her womb but also in her heart and mind. She experienced Life within her not merely in the biological sense but because she was acknowledged by God and was an active agent in God's saving work. The breath of God, the power of God, the light and wisdom (*sophia*) of God, had come upon her as it comes upon those women who claim that gift: 'Come, Holy Spirit.'

The church has always insisted that God is Spirit and therefore not subject to the limitations of gender. It is more sound theologically of course to ascribe neither male nor female characteristics to God, for these are mere allegories.[9] The church was, in fact, only half wrong: it ascribed only male identity to God and ignored the female.

## The Spirit of Life as Liberator

Feminist liberation theologians like Alwyn Marriage, Elizabeth Johnson and, nearer home, Mercy Amba Oduyoye are offering alternative ways of speaking about the Spirit of God. The enthusiasm with which that route is being followed indicates that there is more at stake here than merely putting labels such as 'mother' on the Spirit of life. There is a life-and-death struggle for freedom. It is a freedom not only to be and to become but also to serve in love for the sake of God's reign. In other words, Spirit-freedom is never a private affair; it results in being sent or missioned.

Another feature of Spirit-freedom is that it paves the way for even greater liberation. The Black liberation theologian Sabelo Ntwasa writes: 'Black Theology as it struggles to formulate a theology of liberation relevant to South Africa, cannot afford to perpetuate any form of domination. If its liberation is not human enough to include the liberation of women, it will not be liberation.'[10]

That, in my opinion, is an 'enlightened' statement, for in the past, liberation theologians did not take the plight of women seriously. Leonardo Boff, a liberation theologian from Latin America, advances a step further still. He appropriates the Spirit imagery of certain feminist theologians and develops it in his book *The Maternal Face of God: The Feminine and Its Religious Expressions*. Here is an extract for your consideration: 'The Spirit, the eternal feminine, is united to the created feminine in order that the latter might be totally and fully what it can be.'[11] The Spirit grants us the freedom, says Boff, to be our best and most capable selves. But note also that Boff was himself liberated not only to identify with the 'feminine' Spirit of God but also to acknowledge the feminine spirit within himself, to claim the *anima* (feminine principle) hitherto ignored.

The Spirit of life is gift and the giver of gifts. She speaks to the oppressed and oppressors alike, for the former can become accustomed to their oppression and passively succumb to it; the latter may plead ignorance and persist in oppressing. On that account one ought not to see the gifts or the fruits of the Spirit of life in isolation. Besides freedom, the oppressed may need fortitude[12] to hold their ground and resist the oppressor; while on the other hand knowledge, counsel and fear of the Lord may serve to free the oppressor. Paul writes: 'From the beginning 'till now the whole creation, as we know, has been groaning in one great act of giving birth; and not only creation, but all of us who possess the first fruits of the Spirit, we too groan inwardly as we wait for our bodies to be set free' (Rom. 8:22–23).

Clearly it is not merely 'the body' that stands in need of life-giving freedom – we wrestle with or against prejudices, poverty, alienation, fear, anxiety, oppressive social structures and violence. Freedom from alienation, for example, is one of the great themes of our times. People are at enmity with and estranged from one other on the basis of sex, race, social status, religion or political persuasions. The phrase 'born free' is therefore something of a misnomer. Few if any people enter the world without some 'sting in the flesh', some handicap, some obsessive habit, some oppressive force placing limits on their freedom. All the more reason therefore to be aware of the possibilities for breaking those vicious cycles. Once again we need to pray: 'Come, Holy Spirit, giver of freedom, renew the face of the earth.'

The Spirit has often been described as the love which exists between God and the *Logos*. Those who are born of the Spirit can feed on that same Spirit and grow in love. In other words, the Spirit of life does not merely 'beget' offspring, she also nourishes and guides them towards maturity, giving them opportunities 'for the hidden self to grow strong' (Eph. 3:16) so that rooted and grounded in Christ's love they might be nourished and filled with 'the utter fullness of God'. In other words, life in the Spirit presupposes growing up and reaching spiritual maturity.

One cannot say everything about the Spirit of life in one short chapter but I would like to include one final key notion, namely a reflection on the breath of the Spirit that is God's *ruach* (the Hebrew word for life-giving breath).

## The Breath of the Spirit of Life

In the natural order the birthing process means leaving the darkness of the womb and coming into the light, into a new and greater world. The new-born creature gasps for breath, and thereafter a new and more independent form of existence begins.

Let us return to the book of Genesis, this time to Genesis 2:7. The human person having been fashioned from the dust of the earth, the breath of God was poured into its nostrils and a living being was created. In some mysterious way, not only were women and men imaged in God's likeness but the breath (Spirit) of God was given to them. That vital element was added to the material parts of the human body and they became living body–souls.

If the weakness of human persons lies in the fact that they came from dust and would return to dust, then their strength lies in the fact that they are now living souls with God's Spirit in them. That divine image and life can never be snuffed out.

'The Spirit of God has made me, and the breath of the Almighty gives me life', said Job confidently (Job 33:4). Donald Gelpi points out, in his fine book *The*

*Divine Mother: A Trinitarian Theology of the Holy Spirit,* that 'the breath' is a free gift from the very lips of God and that 'there is a sense in which it continues to belong to the Lord of life'.[13] We are living on borrowed breath!

The divine *ruach* has been linked with religious consciousness or enlightenment and also with the interior and spiritual life. It has been identified with 'practical wisdom' (Gen. 41:38), which could make a chancellor out of the boy-prisoner Joseph. That same breath of the Spirit would raise up charismatic leaders and prophets who collectively would mobilise and support Israel in her darkest hours (Nah. 17:30, Judg. 3:10, Deut. 34:9). The breath of the Spirit of life could seize hold of a woman or man, as it did at the anointing of David and, more significantly, it 'stayed with him from that day on' (1 Sam. 16:13).

In all cases the living breath of the Spirit empowers believers, making them sensitive to the workings of God in their lives. It enables them to be faithful to their covenantal relationship with God. It illumines their minds and their hearts. Under the influence of the breath of the Spirit of God, prophets found a wisdom, which the ignorant described as 'ravings' (Hos. 9:7). In some cases the breath brought not only illumination but also extraordinary courage. The prophet Micah could say without batting an eyelid: 'I am full of the strength of the breath of Yahweh, of justice and courage, to declare Jacob's crimes to his face and Israel's to his' (Mic. 3:8). The same breath was capable of keeping chariot wheels in motion (Ezek. 1:22). What a saving for the horses!

Psalm 139:7 says that there is no escaping from the breath of God. But the pursuing *ruach* is clearly neither antagonistic nor vindictive, merely watchful as a benign and protective presence, a presence that alleviates anxiety and engenders peace, inducing holy living. It is life-giving not only for humankind but also for all of created reality. 'You give breath, fresh life begins, you keep renewing the world' (Ps. 104:30). All creatures depend on that life, for should the divine *ruach* stop they would simply die.

In the New Testament the Greek *pneuma* replaces the Hebrew *ruach*. This *pneuma* was the Breath of the Risen Lord, whom Paul repeatedly witnessed to. That was the life-force which had transformed Paul's existence (Rom. 1:3—4) and which would empower the early Christian community (1 Cor. 3:1—3). The *pneuma* was, moreover, gracious and the giver of freedom (Rom. 8:14—15). The *pneuma* also bestowed numerous gifts: love, joy, peace, patience, kindness, goodness, trustfulness, gentleness and self-control. Paul adds: 'Since the Spirit [*pneuma*] is our life, let us be directed by the Spirit' (Gal. 5:26), but each one according to the particular gifts granted to each.

Like Christ who was crucified and rose again, members of the early Christian community were conscious that they might have to die violently. It was the *pneuma* of God that empowered them not only to face martyrdom for Christ's sake but to do it joyfully.

## Conclusion

I would like to end on a hopeful note. The Spirit of life is the strength of those who have no strength. In obvious and less obvious ways this same Spirit has been at work from the beginning, preparing for new creations and for the birth of a new humanity. Liberation theologians, like José Comblin, do not hesitate to say that she 'leads the struggle for the emancipation and fulfilment of the people, of the oppressed'.[14] Furthermore, the Spirit acts in history in women and men who carry the Spirit within themselves and who awaken the poor to freedom, to self-respect, to speaking out, to building community life creatively. Prompted by the Spirit, expressions of spirituality are born often out of situations of struggle and of near-despair. The Spirit moves, touching people gently from within, putting marrow into dry bones and passion into anaemic souls, compelling them to render service in love, a service which bears much fruit. The fecund Spirit of Jesus still continues to brood over the earth and a voice is still heard saying: 'Let there be life.'

[1] Frederick D. Brunner, *The Holy Spirit: Shy Member of the Trinity* (Minneapolis: Augsburg Publishing House, 1984), p. 14.

[2] Ibid., p. 17.

[3] See John 1:1–8.

[4] C. Westermann, *Creation* (Philadelphia: Fortress, 1974).

[5] Elizabeth Johnson, *She Who Is: The Mystery of God in Feminist Theological Discourse* (New York: Crossroad, 1993), p. 130.

[6] P. G. Allen, *Grandmother of the Sun* (Boston: Beacon, 1986), p. 22.

[7] Alwyn Marriage, *Life-giving Spirit: Responding to the Feminine in God* (London: SPCK 1989), p. 97.

[8] Elisabeth Schüssler Fiorenza, *In Memory of Her* (New York: Crossroad, 1987), pp. 140–141.

[9] We can only speak in allegories (comparisons) when we speak about God – God is a mother/father, the Spirit is a Comforter, Jesus is the Good Shepherd. As human beings we have no alternative!

[10] S. Ntwasa and B. Moore, 'The Challenge of Black Theology in South Africa' in G. S. Wilmore and J. H. Cone (eds.), *Black Theology* (New York: Orbis Press, 1979), p. 430.

[11] Leonardo Boff, *The Maternal Face of God: The Feminine and Its Religious Expressions*, translated into English by R. Barr and J. Diercksmeier (Maryknoll: Orbis Press, 1987), p. 101.

[12] Among the Spirit's gifts are wisdom, understanding, counsel, fortitude, knowledge, piety and fear of the Lord.

[13] Donald Gelpi, *The Divine Mother: A Trinitarian Theology of the Holy Spirit* (New York: University Press of America, 1994), p. 45.

[14] José Comblin, *The Holy Spirit and Liberation* (Maryknoll: Orbis Press, 1987), p. 185.

## Select Bibliography

Allen, P. G. *Grandmother of the Sun*. Boston: Beacon, 1986

Boff, Leonardo. *The Maternal Face of God: The Feminine and Its Religious Expressions*, translated into English by R. Barr and J. Diercksmeier. Maryknoll: Orbis Press, 1989

Brunner, Frederick D. *The Holy Spirit: Shy Member of the Trinity*. Minneapolis: Augsburg Publishing House, 1984

Comblin, José. *The Holy Spirit and Liberation*. Maryknoll: Orbis Press, 1987

Fiorenza, Elisabeth S. *In Memory of Her*. New York: Crossroad, 1987

Gelpi, Donald. *The Divine Mother: A Trinitarian Theology of the Holy Spirit*. New York: University Press of America, 1994

Johnson, Elizabeth. *She Who Is: The Mystery of God in Feminist Theological Discourse*. New York: Crossroad, 1993

Marriage, Alwyn. *Life-giving Spirit: Responding to the Feminine in God*. London: SPCK, 1989

Westermann, Claus. *Creation*. Philadelphia: Fortress, 1974

# 7

# Trinitarian Experience and Doctrine

## BRIAN GAYBBA

The doctrine of the Trinity, which puts the Christian view of God in a brief formula, can lay claim to being *the* most important of all Christian beliefs. This chapter will attempt to make clear why this is so.

The chapter has two main parts. The first sketches the historical development of the doctrine, and provides a brief outline of it in its classic form. The second explains part of the relevance of the doctrine to Christian belief and practice.

### The History of the Doctrine

Scripture does not talk about three persons in one God. But it does talk about Father, Son and Spirit in such a way that the development of some sort of trinitarian view of God was inevitable. By a 'trinitarian view of God' I mean a way of thinking that regards not only the Father but also the Son and the Spirit as being in some way or other part of the divine side of things and as having distinct roles to play in humanity's creation and salvation. In this section I will trace the broad outlines of that development, from its emergence in apostolic times to its consolidation in a fifth-century creed.

It is especially in those parts of the New Testament that speak about the risen Lord that we see a trinitarian view of God developing. Let me mention just some of the texts illustrating this.

In 2 Thessalonians 2:13–17, written barely twenty years after Jesus' death, we find Paul associating all three with the divine work of our salvation. A few years later we find in Galatians 4:6 an even more developed trinitarian mentality. Here we see all three helping people to share in the Son's relationship with the Father. Moreover, the Spirit — *God's* Spirit — is clearly described as *Jesus'* Spirit. This is a further way of associating Jesus with the divine. But it also reinforces the idea that there is a distinction between the Spirit and God (that is, between the Spirit and the Father) that was not really envisaged in Israelite religion as described in the Hebrew Bible.

Moving on to a slighter later period, we find in Ephesians 4:3–6 a text that stresses their contribution to the church's unity and therefore their own unity with each other, an idea that surfaces again in 1 Corinthians 12:4–6. Further examples of 'trinitarian' texts can be found in 2 Corinthians 1:21–22, 3:3 and 13:14. The last is particularly interesting because it is evidence of the three coming to be named together in liturgical formulae that will be used over and over again.

The above texts (and others such as 1 Peter 1:2, Jude 20:21, Revelation 1:4–5 and Hebrews 6:4) all come from sources that concentrate on the life of the infant church after Pentecost. However, examples can also be taken from the gospels. Jesus' baptism, clearly a key revelatory event for the early Christians, is one such example (see Matthew 3:13–17 and parallel texts). Let me close this section by referring to two others.

The first is from the gospel of John, 15:26–16:15, where Jesus speaks of his relationship to the Father and to the Spirit. It is a text that not only underscores the close unity Jesus has with the Father, but also elucidates the respective relationships between all three. The Father is the source of all, the One who sends not only the Spirit but also the Son. The Father gives all he has to the Son, including the Spirit. The Son therefore can also send the Spirit, and does so. Moreover, since whatever the Father has belongs to the Son, whatever the Spirit brings is derived from the Son.

The second text is from Matthew's gospel – 28:19 – and is, by common consent, the high point of the development of a trinitarian mentality in apostolic times. It is also a formula that has entered into the church's baptismal liturgy. In this text, written probably as late as AD 85, the three are named alongside each other as though all were equal, the only differentiation being their ordering.

In early post-apostolic times the custom continues of associating Father, Son and Spirit with each other in the way we have just seen. Barely fifty years after the end of the apostolic period (*c.* 155) we can see the outlines of a formula developing that will become customary in the church: 'to the Father . . . through the Son . . . and the Holy Spirit' (see for example Justin Martyr's *Apology* I, 65). And only twenty years later (*c.* 180) we find Theophilus of Antioch describing the three as a 'triad', that is to say a 'threesome'. The term 'triad' did not enter into Western theological thought. But a similar term coined about sixty years later by the African scholar Tertullian did – 'Trinity'.

Tertullian also coined the phrase 'three persons in one substance', to bring out the fact that the distinction of persons did not imply dividing the divine substance between them. God was one in substance but three in the way in which that substance was shared. About a century later, theologians from the East came up with a similar formula: 'three hypostases in one substance'. It was coined by a group of theologians known as the Cappadocians, since they were all born in Cappadocia. The basic idea behind both formulae was that the one, undivided Godhead was shared in three different ways.

In the fifth century in the West, a creed was composed that spelt out all the implications of the formula. It also highlighted the core Christian beliefs that necessitated some such formula: Father, Son and Spirit are distinct realities and each fully God. Nevertheless, there is only one God. The creed is known as the *Quicumque*, after its opening word, and also as the Athanasian Creed, after Athanasius, who was at one time wrongly believed to have been its author.

It should be clear by now that the Christian doctrine of the Trinity has its roots in Scripture and is not, as some have tried to argue, derived from pagan polytheistic or philosophical ideas. However, philosophical ideas provided early Christian thinkers with tools for trying to understand how a single divine substance could be shared by three without being divided. We turn, then, to some of those ideas and the models built with them.

The Apologists tried to use Stoic ideas about *logos* to understand the relationship between Jesus and the Father, especially to explain how they could be part of one undivided divinity and yet distinct from each other. *Logos* means reason or word. The Stoics distinguished between the 'immanent *logos*' and the 'expressed *logos*'. The former is reason in an inactivated state, while the latter is its activated expression. Applied to God, the divine *logos* was merely immanent within the Godhead until the moment of creation, when it became activated, a *logos* expressed in the order and harmony in the world.

Prior to creation, the Apologists argued, the Son was only immanent — that is, not clearly formed — within the Godhead. With creation, however, the Son sprang forth within the divinity as an idea springs forth within our minds, thereby becoming the 'expressed *logos*'. There were now two clearly distinct realities within God: the thinker (the Father) and the expressed thought (the Son).

As can be seen, the basic idea here is to compare the Son to an idea springing forth from the mind of God. This way of picturing the relationship between Father and Son became part of classic Western trinitarian theology, as a result especially of Augustine's 'psychological model'. It was an attractive model precisely because Scripture itself refers to the Son as the *logos* or 'word' of God, with God from the beginning, expressing the mind of God perfectly (John 1:1–14). The Apologists' version of it had for many the drawback that it seemed to deny the eternity of the Son's existence — since the Son springs forth clearly only at creation. But the model itself was to remain. As regards the Spirit, this was seen as some sort of effluence flowing from God. However, the Apologists had no intellectual model within which to place the Spirit.

Later in the same century we find Irenaeus of Lyons extending the Apologists' model to the emergence of the Spirit too. He does so by distinguishing within God the capacity for reason (God's latent Word) and the capacity for spiritual activity (God's latent Wisdom). At the moment of creation and redemption these latent capacities are activated, and in their activated, expressed form are known as the Son and the Spirit respectively. Thus activated, they can be compared to 'hands' used by the Father for our creation and redemption.

Writing in the third century, Tertullian also used the Stoic idea of the emergence of the *logos* from an immanent to an expressed state in order to explain how the Son could be both divine and yet distinct from the Father. However, he also used other models or images, all of which bring out a further point, namely the relationship between Son and Spirit. For he uses images that evoke the idea of a process beginning with the Father, moving *through* the Son and ending up in the Holy Spirit: a fruit derived from a shoot which in turn grows from the root; a channel of water drawn from a river whose source is a spring; a point of light at the end of a beam that originates in the sun.

Origen lived at the same time as Tertullian but was an Eastern thinker. The model used by him was drawn from the emerging Neoplatonic philosophy of the time. The overarching idea is that goodness has a built-in drive to share itself. This impulse to share moves the original, undifferentiated, divine One to produce Mind. From Mind there emerges Soul. Soul has two levels, a higher and a lower level. From the latter, matter is produced. Origen fitted his trinitarian thought into this scheme. The Father is identified with the One. To produce the world, he first produces Mind, the Son. And just as Soul flows from Mind, so too the Spirit proceeds from the Father *through* the Son — a point Tertullian made in another way.

As we saw, the Cappadocians bequeathed to the East the formula 'three hypostases in one substance'. Moreover, they distinguished between them as follows: a *hypostasis* is a particular way in which a substance exists. The difference between the two is therefore the difference between the particular (*hypostasis*) and the general (substance). Father, Son and Spirit are portrayed as three particular ways in which one and the same divine substance exists. To illustrate the difference between the general and the particular, Basil of Caesarea appealed to the example of humanity shared by several individuals. We all share fully in the substance known as 'humanity' but we are all different realisations of it. We are all human beings. But we are all different ways of being human.

Of course, this was only an analogy. If it were applied to God too literally, one would end up with three gods. But it does illustrate the basic point the Fathers were trying to make, namely that one and the same divine substance can have three different and quite distinct (though not separate) ways of existing *simultaneously*. To make the same point more crudely: the one undivided Godhead exists simultaneously in three different 'shapes' — as Father, Son and Spirit.

The Cappadocian model, therefore, is of a single substance having three different and yet simultaneous ways of existing. What differentiates each way is either the fact that it is the original, underived way (the Father) or one of the two ways in which it is derived from that original position (Son and Spirit). The more accurate model, then, is as follows: a single undivided substance, existing simultaneously in three different ways, each of which is unceasingly flowing either into or out of the others. The flow is known as the divine *perichoresis* or *circumincessio*.

In trying to deepen his understanding of the Trinity, Augustine took as his starting point the fact that, according to the Scriptures, humanity has been made in God's image and likeness. The best place to look for a model or image of the Trinity, therefore, is within ourselves, at our spiritual natures. In pursuing this line of thought he developed several 'psychological models' (as they came to be called) of the Trinity. The main ones all revolve around the capacity of the human mind to know and love.

The aspects of the mind that Augustine eventually singled out were the following: its ability to be aware of itself (which he called 'memory'), to understand itself (which he called 'understanding') and to love itself ('love'). Here we have an undivided spiritual reality (the human mind) that can exist in three distinct but related forms: self-awareness, self-understanding and self-love. This provides us with a model of a God whose self-awareness (Father) giving rise to self-understanding (Son) is completed in an act of self-love (Holy Spirit).

The earliest models began by focusing on the divine mind. Augustine balanced this out by bringing in the divine capacity to love. In the twelfth century we see Richard of St Victor moving to the other extreme and focusing exclusively on love. In doing so, he gave rise to what has been called the 'family model' of the Trinity, because it pictures the love of two persons for each other producing a third, almost as an offspring.

Richard's starting point is the idea that God will automatically love in the fullest possible way. God's initial drive to love results in the following structure within the Godhead: a love that is given freely ('gratuitous love') and a love that is received ('indebted love'). However, love shared only by two is not yet perfect, since perfect love leads lovers to turn away from each other so as to share their love with a third. Hence gratuitous and indebted love – Father and Son – produce what Richard calls a 'co-beloved'. Love in this third form is the Holy Spirit. It is a love that is *purely* received, since it issues in no further forms of love.

The Scriptures provide not only the basic raw material from which some such doctrine as the Trinity had to emerge but also a clear indication of the relationship that existed between the three. The Father always appears as the source of both the Son and the Spirit, as the one who sends the Son and sends the Spirit. As regards the relationship between the Son and the Spirit, the Spirit is repeatedly referred to as the Spirit of the Son and not vice versa: the Son, too, sends the Spirit but the Spirit is never spoken of as sending the Son.

Hence, Christian thinkers always spoke of the Son as proceeding – that is, coming – from the Father. As regards the Spirit, however, a dispute arose between East and West that was to become a major point of division between them. The West believed that the Spirit's dependence on the Son can only be due to the fact that the Spirit proceeds or flows from not only the Father but also the Son. This is the doctrine known as the *filioque*, a Latin word meaning 'and from the Son'. The Greeks, on the other hand, believed that the Spirit flows only from the Father, even though the Son has a role in giving the Spirit to us and even in shaping the Spirit's identity. The dispute continues to this day.

By the end of the fifteenth century, the typically Western theology of the Trinity was more or less complete. Indeed, its basic outlines had already been shaped as early as the sixth century. This is therefore a useful place to pause and summarise the main elements of that theology.

The classic formulation of the doctrine of the Trinity is that there are three 'persons' in one undivided God. Each of the 'persons' is fully divine, none is 'more' God than any of the others. This means that a distinction must be made between 'person' and 'nature'. 'Nature' refers to the one undivided divine substance. 'Person' refers to the way in which that undivided substance is shared or, more accurately, to a particular way in which it exists. As used here, therefore, 'person' is a term that does not refer (as we normally do) to someone who has his or her own separate nature, mind and will. On the contrary the divine three share fully one undivided nature, one undivided mind, one undivided will. The *whole* of the divinity – mind, will, consciousness – exists in three inseparable and undivided ways: as the unbegotten origin of all else (the Father); as the begotten expression of all that the Father is (the Son); and as (according to one stream of thought) the bond of love between Father and Son or (according to another stream of thought) the result of a single act of love on their part.

The three unique ways in which the divine nature exists or (as it is technically put) 'subsists' are derived from a process within the divinity that sets up a relationship between each of them. It is this relationship that distinguishes Father, Son and Spirit from each other. Indeed, it is this relationship that creates their very identity. Thus the Father *is* the divine nature existing as source of the Son, while the Son *is* the divine nature existing as flowing from the Father as the Father's image. The Spirit (in Western theology) *is* the divine nature existing as a love that flows from both Father and Son.

The term 'procession' here simply means the coming forth of one divine person from another. Christian tradition — both East and West — has always distinguished two processions. The first is the procession of the Son from the Father. The second is the procession of the Spirit, which in Western theology is from Father *and* Son.

The term 'procession' itself is a biblical term. It is used of the Holy Spirit's coming forth from the Father in John 15:26. Although it was originally applied only to the Holy Spirit, it came to be used in Western theology as a generic term referring to the coming forth of both Son and Spirit. Other terms were used for distinguishing between them — the Son's procession was called 'generation', the Spirit's 'spiration'.

As noted above, the Son proceeds from the Father. That, and that alone, is what is demanded by Christian orthodoxy. However, the West developed a speculative explanation of the Son's procession, one that connected it with God's mind. As refined by Thomas Aquinas, the Son proceeds from the Father's intellect, as a mental image proceeds from our intellect. This idea also meshed very well with biblical references to the Son as the 'Word' of God (John 1:1ff.), the 'image of the invisible God' (Col. 1:15) and 'Wisdom' (see 1 Cor. 1:24). 'Word' and 'Wisdom' evoke ideas of a mind at work, and 'Word' also evokes the idea of the creation of a mental image.

As regards the Spirit, the West saw the Spirit as proceeding from an act of the divine will as possessed by Father and Son. The Spirit proceeded as the love or result of the love that flowed from Father and Son.

This way of understanding the divine processions was also very attractive because it seemed to make so much sense. God is a spirit, and a spirit has two basic activities: knowing and willing. That the Son should be spoken of in Scripture as the image or Word of the Father, while the Spirit is connected with divine action or love, seems to be well explained if one sees the former as proceeding from the divine mind and the latter from the divine will.

Since the divine persons share a single nature, they are said to 'be in' or 'flow into' each other. This is referred to as the divine *perichoresis* (a Greek term) or, to use its Latin equivalent, *circumincessio*. The rational grounding of this doctrine is simply the fact that they share one nature. However, a biblical ground was also found in Jesus' words in John 10:38.

Precisely because all that distinguishes the divine persons from each other is their mutual relationships, everything else is held by them in common. Hence, every divine action which has an effect beyond the borders of the divinity (*ad extra divinitatem*) is performed by all three acting in unison. This is a sound principle. However, it came to be distorted in Western theology by saying that one could not really distinguish the Father's contribution from that of the Son (apart from the Son's taking on a human nature), or either's contribution from that of the Spirit. Modern theologies of the Trinity have corrected this distortion.

We can now look back and see that what has developed is not simply a particular theology but a Christian *dogma*. In other words, the Trinity has become an unquestioned part of the faith of the church. The doctrine therefore has the merit of presenting a clear expression of what Christians believed were the full implications of the relevant biblical data.

On the negative side, however, we have witnessed the price paid for that clarity: the isolation of the doctrine from its roots in the involvement of Father, Son and Spirit in our salvation. Trinitarian theology had become exclusively a theology of the 'immanent' Trinity — that is, the Trinity considered solely as an inner divine reality, where all the attention is focused on the relationships between Father, Son and Spirit and on the problem of maintaining both their distinction and the divine unity. This 'immanent Trinity' became divorced from the 'economic' Trinity, which is the Trinity as involved in the 'economy' of salvation. Not surprisingly, the Trinity ceased to have any practical relevance for Christians. It contributed nothing to their experience of salvation and did not enter in any meaningful way into their prayer life. It functioned mainly as the supreme 'mystery' of their faith.

In the twentieth century, theologians have come to stress again the unity of the economic and immanent trinities. Perhaps the most renowned of the attempts to do so is that of the German theologian Karl Rahner, who loved to say that the immanent Trinity *is* the economic trinity and vice versa. Let us now see what a theology of the Trinity looks like that takes this principle seriously.

## Taking God's Incarnation Seriously: The Trinity As a Divine–Human Reality

As far as we are concerned, the only 'inner divine life' we know of is the relationship between the Father, the man Jesus Christ and the Spirit binding them to each other. Even if one believes that there was an inner life within God before Jesus appeared on this earth, Jesus' coming has changed that inner life forever. For Jesus' coming means that God no longer has any life that is unrelated to human beings. The Son is and remains for all eternity both a human being and part of God's own very being. The Spirit flows for all eternity from both the Father and a human being (if one subscribes to the Western *filioque*). In short, there is no such thing as a Trinity apart from humanity. What God's inner life would have looked like apart from the man Jesus of Nazareth is of no interest or relevance to us. For the fact is that the only Trinity Christians know of is one in which a human being — Jesus — is one of its members.

This is the deep truth embedded in Rahner's insistence that the immanent Trinity *is* the economic Trinity and vice versa. God's own trinitarian life is an incarnate form of life. When the Word became flesh, what became incarnate was not simply a single person but a network of divine relationships. All this implies that God's inner life became something visible, something that was seen by people.

To appreciate this point, let us dwell for a moment on Jesus' baptism. There we see the Father proclaiming Jesus to be his beloved Son, and his Spirit descending on Jesus. But what we are witnessing is not simply the relationship between a human being and God, but God's own inner life exposed, made visible. We are witnessing an event taking place within the divinity. Moreover, that incident enables us to understand that the rest of Jesus' life was a life being lived within the divinity. The rest of Jesus' life was the living out of the relationship between Father, Son and Spirit. The rest of Jesus' life was the living out of God's own love life.

But that is still not all. When we think of Jesus' life as the living out of God's own love life we must not look simply at Jesus' relationship with his Father and his possession of the Spirit. For Jesus stands before his Father not simply as a divine person unrelated to anything outside of the divinity but rather as a human being who has a mother, a foster-father, close relatives, distant relatives, friends, a nation — an entire world filled with joys and sorrows. All of these other links are part of his and therefore part of God's own love life. Granted they can never be part of God in the same sense as Jesus is. But to the extent that they are part of Jesus' world they are also part of God's world. They are a visible part of God's inner life.

God became part of humanity's world so that we can become part of God's world. The doctrine of the Trinity is a doctrine that God is a community, a community of Father, Son and Spirit. Humanity, created as it is in God's image (Gen. 1:26–27), is also a community. God's plan was not that the two communities should each have their own group area but rather that they should be fully integrated. That was why the Word became flesh and the divine Spirit of love was poured out on all at Pentecost.

The idea that our life is part of God's inner life and vice versa is central to Christianity. It is the whole point of the doctrine of the Trinity. It is summed up in that famous text from 2 Peter 1:4: 'Do you not know that you are sharers in the divine nature?' In time this came to mean in both East and West that somehow or other our own being was transformed by God's presence, just as iron glows when placed in a fire. However, the fuller biblical picture is that we share in God's love life. We become, in a real sense, part of the Trinity. For the Father becomes *our* father, the Spirit of love *our* Spirit of love, binding us all to each other.

The church is meant to be the place where we can see and experience this divine—human community taking shape down the ages. For it is only in the church that we have a community of people who publicly proclaim Christ as their brother, the Father as their father and the Spirit as the love binding them to each other. The church is called to *be* something before *doing* something: to be the visible embodiment through the ages of the ongoing life of the economic Trinity.

But even in the church this divine—human community is only a shadow of what it is meant to be. It can only become fully what it is meant to be by going through the same process of death and resurrection that Jesus did. Only then will we be freed not simply from all sinful influences but also from the limitations of space and time, as we experience them. Only then will our humanity be so transformed that at last we will be able to be 'inside' each other as Father and Son are. Only then will we be able to be present to each other in the Spirit as Father and Son are present to us now. Only then will we share as fully as a creature can in the Trinity's *perichoresis*, the unending flowing into and out of each other.

The doctrine of the Trinity thus clearly affects the way in which we view salvation. In the past salvation was viewed individualistically. That is to say, all the emphasis was on the individual's relationship with God, and with a God viewed pretty much as a single individual. However, if God is a community of Father, Son and Spirit, then salvation implies being inserted into the life of a community. To be saved means not simply having one's personal sins forgiven or getting into heaven but rather to share in the life of a community.

Moreover, if this community is not simply a divine community but a divine—human community, then to be saved is to be made part of a family that includes not only Father, Son and Spirit but also neighbour. Love of God and love of neighbour are not merely inseparable. They are part and parcel of one and the same love. For the love that binds all the members of this divine—human community to each other is formed within them by the Love that is Holy Spirit.

Hence, building up human community can be part and parcel of the very experience of salvation. When we reach out to the poor, the lonely, the oppressed and treat them for what they are, namely our brothers and sisters, we are enabling them to experience not simply human love and caring but also what it means to share in God's own community life. We are enabling them to experience an important dimension of salvation.

It has become somewhat fashionable in theological writings to argue that a trinitarian model of God pushes one in the direction of democratic, egalitarian structures, while viewing God as a single person (called the 'monarchical' model, viewing God as a monarch) pushes one in the direction of authoritarian, hierarchical structures. The general drift of the argument is that to conceive of God as a single person, Lord of the universe, is to have a model that legitimates autocratic structures in both church and state — pope and king. Conversely, to conceive of God as a community of coequal persons is to have a model that demands democratic, egalitarian structures — a congregational one in church affairs and a socialist one in the political realm.

A good deal of confused thinking occurs here. For the truth is that both monarchical and trinitarian models of God can support democratic and undemocratic structures. One must not forget that it was ancient Israel's very monarchical view of God that was the inspiration behind its originally federalist and egalitarian social structures. Moreover, the doctrine of the Trinity is not simply the doctrine that there are three coequal persons in one God. It also asserts that there is a definite order amongst the persons — the Father comes first, whom the Son obeys in all things, and the Spirit witnesses to the Son and not to herself.

What is far more important than the mere structure of our model — monarchical or trinitarian — is the way God acts, especially in relation to human beings. And it is here that the doctrine of the Trinity has an undeniable advantage as a theological basis for reflecting on social structures. For the Trinity teaches us that God is structured along the lines of a self-emptying love. The Father shares everything with the Son, who gives himself totally to the Father (John 5:19ff.). The Spirit is the love that turns that ceaseless flow from Father to Son and back into something more than merely physically sharing a divine 'substance'.

If God is structured like that, then our ecclesiastical and political structures must reflect self-emptying, mutual service, love and, above all, sharing. For the real value of the Trinity as a socio-political model is to be found in the total sharing that is the very foundation for the distinction between the divine persons.

Since, in our sinful world, monarchical structures usually tend to block this idea of sharing and entrench the privileges of those in authoritarian positions, a more democractic, indeed socialist-type structure would seem to reflect more easily the God that Christians believe in. However, whether that is so in a particular situation will depend very much on that situation. What is crucial is that Christians should oppose any social structures that work against rather than for a social climate in which the emphasis is on mutual belonging, service and sharing. If humanity's destiny is to be as one with each other ('inside' each other!) as Father and Son are, then any church or state structure that reflects that ideal, however dimly, is to be supported. On the other hand, structures that entrench radically contradictory ideals (apartheid or self-aggrandisement at the expense of others, for example) are to be opposed.

Church structures, in particular, should be subjected to a piercing criticism by Christians. It is very difficult for Christians to point convincing fingers at inadequate or sinful political or economic structures if the way they structure their own togetherness in Christ reflects more of a concern for power, domination and self-centredness than the Trinity, whose life they are telling the world they share.

Finally, I would like to say something about integrating the doctrine of the Trinity into the way we practise our Christianity. Let me begin with prayer. Many Christians pray to God as though the doctrine of the Trinity did not exist. They address their prayers simply to 'God', without reflecting on which of the divine persons they are talking to.

If we take the doctrine of the Trinity seriously, it will mean becoming conscious of the persons in our prayer life. Moreover, it will mean becoming conscious of the different relationship we have with each of them. To make a conscious effort to alter our prayer habits so that we relate in a different way to Father, Son and Spirit will make the Trinity come alive for us. One will actually begin the process of living one's incorporation into God's own communal life.

Taking the Trinity seriously also means taking seriously the fact that other human beings are our brothers and sisters. It means trying to transfer some of the family feelings we have for our own blood brothers and sisters to the wider community. I say 'some of the family feelings' because it should be obvious that it is physically impossible to relate to a large group of human beings in exactly the same way one can relate to the smaller group of one's own blood relatives. Moreover, it is only in the small group that one is able to learn the skills of loving and accepting that are so important for the stability of the larger group. However, taking seriously our insertion into the life of the Trinity means taking seriously the fact that experiencing our earthly parents and siblings is meant to be the beginning of a broader and deeper experience. This is the experience that the whole of humanity is — as intended by God — a single family in which all are brothers and sisters of each other, sharing a Love that flows out of and back to our common divine parent through our brother, Jesus Christ.

The two families — our own and that of wider humanity — are not meant to be opposed. The one should feed into and support the other. However, should they clash, one cannot without further ado choose one's blood family. The needs of the wider one could well demand that in a case of irreducible conflict we choose it. This was why Jesus said that a consequence of his coming could well be that family members are set over against each other (Matt. 10:34). This was why he said that we had to love him more than father, mother, brother, sister (Matt. 10:37ff.). This was why he himself made it clear that his own brothers and sisters were far broader than the narrow circle of those who came to call him on a particular occasion (Matt. 12:50).

Our world is one in which systems such as apartheid are roundly condemned. But it is still a world in which national interests are regarded as being so important that they attempt to demand all our loyalty. Indeed, national interests are repeatedly appealed to in order to block moves that would lead to a more just international system. The United Nations does provide some forum for counteracting this tendency. But the time still has to come when Christians allow the doctrine of the Trinity to cast a sufficiently critical light on nationalism so as to condemn many of its forms with all the ferocity with which apartheid was condemned. For much of contemporary nationalism is really just apartheid writ large and dressed up in an acceptable way.

Part of a Christian's spirituality, therefore, is to see not only the family but also the nation-state as but a sign of a larger reality. And it is this larger reality, the establishment of a divine—human community, that operates as a final, absolute yardstick against which all lesser loyalties must be measured. Family loyalties and national loyalties do indeed have their place, an extremely important place. Without them we cannot grow in the experience of loving and sharing. However, they are but embodiments of a larger reality and it is the larger, trinitarian reality that is of ultimate importance.

Note that I said that it is the larger, trinitarian reality that is of ultimate importance — and not simply that it is God, the Trinity, that is of ultimate importance. The reason is, once again, that we cannot separate the immanent and economic trinities. Humanity is part of God's inner life, for Jesus was and remains forever a human being. And by the same token, God is part of humanity's life. This means that we cannot separate God and humanity and say that the former is of ultimate significance while the latter has only relative value. Belief in the economic Trinity means that we can no longer separate the two. Certainly it is possible to separate individual human beings from the economic Trinity and from the broader divine—human community centred on the economic Trinity. The doctrine of hell is the doctrine that this awful possibility exists. But it is not possible to separate the human from the divine and give ultimate significance only to the latter.

This is why Jesus regarded love of neighbour and love of God as being inextricably linked, so much so that one could say that they are of equal importance (Matt. 22:38—39). It is why he was able to say that God's sabbath — Sunday! — was established for humanity's needs (Mark 2:27). The doctrine of the Trinity means that love of neighbour, too, has ultimate significance.

With that we have come to the end of this brief survey of the doctrine of the Trinity in Christianity. As can be seen, it is a doctrine that the infinite reality called 'God' is a community. It is a doctrine that this God has created the community of humanity for the purpose of sharing in that inner divine life. It is a doctrine that points us to the basic values necessary for sharing in it: self-emptying, even to the point of the Cross. It is a doctrine that tells us that God and humanity cannot be separated, with absolute value being given to the former and relative value to the latter. Rather it teaches us that the two have become so completely one that the best image for what the future holds in store for us is that we will be 'inside' each other — as Father, Son and Spirit are.

## Select Bibliography

Boff, L. *The Trinity and Society*. Maryknoll: Orbis, 1988
Gunton, C. E. *The Promise of Trinitarian Theology*. Edinburgh: T. & T. Clark, 1991
Hill, E. *The Mystery of the Trinity*. London: Chapman, 1985
Hodgson, L. *The Doctrine of the Trinity*. London: Nisbet, 1943
Kelly, A. *The Trinity of Love*. Wilmington: Glazier, 1989
Kelly, J. N. D. *Early Christian Doctrines*. London: Black, 1968
LaCugna, C. M. *God for Us: The Trinity and Christian Life*. San Francisco: Harper, 1991
Moltmann, J. *The Trinity and the Kingdom of God*. London: SCM, 1981
Panikkar, R. *The Trinity and the Religious Experience of Man*. London: Darton, Longman and Todd, 1973
Rahner, K. *The Trinity*. London: Burns and Oates, 1970

# PART THREE
# Creation and Redemption

# 8

# The Wonder, Agony and Promise of Creation

## FELICITY EDWARDS

The Christian belief that God made the world enhances confidence that God is on the side of life and fulfilment. Yet today there are aspects of creation which give us good reason to be terrified. Most basically, for instance, the soil on which life depends will soon be unable to support the people living on it. Agricultural land is turning into desert. Each year 24 billion tons of topsoil are lost. The United Nations calculates that in a mere six years time, by the year 2000, the population of the planet will be 6.35 billion and by 2020 it will be 8.5 billion, 7 billion of whom will be living in the so-called third world with very little chance of obtaining even minimum nutrition.[1] Right now, through exploitation and mismanagement, we are killing off many natural systems of which we humans are a part. Particularly during the last forty years we have been poisoning not only the soil but also the water and the air. We are at present changing the chemistry, the biological systems and even the temperature of the planet, as well as consuming non-renewable resources at an alarming rate.[2]

These are aspects of what is called the ecological crisis. It is a crisis of global dimensions, and we in South Africa are inevitably part of it. Ecology studies 'the relation of living organisms to their surroundings, their habits and modes of life'. The term 'ecology' comes from the Greek *oikos*, meaning a house or place to live.[3] Ecological insight is crucial for a theology of creation today.

It is accepted that theology must be both contextual and liberating. Ecology emphasises that the context of theology is the whole planet, and all the systems in it, as well as our own very specific situation. We can use ecological insights not only to understand but to liberate and transform ourselves, others and the environment. Ecology speaks of the world as a complex dynamic web of interdependent relationships.[4] It studies in detail these interrelationships and linkages, showing how change in any one part affects the whole and how the condition of the whole affects every part within it. So we are becoming aware that people, societies, animals, plants and the earth itself are not static and separate but are dynamic, constantly changing, and together make up the world in which we experience our personal and social identity. In this way ecology, although starting as a branch of natural science, opens onto the ethical, political and religious dimensions of life.[5]

Studies of our ecological crisis demonstrate that to a large extent the unsustainability of the earth and its major ecosystems is linked to socio-political injustice and human exploitation world-wide. But returning to traditional concepts of social justice will not be enough. These are going to have to be revised and enlarged to deal with the problems posed by failure to see the need for an ecologically sustainable society.[6]

This crisis is global and it calls for response. The rallying cry is 'Think globally, act locally now'.[7] We are looking to an ecological theology of creation. This is linked to a spirituality which goes straight to the question of personal and social identity: 'Who am I?' 'Who are we?' 'What is the world, and what is it or who is it that grounds and supports the existence of all that is?' The ecological problem is linked to the fact that most of us do not know who we are or what the cosmos is, and we are not aware of the severity and urgency of the global crisis.

A contemporary ecological doctrine of creation requires ideally that we re-vision who we are, what the world is, and how all this relates to God. It also requires that we move from this renewed vision to *experiencing* creation differently.

Theology and spirituality are interrelated in such a way that a contemporary theology of creation feeds into and is informed by lived ecological spirituality. This is both threatening and exhilarating. It is threatening in that we must be prepared to be changed, and perhaps to let go of cherished old patterns, both of how we perceive and of how we act, in order that new perceptions and actions may be possible. The good news is that as we begin to grasp the new vision of reality and begin to act appropriately, so energy becomes available to do what has to be done. And as we act, so there is exhilaration, transformation, liberation, new creation. That is what the wonder, agony and promise of creation are about.

## An Ecological Theology of Creation

There are three stages in the history of the doctrine of creation.[8] First, the biblical traditions and ancient cosmologies were combined, giving rise to a religious cosmology. Then, developing science emancipated itself from this religious cosmology, while theology retreated from all interest in cosmology, and the doctrine of creation was reduced to personal belief in creation. The third stage is the present transitional one where, pressured by the ecological crisis and the urgency of finding a new direction that will make global survival possible, theology and the sciences are moving fast and moving together towards an 'ecological awareness of the world'.[9]

In Genesis the two 'creation stories' express profound experience of createdness and, in story form, refer to 'the beginning'. The first creation story (Gen. 1:1–2:4a) tells of the stages by which the world came to be formed, and each stage up to humanity is declared to be 'very good'. Then man and woman, created in the image and likeness of God, are told, 'Be fruitful and multiply, fill the earth and subdue it.' Here humans are set apart from nature and, seemingly, put in a position to dominate nature. But as Moltmann points out, the creation of humankind is not the culmination of creation. Rather, the culmination is the

Sabbath, for 'after action comes letting things be, and after creation comes existence. . . The Sabbath is the consummation of creation; without it creation is incomplete. . .'[10] This 'letting be' is extremely important because letting be is precisely what love is in the Christian tradition. Love is linked with attaining full personhood within a just and sustainable world.

In the second creation story (Gen. 2:4b–25) God makes 'man' (*adam* in Hebrew) from the earth itself. God breathes into him the breath of life, making him a living being, and puts him in the garden of Eden to cultivate and take care of it. Then follows the story of the fall (Gen. 3:1–24), where there is a rupture in the relationship between humankind and God, and also between humankind and nature.

These two creation stories are basic to a contemporary understanding of who we are and what the world is. In one story human beings are continuous with nature and are given responsibility for taking care of it. In the other, humans are seen as separate from nature and 'mastering' it, having dominion or lordship over it. What has happened, particularly in Western culture, is that the notion of being separate from nature has predominated and has reinforced the urge to possess, control and exploit. In spite of the fact that Israel was quite clear that the land belongs to the Lord (cf. Lev. 25:23) and that nature is awesome, wondrous and to be sincerely respected, this urge to dominate nature and others has been a major factor contributing to the present ecological crisis. In the process, awareness of our common origin with the earth, and of our shared connectedness with it, has been undermined.[11]

## The Contours of the Doctrine of Creation

The doctrine of creation, as it has developed in the Christian tradition, may be summarised in the following eleven assertions that relate it to other aspects of Christian doctrine and to developing science. Reading this, remember that things do not have to be as they are. The world does not have to be as it is. Transformation is possible. The promise is that the whole of creation will be brought to completion in the ultimate liberation, which is the implementation of all-encompassing love.

Christians assert, first, that the work of creation is the work of the whole Trinity — Father, Son and Holy Spirit — and from the beginning it is the work of love. The Trinity is the well-spring of unconditional love. The source of creation is God the Father. In the beginning, 'The spirit of God' moved creatively over the primeval waters (Gen. 1:2), while the Son is the Word of God, 'through whom all things were made' (John 1:3; cf. Col. 1:16). The Word through whom all things were created is the same Word who became incarnate in the person of Jesus Christ. Because of the incarnation we can make sense of creation, understanding it with our minds and contributing to its order.

Second, Christians claim that it is God alone who creates. The created order is therefore one and good. It is originally a well-ordered whole (*cosmos*) in which every part has its place and in which there is dependability and regularity, based on God's covenant faithfulness (cf. Gen. 8:22, 9:13–17).[12]

Third, creation is of all things. It is creation of space, time and all that is. There is literally no thing, nothing, that is not created by God. 'All things were made through him and without him was not anything made that was made' (John 1:3). All things are from God, through God and in God.

Fourth, creation is ultimately dependent on God. What God creates owes its existence only to the free, loving activity of God, which is the ultimate ground of all actuality. Conversely, if God's loving, creative activity were to be withdrawn for an instant, there would be literally no thing, nothing (cf. John 1:3; Ps. 104:29).

Fifth, although everything is ultimately dependent on God, creation has a degree of independence, of freedom. At the human level this links to freedom and responsibility. God, having created, stands back, as it were, and beholds what God has made, letting it be. This letting be is love.

Sixth, creation is understood theologically by three terms: as being by the Word, out of nothing, and continuous. Creation comes to be as God calls it into being through God's word. 'God said, "Let there be ..."' (Gen. 1:3ff.) and it was so. Speaking a word is a personal act, and God's Word in creation establishes a personal relationship between Creator and creation, the Word finally becoming flesh in the person of Jesus Christ (John 1:1–18).

God calls forth that which does not yet exist. This is most clearly expressed in 2 Maccabees 7:28, which was written in the time between the periods of the Hebrew and the Christian Scriptures (cf. Rom. 6:17; Heb. 11:3). There are two aspects of this doctrine. First, it stresses that God is completely transcendent, such that there is no organic connection between God and the world. Second, it stresses that God is sovereign, and does not have to work with pre-existent material which could offer resistance to, or place limitations on, God's divine will. This doctrine emphasises again that God alone creates; before creation, all there was was God. By creation out of nothing God 'makes room' for created reality.

God's loving creation activity could not be limited to the beginning. God did not create everything at once; rather God continues to create. Here there is included the doctrine of providence: everything is sustained moment by moment (cf. Col. 1:17). God both preserves and innovates. It is important to note that history is being created by God. God, the Lord of history, is doing new things, moment by moment. It is significant that the Hebrew word *bara*, which is 'the unique word for the divine creation, is used much more frequently in the Bible for God's creation of liberation and salvation in history than for the initial creation of the world'.[13] This is also where we come in, for there is a sense in which we are created co-creators with God (cf. 3.2).

Seventh, it is only by faith that we know that the world was created by God (cf. Heb. 11:3). This means that we cannot simply look at the world and read off the fact that it is made by God. This is why we are doing the *theology* of creation, remembering that, while using many different sources, theology is 'from faith to faith'.

Eighth, the purpose of creation is love, unconditional, inexhaustible, innovative love. This love is about life authentically and intensely lived, the eternal life of the New Testament. It is about that wholeness and aliveness which is the glory of God. God makes a universe and ultimately people in it, for love, so that through communion human persons may freely return God's love, ultimately returning themselves to God their source, in their totality. The doctrine of creation, like the doctrine of the Trinity, is the expression of the experience that 'God is love'.

Ninth, along with this is the teaching, based on experience, that every aspect of creation is in some or other way flawed. There is futility, suffering, agony. All creation is subject to dissolution, impermanence, decay, falling away into nothingness. There are natural disasters, moral evil and intense suffering. Creation is experienced as alien and threatening. But this situation is understood in the context of hope. The life, death and resurrection of Jesus Christ have affected the destiny of all creation. The creation itself will be liberated and will be brought into the same glorious liberation (or liberated glory) as the children of God (cf. Rom. 8:19—23). This, wondrously, is to do with the redemption of our bodies (Rom. 8:23) and with the new creation.

Tenth, the creative movement of God through history, through calling and covenant, repentance and reconciliation, suffering and liberation, peaks in the life of Jesus Christ and particularly in his resurrection. 'If anyone is in Christ that person is a new creation' (2 Cor. 5:17). The transformation promised to humankind in the resurrection of Jesus has its counterpart in the transformation of the cosmos. God was in Christ reconciling the cosmos to God (2 Cor. 5:19). So the anguish of the universe groaning in agony is not a hopeless desperation. Rather, to use Paul's image, it is more like the cries of a mother giving birth (Rom. 8:22). The book of Revelation takes up the prophecy of the third Isaiah (Isa. 65:17, 66:22) and presents the great vision of a new heaven and a new earth (Rev. 21:1) where Christ is the Alpha and the Omega, the beginning and the end (Rev. 1:8, 17; 21:6). The basis for a positive and optimistic attitude to creation is linked to the doctrine of the 'cosmic Christ', who is the agent of creation (as in John 1:1—14, Col. 1:16ff. and Heb. 1:3), present in every part of it. He who is the origin of the universe is destined 'to be in all things alone supreme' (Col. 1:18). He who receives the entire 'fullness of God' (Eph. 1:23) descended to our world and ascended again 'in order that he might fill the universe' (Eph. 4:10). In the meantime all creation is eagerly longing for the liberation which is glimpsed in that promise (cf. Rom. 8:20).

Eleventh, the process of creation is eschatological, which means that only at the end of the cosmic process will it be fully completed, known and experienced.

## The Developing Tradition: From Monism to Dualism

The Christian understanding of the doctrine of creation has developed through the course of history. We will consider some of the significant contributions to this developing tradition.

The contribution of Irenaeus (c. 130—c. 200) is particularly significant for today because his theology is very world-affirming and links well with some aspects of contemporary science. Irenaeus was bishop of Lyons, at a time when Gnosticism presented a serious threat to the gospel. Gnosticism took a very pessimistic view of creation, seeing matter and the body as at best neutral and at worst evil. To be saved one had to escape from matter. Salvation was thus totally disconnected from creation. Irenaeus's work deliberately relates creation and salvation. He saw in the empirical world all kinds of separations and alienations, and he speaks of the work of Christ as having achieved the reuniting of all things unnaturally separated. This reunion is brought about in the person of Christ by the process of *anakephalaiosis* or recapitulation, which means both 'gathering up to a head' and 'gathering up again'. This doctrine is based on the New Testament, especially Ephesians 1:9,10, where it is said that 'all things, things in heaven and things on earth, are united, gathered up to a head in Christ'.

Irenaeus emphasised Christ's true humanity in such a way as to highlight a crucial part of the gospel: because Christ took our full humanity, the whole of physical matter and the cosmos are redeemed and liberated in him. Through his whole human life and death Christ dealt with Adam's sin. But Christ did more than that. Irenaeus regarded Adam more as the adolescent of the human race than a fully mature person. So, in recapitulating in himself the whole history of humankind, Christ was able to bring humankind to a maturity far beyond the immaturity of Adam. *Anakephalaiosis* is thus a recapitulation of the evolution of the cosmos and of humankind in the person of the incarnate Christ, such that the kingdom which Christ proclaimed is not simply a return to a primordial pre-fall state, but is a forward-moving, creative fulfilment which takes in the whole of creation. 'The glory of God', said Irenaeus, 'is a fully living person.'

The teaching of Thomas Aquinas (1225–1274) is representative of the positive and comprehensive world-view of medieval theology. For him creation is orderly, hierarchical and dependent on God. He emphasised the relatedness of creation to God. God *is* being and, as such, is the creative giver of all existence. This means that creatures are to be seen not simply in their horizontal relation to one another, but in their coming forth from God, receiving being continuously from God. It is not as if God acted initially to create creatures and then left them to get on with it, as it were. Rather, the creature continually receives existence from God, 'the principle of its very being'.[14]

For Thomas the world was 'sacramental'. This means it was to be looked through contemplatively, as it were, to the presence of the transcendent God in it. The goal of life was to see God, and to ascend to God, to be united with God above. Thomas's theology of creation, therefore, has a certain ambiguity about it: it affirms nature but at the same time denies it. For instance, one of his famous sayings is that 'grace does not destroy nature but perfects it'; but he also held that creation would not be renewed at the final consummation. Thomas's teaching bore an enormous influence not only on medieval thinking but on later theology, both Catholic and Reformed.

The Reformers of the sixteenth century started with Martin Luther's urgent question, 'How can I find a gracious God?' They answered the question in terms of the same framework of ascent to God which had been used in the Middle Ages, but their basic point was that because of human sinfulness we are incapable of ascending to God. God himself therefore, in Christ, had to descend to our lowly existence in order to raise us up to God. Grace came to be contrasted with nature, and theology was chiefly preoccupied with God, humanity and human salvation. This shift in teaching had important consequences for the doctrine of creation.

Luther saw the whole creation as the 'mask of God', God being hidden in nature but powerfully present in it. And for Luther 'creation is not a transcendental event at the beginning of time. The divine act of creation is also now.'[15] But paradoxically, Luther's doctrine of the two kingdoms, the kingdom of the world and the kingdom of the church, tended to reinforce the separation between nature and grace, and contributed to the false dualism between socio-political realities and the gospel. So, although the Reformers did value nature, their preoccupation with God and human salvation helped to set the scene for the following major developments in Western thought and practice.

Because humanity had come to be thought of as more important than nature and as basically separate from nature, human domination over nature became an acceptable motivation for action. Nature was seen as the field for moral activity rather than contemplation. Since God was not to be looked for in nature, there arose a sense of freedom to investigate nature as interesting in itself. So there began the practical investigation of the natural world by measurement and experimentation, and modern empirical natural science was born. With modern science there arose technology, which applied the findings of science to a wide range of practical fields, including rapidly expanding industrial development. At this stage Western thought came to regard nature as capable of being understood without reference to God.

Arising out of a Christian interpretation of reality current at the time, modern science and secularism have shaped the mentality of the West and have deeply penetrated the Christian perception of reality. Key figures here are René Descartes (1596–1650), Galileo Galilei (1560–1642), Isaac Newton (1652–1727) and Charles Darwin (1809–1882). The view of humanity, nature and the world with which most people operate today is known as the Newtonian world-view.

Prior to Descartes the human person had been understood as an integrated being consisting of body and soul. On the basis of Aristotle's notion of form and matter, it was held that the soul was the form of the body. Descartes, by contrast, taught that there are two entities, mind and matter, completely separate from one another. Matter, including the body, is extended outside of us, while the mind is an observer, looking out on the material world. The radical dualism of this Cartesian analysis still largely determines our experience today.

Galileo's discoveries in astronomy, particularly through his empirical approach, confirmed the new cosmology of Copernicus. Copernicus had revolutionised astronomy with his theory that the sun rather than the earth is the centre of our star system. Galileo's views were taken up by Isaac Newton.

The work of Isaac Newton laid the foundation for all modern science. Newton held to the view that nature can be described completely in terms of particles in motion.[16] Combining experimentation and mathematics, he set out the basic laws governing mass and motion, which we know today as Newtonian mechanics. Newton's method in physics was so highly successful that it rapidly became metaphysics, a form of which is the world-view prevailing today.

In the Newtonian world-view the universe was thought of as being like a huge machine working according to the mechanical laws which Newton had so successfully described, like a clock made up of moving parts. Its constituent elements comprised material particles, small, solid, indestructible objects – the building-blocks out of which all matter is made. These particles were thought to be moving in absolute space, as in an empty container. Changes were measured in terms of absolute time, which flowed smoothly from past, through present, to future. The method of investigation was to take the object to pieces if possible, and analyse the parts, on the assumption that the whole could be understood completely in terms of its parts.

It was held not only that this Newtonian mechanistic world-view gave a complete view of reality, but that this was the only possible view of reality. Accordingly, everything that could not be dealt with objectively by Newtonian science was excluded from reality. Human subjectivity, including values, feelings, intuition and the will, was left out. What of God the creator? If the universe is like a clock or watch it is acceptable to think that there had been a watchmaker, but once the watch has been made and working, the watchmaker is of little significance. Mechanical consistency implies a deterministic universe. So while Christian faith still held that the world had been made by God 'in the beginning', the concept of God came to be consistently excluded from the mechanistic, materialistic, deterministic world-view of the modern age.

One compromise between science and theology was the view that where science could not provide an explanation, theology would take over, positing a God who must have acted in a special way. This is known as 'the God of the gaps' theory. It is both bad science and bad theology, because, as scientific explanations emerged to account for the 'gaps', so the concept of God became increasingly marginalised.

In the Newtonian world-view religion was reduced to the relationship between the individual and God. Nature was not included in redemption. This reinforced individuality and separateness, rather than encouraging personhood and relatedness. With this came the fully fledged domination–submission pattern of social relations, Christianity being linked with imperialist expansionism, which involved not only domination of human populations but also the destruction of natural environments.

## An Ecological Understanding of Creation

The context of the doctrine of creation today is global as well as local, and scientific as well as theological. What is needed is a dialogue between global realities and specifically local issues, and between theology and the findings of science, integrated with appropriate spirituality and praxis, and working with the interrelationship between inner reality and outer world. This final section indicates some of the steps on the way ahead. We begin by some reflection on the scientific paradigms of Cartesianism and Newtonianism.

A paradigm is a shared world-view. It includes the concepts, values, perceptions and practices shared by a community and is the particular vision of reality in terms of which the community organises itself. Within the Newtonian paradigm, there is intense fragmentation and a deep sense of separateness. Human persons are experienced as separate from one another and separate from 'nature'. The mind is separate from the body and the material world. The particles of which matter is comprised are all separate from one another. Science is carried out by observers who are separate from their experimental material. Religion is separate from science. If God exists at all, God is outside of the world and separate from it. These separations are unhelpful and in most cases actually wrong.[17] Because we think in terms of fragmentation and separateness we have become conditioned to perceive creation as actually being this way. The sense of meaninglessness which this generates is deeply dehumanising.

Recently a new paradigm has emerged in science, offering a new view of the nature of reality. We are now in the process of shifting to a new participatory paradigm in which unity, wholeness and interconnectedness are more primary than separateness. This new paradigm has arisen particularly in relation to the findings of relativity theory and quantum physics, which have shown that Newtonian principles do not apply in all circumstances. This means that it is a serious error to mentally construct the world in Newtonian terms. Einstein's theory of relativity has shown that the notions of absolute space and absolute time no longer hold. Quantum physics has shattered other basic notions of the Newtonian world-view, namely the existence of elementary solid particles, local causality, and the ideal of an objective description of nature. The materialism, determinism and objectivity of the old paradigm are giving way to a much more accurate and viable alternative.

In the new scientific paradigm wholeness is fundamental and is prior to separateness. Parts have their meaning and are to be understood in relation to the whole. At the same time it is recognised that there are no separate parts; what we consider a part is rather 'a pattern in an inseparable web of relationships'. Instead of mechanical laws relating solid particles of matter, 'every structure is seen as the manifestation of underlying process. The entire web of relationships is intrinsically dynamic.'[18]

Within this new paradigm the relationship between science and theology has a new creative confidence. Three things in particular are being recognised. First, that science can enhance the sense of God instead of undermining it. Second, theology must not attempt to judge scientific theories or provide theological answers where scientific answers are required. Third, while theology must not uncritically mesh with the latest scientific theories, it is a serious mistake to teach a view that patently runs counter to the findings of science. So theology and the sciences are now moving creatively together towards what Moltmann calls 'the ecological awareness of the world'.[19]

The new paradigm makes a radical difference in how we consider the God—world relationship. In both paradigms we use models to point to the reality. In the old paradigm the difference and distance between the creator and creation were stressed and God's transcendence was emphasised at the expense of God's immanent presence within the created realm. So there were two main types of model in this old world-view: the monarchical model, where God is the absolute monarch exercising power over creation from above down; and the model of God as maker of creation, as a potter, clockmaker or artist. These models are theistic. Even when God's loving concern is stressed, once the work of art is created God is no longer involved. Creation is product, not process. The extreme form of the maker-type model is deism, which holds that, having created the world, God retires, as it were, and has no on-going involvement in creation.

With the new understanding of reality it is appropriate to use the term 'panentheism' to speak of the relationship between God and creation. Panentheism expresses the fact that all things are in God and that God is in all things. This is to be distinguished from pantheism, which equates God and the world. Panentheism means that God is both totally transcendent and totally immanent within the whole dynamic world process. God's transcendence is not spatially 'above', but is perhaps better thought of as 'a transcendence inward ... a continually receding centre of creation that is hidden within creation'.[20] God's immanence, then, is to be understood as God's total presence, activity and accessibility in creation. This immanence, which even embraces God's hiddenness, is in everything that happens, in every part of the flow of cosmic reality and in every human experience within it. Thinking theologically in panentheistic terms resonates with contemporary physics, with the new biology and with the insights of ecology. To generate appropriate new models we need symbols, imagination and intuition.

The new wholeness paradigm in science opens the way for the development of a radically therapeutic doctrine of creation. We are led to a holistic, organic and ecological approach to reality. In the new paradigm creation is no longer 'perceived as a machine made up of a multitude of separate objects, but appears as a harmonious indivisible whole, a web of dynamic relationships that include the human observer and her or his consciousness in an essential way'.[21] The whole of creation is process, not product; a process of mutual interconnections, patterns of energetic activity in which every 'part' is in some way within every other part.

By faith we know that all this is coming into being, moment by moment, through the loving creative activity of God. God is involved in the entire process, and is accessible in every part, in every concrete experience. Instead of being only externally related, each person is not only external to the other but, as in God, so also within the reality of every other. This fact is the only possibility for authentic compassion (literally, suffering with), as we experience the suffering, anguish or joy of the other as our own. We can know that God, present in the whole process, experiences the suffering of every person, of every part. Within the empowering energy of this felt sense of createdness it is possible to love with the love of Christ, whose command is 'Love one another as I have loved you' (John 13:34).

Because of the new experience of the wholeness of creation it makes sense to move away from the previous anthropocentric approach to reality. All creation, non-human as well as human, is to be liberated. The incentives of biblical revelation and ecological insight coincide.

At the same time, within the new paradigm human input is even more crucial. Creation is still open and in the process of being created. Luther spoke with great insight of human persons as being 'created co-creators with God'. Because consciousness and matter are not separate but are two aspects of the same reality, it makes complete sense to experience prayer as the co-operative opening up of creation to God. And because everything is coming into being moment by moment, there is the possibility of authentic transformation, forgiveness, reconciliation – literally, new creation. As we live with this participatory awareness, on the space—time edge as the future becomes the present, instead of obstructing God's love we allow God the freedom to make all things new. Response to the prophetic invitation to 'love tenderly', 'act justly' and 'walk humbly with God' (Mic. 6:8) results in the creative coincidence of personal, social and cosmic dimensions.[22] This means learning 'to shift the perceived causes of our global dilemmas from exclusively "out there" in the world and other people, to both "out there" and "in here" within us'.[23] 'We perceive in order to participate.'[24] Opening to such transformation of mind and intention supports the unquenchable urge of the earth to come to fulfilment, and nurtures renewed compassion and justice, caring redistribution of resources, healing of the land, and reconstruction in the social, political and economic structures of our context. And we shall be conscious, fully alive, creative participants, moment by moment, in the divine—cosmic—human process of all that is.

[1] D. Maguire, 'The Power That Moves the Stars', *Creation*, 6:3 (1990), p. 29.

[2] T. Berry, *Befriending the Earth: A Theology of Reconciliation Between Humans and the Earth* (Connecticut: Twenty-Third Publications, 1991), p. 5; S. McDonagh, *To Care for the Earth: A Call to a New Theology* (London: Geoffrey Chapman, 1986), p. 21.

[3] D. Carroll, *Towards a Story of the Earth: Essays in the Theology of Creation* (Dublin: Dominican Publishers, 1978), p. 161.

[4] F. Capra and D. Steindl-Rast, *Belonging to the Universe: Exploring on the Frontiers of Science and Spirituality* (New York: Harper-Collins, 1991), p. 159.

[5] Carroll, *Towards a Story of the Earth*, p. 161.

[6] C. Birch, W. Eakin and J. B. McDaniel (eds.), *Liberating Life: Contemporary Approaches to Ecological Spirituality* (Maryknoll: Orbis, 1990), p. 2.

[7] McDonagh, *To Care for the Earth*, p. 46.

[8] J. Moltmann, *God in Creation: A New Theology of Creation and the Spirit of God* (London: SCM, 1985), pp. 33—34.

[9] Ibid., p. 34.

[10] J. Moltmann, *Creating a Just Future: The Politics of Peace and the Ethics of Creation in a Threatened World* (London: SCM, 1989), pp. 84—85.

[11] Capra and Steindl-Rast, *Belonging to the Universe*.

[12] But see assertion nine below.

[13] Moltmann, *God in Creation*, p. 208.

[14] *Summa Theologiae*, 1a, q.45 art.3(c).

[15] H. P. Santmire, *The Travail of Nature: The Ambiguous Ecological Promise of Christian Theology* (Philadelphia: Fortress Press, 1985), p. 129.

[16] I. G. Barbour, *Issues in Science and Religion* (London: SCM, 1966), p. 36.

[17] R. McAfee Brown, *Spirituality and Liberation: Overcoming the Great Fallacy* (London: Hodder and Stoughton, 1988), p. 26.

[18] Capra and Steindl-Rast, *Belonging to the Universe*, pp. xii, 159.

[19] Moltmann, *God in Creation*, p. 34.

[20] Capra and Steindl-Rast, *Belonging to the Universe*, p. 98.

[21] L. Dossy, *Space, Time and Medicine* (Boulder and London: Shambhala, 1982), p. x.

[22] Carroll, *Towards a Story of the Earth*, p. 71.

[23] D. E. Walsh, *Staying Alive: The Psychology of Human Survival* (Boston: Shambhala, 1984), p. 3.

[24] Moltmann, *God in Creation*, p. 3.

*Select Bibliography*

Balasuriya, T. *Planetary Theology*. Maryknoll: Orbis, 1984

Birch, C. W. R. Eakin and J. B. McDaniel (eds.) *Liberating Life: Contemporary Approaches to Ecological Theology*. Maryknoll: Orbis, 1990

Capra, F. and D. Steindl-Rast. *Belonging to the Universe: Exploring on the Frontiers of Science and Spirituality*. New York: Harper-Collins, 1991

Carroll, D. *Towards a Story of the Earth: Essays in the Theology of Creation*. Dublin: Dominican Publishers, 1987

Fox, M. *A Spirituality Named Compassion*. San Francisco: Harper and Row, 1990

Granberg-Michaelson, W. (ed.) *Tending the Garden: Essays on the Gospel and the Earth*. Grand Rapids: Eerdmans, 1987

Moltmann, J. *God in Creation: A New Theology of Creation and the Spirit of God*. London: SCM; Philadelphia: Trinity Press International, 1985

Moltmann, J. *Creating a Just Future: The Politics of Peace and the Ethics of Creation in a Threatened World*. London: SCM; Philadelphia: Trinity Press International, 1989

Peacocke, A. R. *Creation and the World of Science*. Oxford: Clarendon Press, 1979

Shinn, R. (ed.) *Faith and Science in an Unjust World*, Vol. 1. Geneva: World Council of Churches, 1980

# 9

# The Broken Human Image of God

ADRIO KÖNIG

Christian anthropology is part of the doctrine of creation. It asks what specific contribution can theology make to our self-understanding. It cannot be the same kind of contribution as that of disciplines like biology, sociology or psychology, all of which are focused on some particular aspect of the human being. Theology can attempt an overall view that integrates all other perspectives.[1] The holistic perspective to be developed here is that we are relational beings who only come into our own in relationships of love. We cannot be truly *human* without such relationships. The doctrine of sin must also be discussed in conjunction with anthropology. Sin may be seen as the opposite of our humanity, a distortion of what God meant us to be.

Two concepts will be used to structure our view of humanity: 'covenant partner' and 'image'. Both refer to our relationship with God: we are created in God's image and to live in a covenant relationship with God. This means that it is necessary to build our view of human beings on our knowledge of God. Theologians have used other approaches, including building on Adam before the fall (the traditional Reformed position); on Christ;[2] or on one or more focal biblical concepts of humanity, such as love and freedom,[3] obedience,[4] or on humanity in the presence of God.[5] I have dealt elsewhere with the problems involved in these common approaches.[6]

An anthropology derived from our view of God is a consequence of viewing human beings as covenant partners and the image of God. The fact that we are God's covenant partners implies that we are different from God, whereas the idea that we are God's image implies that we are somehow similar to God. By using covenant partner and image as our main building-blocks, we are able to construct a relational view of human beings. We are created to live with God, with other people and with nature.

As God is love, love must be seen as the essence of human nature. Our relationships will not be enriching or fulfilling unless they are lived in love. Love in each relationship will have a characteristic content. While love for God includes worship, and love for an enemy does not, all forms of love contain the elements of commitment and caring. The theologian Karl Barth called love 'self-giving', a movement away from self towards another, not for the sake of self but for the sake of the other.[7]

## Covenant Partner

Living in covenant with God means that people live in a special relationship with God. The Bible mentions a number of covenants: the covenants with Noah, Abraham, Joshua and David, the old covenant and the new covenant. Each of these covenants has its own character, but two things common to all is that they involve both God and human beings, and that God always takes the initiative and determines the responsibilities of each party. In general it is a matter of mercy on the part of God and responsibility on the human side. The most important covenant in the Bible is the Abrahamic covenant with its formula: 'I shall be your God and you shall be my people.' This, in essence, is also the new covenant. This study assumes that all these covenants are merely different expressions of the same covenant, the basic relationship between God and humanity.[8] Certain characteristics of this covenant may be deduced from the Scriptures.

The covenant is a relationship between unequal partners: God and human beings. God takes the initiative; we have to respond to God's Word.[9] God determines the content of the covenant: 'I shall be your God and you shall be my people.' This means that God takes responsibility for us, that God will lovingly protect, bless, guide and redeem us, and that we should respond to God with love and obedience, with honour and service. This covenant is furthermore a covenant of grace, because we are sinners who do not deserve to be children of God or to live under God's care.

Hence by covenant we mean more than just a relationship. It means a fixed relationship, one which we can count on, since the God who instituted it is faithful, even when we are unfaithful. We dare to confess our sins again and again, because we know that God in Christ has atoned for our sins and wants to forgive us.

The covenant partners are unequal. We are not God's equals, we are God's creatures. Moreover, we are sinners whereas God is holy and hates sin. And yet these unequal partners somehow fit each other. Our gratitude fits God's grace, our obedience God's authority, our faith God's faithfulness, our hope God's promises. Thus from the fact that we are God's covenant partners we deduce a whole range of human attributes, which we call *complementary* attributes, as against *analogous* attributes, which we will deduce from the fact that we are the image of God.

Though God is infinitely greater than we are, there is an appropriate way in which we should respond to God's covenant initiatives: obedience in response to authority; gratitude in response to grace; faith in response to faithfulness, and so on.

What does all this mean? It means, in the first place, that our relationships are extremely important. They are essential to our humanity. While we cannot be reduced to relationships, since we exist over and above (or rather on the basis of) them, and enter into them,[10] we can only come into our own in relationships.

In the second place, the covenant is a relationship between unequal partners in which God takes the initiative and we respond. Therefore we are responsive, responsible (response-able) beings; we neither exist in our own right, nor have any sovereign claim to our lives. We are under authority and live by grace. We ought therefore to be humble, looking up to God.

Thirdly, as God takes the initiative in establishing the covenant it is *God's* covenant with us (Gen. 17:2, 4, 7), rather than *our* covenant with God or even *the* covenant between God and ourselves. This is cause for gratitude, for God will uphold the covenant and go to great lengths to prevent human faithlessness from destroying it. Israel was continually unfaithful to God, but time and again God took new initiatives to maintain the covenant and win Israel back. In Jesus God comes to us, not primarily to fulfil God's side of the covenant (since God is always faithful), but to fulfil *our* side, the side *we* have broken. Jesus comes to end *our* hostility. He offers to God the obedience and righteousness we owe. The profound meaning of the fact that the Son of God became human is that he came to do what humans had neglected to do.

The anthropology developed here deliberately bases our humanity on our relationship with God. To be human means to be in the presence of God (Ebeling) and responsible to God (H. Berkhof). We live our entire lives in the divine presence, so that all other relationships must be measured by the will of God. It is all a matter of God's authority and our obedience. This introduces a critical element into our life in society. When it comes to evaluating a course of action, the final question should never be, 'Will it work?' Nor should it be, 'Will it make us happy?' Nor, 'Is it profitable?' Rather, the final question should be, 'Is it right in the eyes of God?' And while there will not always be an instant answer ('The Bible says . . .'), the question opens up the possibility of a dialogue on what is right.

If we are essentially covenant creatures, all our relationships must be covenant relationships. Therefore we are also in a covenant relationship with one another and with nature, and so these relationships should also be conducted in love.

A need for belonging is a common social phenomenon. Membership of a group is a source of identity and security. As sinners, however, we tend to form groups that exclude and even oppose other groups. Apartheid, on the face of it, identified a wide range of groups (whites, blacks, coloureds, Indians and so forth), but in the end it all boiled down to just two, 'whites' and 'non-whites'. Not only have these two groups become more and more antagonistic, but the whites who hold power have increasingly used it to benefit themselves and to disadvantage and exclude blacks. While group-forming did indeed confer identity, first on whites and later on blacks, it was an exclusive, hostile identity.

The Bible provides critical perspectives on the issue of such groups of people. Two groups in particular come to the fore: Israel in the Hebrew Bible and the church in the New Testament. While both groups confer identity, neither is exclusive. God formed the people of Israel from the descendants of Abraham to be a blessing to all nations (Gen. 12:3). The prophets viewed the eschatological Israel as the light to the nations, drawing them to Jerusalem so that together they could serve God (Isa. 2:2–4; Mic. 4:1–2). The Hebrew prophets related Israel's failure to be the people of God to its exclusivity, to its 'laager mentality' and to its mistaken understanding of election. They indicted Israel for believing that its election meant the rejection of other nations. While Israel as a group did have its boundaries, the divine purpose was that it should constantly expand these boundaries to include the Gentiles.

The same applies to the New Testament grouping, the church. It is the new form taken by the people of God, both Jews and Gentiles who have come to believe in the Messiah Jesus as Lord. This group, too, has boundaries (faith in Jesus Christ), and derives its identity from commitment to Christ. But likewise this group is called to expand its boundaries, to include all people who come to faith in Jesus Christ.

## Image of God

Every person is intended to be the image or representative of God. This is the most common human trait in theological concepts of humanity. We find it in the first creation story in Genesis 1, and even though it does not play an important role in the rest of the Hebrew Bible, it is conspicuous in the New Testament. Furthermore, the human being as the image of God can be linked with the anthropomorphic way in which the Bible speaks of God and the fact that, in Jesus, God becomes a human being. This is evidence enough that humankind as God's image is indeed a crucial Christian anthropological concept.

The statement in Genesis 1:26–28, 'Let us make man in our image, in our likeness', appears in the context of the first creation story. The creation of humankind comes at the end of a long list of things created by God and clearly forms the climax of creation. The importance of humans is further emphasised by the fact that God takes counsel before creating them. Furthermore, human beings are alone in receiving an extensive divine commission as to their responsibility for reality. Added to this is the statement under discussion: only of human beings is it said that they were created in the image of God.

In the context of Genesis 1, this is a rather strange statement. It brings humanity very close to God. Yet this creation story posits a clear distinction between the creator and the things created. Every created thing to which people might tend to ascribe divinity is deliberately de-divinised. Light, the sun, the moon, all of which were prominent deities in the religions of Israel's neighbours, are expressly described as created things. Nothing is divine except God. A clear distance and difference is set up between God and creation.

At the same time, a very close link is postulated between God and humanity. Human beings are close to God, they are created as God's image and representatives. This theme of the closeness between God and humans runs throughout the Bible. God speaks to us, calls us back from our mistaken ways, warns and punishes us, reconciles and saves us, sanctifies us, communes with us and eventually glorifies us. This is a relationship that is never even hinted at between God and the rest of creation. Like the concept 'covenant', then, the 'image of God' emphasises the fact that people are relational beings and that we are essentially determined by our relationship with God.

Western Christianity has over-emphasised that God has given humanity dominion over creation (Gen. 1:26, 28), as though the rest of creation is at our disposal to use, exploit and pollute as we like, simply to get richer and live ever more comfortable lives. We have forgotten that we are still part of creation, and must live in the closest possible harmony with the rest of creation. Reading Genesis 1 more carefully reveals this link with creation. We are created as part of the same process that produced the rest of creation. We were even made on the same day as the land animals. According to Genesis 2:7, we were made out of a component of the earth (dust). It is significant to note that the Hebrew words for our 'dominion' are gentle words, originally applying to the domestication of animals. Rather than giving licence for humans to exploit nature, they say: 'Tame the animals so that they can serve you, and then look after them.' That, after all, is how God rules us: with a gentle hand. And as God's image, we should act accordingly.[11] These views will have to receive far greater emphasis if we are to understand our position as an essential part of nature.

One further facet of the cultural—historical situation of Israel concerns us here. The concept of the image of God was known to some other peoples as well, but they used it to refer exclusively to the king.[12] He was often associated directly with the gods. His decrees were as unassailable as those of a god, and he was often held to be of divine descent. It was in this capacity that he was considered the image of the gods.

While Israel assigned a special position to the king, *all* people were created in the image of God. This gave to all special value and a position of equality. It is therefore not surprising that a particular emphasis on freedom, equality, and the rights and duties of all people should have developed in the Judaeo—Christian tradition.

A final question about this creation story concerns whether it is dealing with the creation of a single human being, or of humanity as a collective concept. This links up with the further question about whether it is the individual or the human race as a whole that is created in the image of God.

Biblical translations differ as to whether Genesis 1:26—27 refers to a single person or to more than one. Towards the end of verses 27 and 28 we find only the plural: 'men' and 'they'.[13] In fact we have no choice: the biblical expression 'man' is a collective term, since two people at least ('man' and 'woman' — Genesis 1:27) are needed to make up 'man' (humankind). Any single person forms only half of this concept, and the 'man' by himself is 'not good' (Gen. 2:18). It is in this context that we note that 'woman' was created as an equal partner to 'man' (Gen. 2:20) and that the man spoke of her as 'like himself' (Gen. 2:23). These are strong statements favouring the equality of men and women, especially if we remember that they were made in a cultural situation where women were considered inferior (often no more than chattels or possessions — Exodus 20:17).

But what precisely do we mean by 'image of God'? This question can be understood as either, 'Which *part* of a human being constitutes the image?' or, 'In what sense is a human being (as a *whole*) the image of God?'

In the course of its history, Christian theology has frequently opted for the first interpretation: part of the human being is the image of God. Such approaches divide the human being into two dissimilar parts: a 'higher' part, usually called 'the immortal soul' (which includes the mind and will), and a 'lower', mortal, earthly part called 'the body'. This inferior part could not be the image of God.

Most Christians accept almost uncritically that the Bible says we consist of these two dissimilar parts. It sometimes comes as a shock to discover that this is a Platonic or Neoplatonic concept, quite alien to the Bible. The Bible uses such words as body, soul, spirit, mind or heart not as fixed 'components' of a human being but with a wide range of meanings. Sometimes 'body' means the entire person (as in older translations of Romans 12:1) while 'soul' often refers to the throat or mouth (Isa. 5:14; Jer. 4:10; Hab. 2:5, NEB). According to the Bible, a human being does not consist of parts but is a whole that can be viewed from different angles. Genesis 2:7 does not mean that God fashioned a 'body' from the dust (soil) and then put a 'soul' into this body, as older translations would seem to imply. Rather, it says that the Lord fashioned a human being from the soil and then brought this person to life.

This dualistic view of humanity is part of a philosophy and world-view which regarded the gospel as concerned with the salvation of the soul. Life on earth and people's concrete circumstances are viewed as of little account. The gospel is equally concerned with social issues, with how people are treated, with justice and injustice. A dualistic anthropology informs the gospel and must be replaced by a more holistic approach.

As regards the image of God, nowhere in the Bible do we find the notion that this is restricted to some part of the human being. The person as a *whole* is the image of God; indeed, the image of the *whole* God.[14] That brings us to the second understanding of the question. In what sense, then, are we the image of God?

Some theologians have seen the image of God as referring to our dominion over nature, while others have seen it as our existence as men and women.[15] Although these views have valid insights, both are unduly restricted. As little is said about the 'image of God' in the rest of the Hebrew Bible, it is more helpful to consider what the image means in the New Testament.[16] Two issues call for consideration: the repeated references to Christ as the image of God, and the association of our new life with this image.[17] It is not strange that these two matters are associated with the image, since Christ is himself our new life (Col. 3:4). Interpreting the creation of human beings in the image of God in terms of re-creation in Christ (the image of God) means that we are re-created or redeemed in order to live a new life. The Bible constantly interrelates creation and re-creation.[18]

The New Testament contains a number of references to the image of God. It is said that Christ is the image of God (2 Cor. 4:4; Col. 1:15; Heb. 1:3); that we are transfigured into the likeness of Christ (Rom. 8:29; 2 Cor. 3:18); and that we are and must be fashioned anew according to the image of God (Eph. 4:24; Col. 3:10). There is also the statement that we should take the shape of Christ (Gal. 4:19). Thus while the covenant emphasises the difference between us and God, the image emphasises that there is some sort of similarity between us and God. A modern translation of Galatians 4:19 might read as follows: 'people must see in you who Christ is.'

What constitutes this similarity or likeness? The exhortations in the New Testament contain a number of pronouncements that urge us to be *like* God or *like* Christ. We must be like God in forgiving, being merciful, being holy, living in the light, even being perfect as God is perfect (Col. 3:13; Eph. 4:32; 1 Pet. 1:15—16; Luke 6:36; 1 John 1:5—7; Matt. 5:48). In the same way we are exhorted to act like Christ. We must love one another as Christ loves us; we must, like Christ, live in love; we must be pure like him, righteous like him, and men should love their wives as Christ loves us. Furthermore, we are sent as Christ was sent (John 13:34; Eph. 5:2; 1 John 3:3, 7; Eph. 5:25; John 20:21).

A great many other, less direct comparative admonitions (such as Matt. 5:16; John 14:12; Eph. 5:1; Phil. 2:5ff.; 1 John 3:1, 9—10) confirm that we are dealing with a similarity of life, of lifestyle and values. Many of these exhortations readily fit into the framework of the Ten Commandments (cf. Eph. 4:25—5:5), which expresses God's will for the covenant people.

This has certain implications. First, that God created us to represent God on earth. We are to make God visible, to live like God. There is no question of an identity between us and God; the distance and difference implied by the covenant relationship is too great. But we can speak of an analogy despite the difference.

Secondly, there will be a number of human attributes analogous to the divine attributes. Because God is love, we must love; because God is holy, we must be holy; because God is merciful, patient, righteous and faithful, we too must be all of these. Analogous qualities are qualities that show a striking similarity to those of God, yet at the same time are different. Our love differs from the love of God inasmuch as God loves us *despite* our unworthiness, whereas we love God *because* God is worthy.

Thirdly, it is clear that these attributes bind people together. The new life given us by God through Christ is a communal life in which we cannot just experience good feelings and intentions at a distance (as the apartheid ideology supposed) but must live with God and with one another as God's family.[19] It is instructive to compare the fruit of the Spirit with the practices of sinful human nature from this point of view (Gal. 5:19—22). The fruit of the Spirit binds us together, while the practices of sinful human nature estrange us from others, making us a threat to one another. From a different perspective, God is love; and thus as those created in the image of God, we must love God and one another.

For lack of space, the marked connection between image, anthropomorphism and incarnation cannot be dealt with in greater detail. Since we are created in God's image, such that there is a definite analogy between God and ourselves, it is appropriate that the biblical authors speak of God in anthropomorphic, that is in human, terms. Moreover, it is understandable that God could have become human.

We may summarise by saying that there are two basic aspects to the relationship of humanity with God, which flow directly from the nature of God and which define human nature. As covenant partners of God we are different from God and must respond in complementary fashion to the divine initiatives. As the image of God, again, humans must be analogous to God in their lives, values and lifestyle, thereby representing God in the world, loving as God loves.

The essence of humanity is determined by these relationships. This means that people are relational beings, and their relations must be lived in love, because God is love. It means that they must be committed to God, to other people and to nature. Because all have the same human nature, all are equal. Christians will therefore work for an open, free, just society in which people have equal rights and opportunities, in which, above all, they care for one another as individuals and as groups.

## Sin: The Broken Image

As relational beings, humans experience fulfilment in so far as they have good relationships. Sin is the exact opposite: it is to live either in wrong or in broken relationships. In wrong relationships humans might still be bound to one another because of shared hatred, jealousy or enmity against others; but these feelings can never promote fulfilment or a meaningful life. On the other hand, they might simply break off their relationships and live in isolation. This, too, results in a sense of failure. And both situations result in meaninglessness or emptiness. This follows logically from the nature of sin. Sin is meaningless, inexplicable, chaotic, destructive.

Genesis 3 makes important contributions to our understanding of sin. The first is that Genesis 3 does not flow in any meaningful sense from Genesis 2. No-one who has taken the slightest trouble to understand Genesis 2 could think for a moment that Genesis 3 is a continuation of it. Why not? Genesis 2 is a beautiful covenant story. God creates a human being in a rough, inhospitable world. Immediately God makes provision for human flourishing by establishing an idyllic environment. In Genesis 3, however, we find Eve listening to a hideous snake which is bent on defaming this faithful God. Did she know too little as yet about God and his caring love? In that case, how fortunate that Adam was there to curb and correct her. But it does not work out like that. In fact, while Eve still offered a bit of resistance to the serpent, Adam gave in without a word. Quite literally unbelievable.

The story is precisely what sin is like. It does not fit in, makes no sense, cannot be explained. It is even wrong to look for the origin of sin. Origins are explanations which make it possible for us to understand where things come from; but the 'origin' of sin cannot be clarified. Not one single meaningful comment is possible on why Adam and Eve should have listened to the devil.

Sin has remained equally meaningless throughout history. Try to find one sound reason for Israel's consistent faithlessness to the benevolent God who rescued them from the slavery of Egypt and cared for them in the desert day by day. Speaking through the prophet Jeremiah, God exclaims in bafflement, actually in horror, about the sin of Israel. How is it possible? They exchange a bubbling fountain for cracked cisterns that depend on the capricious Palestinian rainfall (Jer. 2). And Isaiah (5:1–7) asks: What more could God have done for this vineyard? How is it possible that it should have yielded sour grapes? And what is more disturbing to rational thought than the crucifixion? What meaning is there in theft and murder, fraud and violence? How can arrogance and quarrelling give meaning to human lives? How can people be made happy by racism and avarice? Sin does not make sense.

All of this reminds us that the biblical story of the human fall into sin continues in Genesis 4 to describe sin against another human being. Too often sin has one-sidedly been seen as sin against God. However, our relationship with God cannot be right if our relationships with our fellow human beings are wrong.

By the same token, our personal relationship with God and with others cannot be right if we live in sinful structures. Sin is not merely a personal matter: people create structures; and because people are sinners, structures and systems can be sinful as well.

A few distinctions might help us to understand. Firstly, there are good structures within which people may sin. Marriage is a good social structure, but a marriage partner can be unfaithful. Secondly, sinful facets can be built into a good structure. Education is essentially a good thing. But if the education that is given is inferior, it means there is a bad component in that structure which must be amended without necessarily removing the structure. Thirdly, a structure can be inherently sinful, such as slavery or apartheid. In this case there is no point in trying to improve it: the entire structure must be broken down and replaced by another.

Apartheid has shown us how powerful sin can be once it has been built into structures. How appallingly difficult it is to break down and replace apartheid! How long, for example, is it going to take us to restore the unity of the church, when residential areas for different races were deliberately placed far apart in the heyday of apartheid? How are we going to rebuild education in South Africa after the devastation caused by Bantu Education?

The question about the nature of sin must be answered in terms of the nature of being human. If people are meant to live their relationships in love, and if love is a movement away from oneself towards others for the sake of those others (Barth), then sin, in essence, is lovelessness and self-love. About lovelessness there would probably be little difference of opinion. Since the entire law of God can be summarised in the two commandments to love, lovelessness is clearly the essence of the transgression of that law.

How are we to understand the injunction to love our neighbours *as ourselves*? Loving ourselves here means a recognition of our worth as created in the 'image of God'. It is self-respect. Self-love, on the other hand, is a contradiction in terms, since love is directed to others and the ultimate form of love is to lay down one's life for another (as Jesus said and did). It is not possible to lay down one's life for oneself. Augustine called self-love the supreme sin. The commandment to love one's neighbour does not include a second commandment to love oneself ('like yourself') but indicates the need to love others out of respect for their worth.

Another problem in the doctrine of sin is whether we should speak of God's punishment for sin, or rather of the consequences of sin. Some traditions lay great emphasis on God's wrath and judgement, and there is much to be said for this. The severity of God's wrath is most clearly illustrated by the Cross, where the Son of God suffered for our sins and experienced being forsaken by God.

In speaking of divine judgement as the consequence of sin, we are emphasising our own responsibility rather than the wrath of God. *We* are responsible for sin and its evil consequences. Sickness, death and hell (to name only a few of the consequences of sin) form no part of God's purpose for creation. These things we have brought on ourselves. God's purpose is to rescue us from them. God heals us, ultimately raises us from the dead, and permits Jesus to suffer the pangs of hell so that we can go free if we trust in him.

As far as sickness is concerned, it does not do to ascribe it directly and uncritically to God. In Jesus we encounter God as the healer of disease and the liberator from the power of evil. Sickness is a precursor of death. Because, according to Israelite religion, death ended the believer's communion with God, the Israelites feared death and pleaded for a long life. They firmly believed that only in this life could they praise God (Isa. 38). That is why the resurrection of Jesus in the New Testament is so decisive a part of the gospel. By rising from the dead, Jesus breaks the power of the last enemy, death. It means that believers who die now, after the resurrection of Jesus, cannot be separated from the love of God even by death (Rom. 8:38–39).

Hell (or eternal damnation) is one of the most difficult concepts in the Bible. It is totally at variance with our modern world-view. Eternal torture is a repulsive idea. It is much easier to reconcile divine mercy and patience with the complete victory of the God of love, breaking down all resistance and saving all people. At the same time, we ought not to let our modern sentiments be the final authority. The concept of hell is not a random, marginal idea in the New Testament. Jesus himself frequently and earnestly warned people against damnation. Since matters such as heaven, hell and judgement are apocalyptic images of a reality that cannot be described in terms of our experience, it is well to handle them circumspectly, taking seriously the warnings of Jesus in this regard.

## Conclusion

The theological concepts of God's covenant and the image of God provide us with an integrated concept of true humanity as constituted by relationships: relationships with God, humanity and nature. Sin is the destruction of these relationships, which results in meaninglessness, alienation and judgement. The good news of the gospel is that Jesus has come as the perfect covenant partner and image of God. He has taken upon himself our responsibilities to make it possible for us to be restored in our relationships with God, humanity and nature.

---

[1] Hendrikus Berkhof, *Man in Transit* (Wheaton: Key Press, 1971), pp. 11ff.

[2] Karl Barth, *Church Dogmatics* III:2 (Edinburgh: T. and T. Clark, 1959).

[3] Hendrikus Berkhof, *Christian Faith* (Grand Rapids: Eerdmans, 1979), pp. 178ff.

[4] J. A. Heyns, *Lewende Christendom: 'n Teologie van Gehoorsaamheid* (Kaapstad: Tafelberg, 1972).

[5] Gerhard Ebeling, *Dogmatik des Christlichen Glaubens* (Tübingen: J. C. B. Mohr).

[6] A. König, *Bondgenoot en Beeld: Gelowig Nagedink*, Deel 4: *Oor die Wese van die Mens en die Sonde* (Pretoria: NGKB, 1991), pp. 45ff.

[7] Karl Barth, *Church Dogmatics* IV:2 (Edinburgh: T. and T. Clark, 1967), pp. 733ff.

[8] Karl Barth, *Church Dogmatics* IV:1 (Edinburgh: T. and T. Clark, 1974), pp. 22ff.

[9] Berkhof, *Christian Faith*, pp. 181ff.

[10] Ibid.

[11] A. König, *Here I Am: A Believer's Reflection on God* (Grand Rapids: Eerdmans, 1982), pp. 173ff.

[12] H. -J. Kraus, *Psalmen 1: Teilband: Biblischer Kommentar Altes Testament* (Neukirchen Verlag, 1961), p. 73.

[13] This takes into account only those translations of the Bible which do not use inclusive language.

[14] G. C. Berkouwer, *Man the Image of God* (Grand Rapids: Eerdmans, 1978), pp. 76ff; H. Bavinck, *Gereformeerde Dogmatiek*, Tweede Deel (Kampen: Kok, 1928), pp. 493, 516.

[15] Barth, *Church Dogmatics*, III:1, pp. 184ff.

[16] Otto Weber, *Grundlagen der Dogmatik*, Erster Band (Neukirchen: Verlag der Buchhandlung des Erziehungsvereins, 1955), p. 622.

[17] Berkouwer, *Man the Image of God*, pp 84, 98ff.

[18] A. König, *New and Greater Things: Re-evaluating the Biblical Message on Creation* (Pretoria: Unisa, 1988), pp. 57ff, 144ff.

[19] Berkouwer, *Man the Image of God*, pp. 98, 116ff.

## Select Bibliography

Barth, K. *Church Dogmatics*. Edinburgh: T. & T. Clark, 1958–1974

Bavinck, H. *Gereformeerde Dogmatiek*, Tweede Deel. Kampen: Kok, 1928

Berkhof, H. *Man in Transit*. Wheaton: Key Press, 1971

Berkhof, H. *Christian Faith*. Grand Rapids: Eerdmans, 1979

Berkouwer, G. C. *Man the Image of God*. Grand Rapids: Eerdmans, 1978

Ebeling, G. *Dogmatik des Christlichen Glaubens*. Tübingen: J. C. B. Mohr, 1979

Heyns, J. A. *Lewende Christendom. 'n Teologie van Gehoorsaamheid*. Kaapstad: Tafelberg, 1972

König, A. *Here I Am. A Believer's Reflection on God*. Grand Rapids: Eerdmans, 1982

König, A. *New and Greater Things. Re-evaluating the Biblical Message on Creation*. Pretoria: University of South Africa, 1988

König, A. *Bondgenoot en Beeld. Gelowig Nagedink, Deel 4: Oor die Wese van die Mens en die Sonde*. Pretoria: NGKB, 1991

Kraus, H.-J. *Psalmen 1. Teilband: Biblischer Kommentar Altes Testament*. Neukirchen Verlag, 1961

Weber, O. *Grundlagen der Dogmatik*, Erster Band. Neukirchen: Verlag der Buchhandlung des Erziehungsvereins, 1955

# 10

# Redemption: Freedom Regained

## JOHN SUGGIT

### The Human Situation

The myth of Genesis 2–3 expresses in dramatic terms the plight of human beings. As God's vicegerents (Gen. 1:28) and as made in God's image, they are called to do great things, and yet they are continually frustrated in their endeavours to achieve them. The story of the expulsion of Adam and Eve from Eden represents their alienation (and that of everyone else) from their true being and vocation. So they find themselves bound and fettered through their disobedience to God and the purpose of their creation. They have lost the freedom which they were created to enjoy as partakers of the freedom which belongs in its fullness to God alone.

The stories within both the Hebrew and Christian Scriptures reflect the constant struggle of human beings to recover their freedom, considered not so much as freedom from what hinders and oppresses them as freedom to become all that God intends them to be. But though the struggle may be seen as that of human beings, the victory is provided by God, who invites and challenges people to accept and share in God's victory. The biblical story therefore is the account of the ways by which God restores to human beings the freedom which they were created to enjoy. The word redemption, which strictly means 'buying back' or 'ransoming', is a useful term to describe the overcoming of the alienation which separates human beings from themselves, from God the source of their life, and from others. By God's act of redemptive love they discover their true being, and that they belong to God.

In South Africa today, many experience oppression and alienation, being excluded from full participation in the society in which they live. The theme of 'the struggle' finds expression among Christians as well as others. The struggle for freedom is understood largely in socio-economic and political terms. On all sides there are demands for the upholding of human dignity and rights, whereby individuals may be protected against oppression and exploitation. At the same time different communities claim the right of self-determination and the maintenance of their own particular culture and way of life, since they know that the freedom of the individual is bound up with that of the community. But in the struggle to find true humanity individuals and communities frequently discover a fundamental opposition between personal welfare and the well-being of the community. How far is it right for the community to subordinate the claims of individuals to the common good? How far can the individual or even groups of people assert their rights in the face of the common will? To what extent will it ever be possible for the different communities and cultures which live in South Africa to form a single people?

These are the sorts of questions which the biblical doctrine of redemption must address if it is to play any serious part in the reconstruction of South African society. Religion ought to be a means of binding people together by virtue of a common faith (the etymological root of the word 'religion' is *lig*, to bind). Only too often, however, religion has been responsible for dividing human beings from one another instead of expressing their common humanity and bringing them together under God.

The purpose of this chapter is to consider the meaning of redemption for the people of the world today, and especially for South Africa. What does the Bible and the Christian church have to say about ways of bringing unity to the human family? To this end a brief review of the scriptural evidence, both in the Hebrew Scriptures and in the New Testament, will be followed by a consideration of some of the various models which theologians have used to describe how God has effected redemption in and through Jesus Christ, and how human beings experience the freedom which this has meant. A final section will attempt to examine possible ways in which the Christian doctrine of redemption may be found of value for the life of this land of South Africa today.

## The Biblical Evidence

The theme which runs through the Bible is that of God's initiative and sovereignty. From the creation of the world to the act of redemption in Christ, it is God who is in control, declaring God's faithfulness and love towards God's people. In the Hebrew Scriptures God is, above all else, the redeemer and saviour, who rescued the people of Israel from Egypt. The story of this rescue became the charter for the life and faith of the people of God, assuming even more importance than the account of the call of Abraham, and certainly since the Exile being regularly recalled and rehearsed in the annual Passover ceremonies. This action of God was regularly described in terms of redemption (Greek *lutrousthai, lutrosis*, representing the Hebrew words *ga'al* or *padah*),[1] as for example in Exodus 15:13, and Deuteronomy 7:8, 9:26, 13:5. A similar theme is found in Deutero-Isaiah (as in 43:1,14; 44:22–23), where God is described as delivering God's people from exile. The use of language connoting ransom indicates the personal activity of God in regaining possession of those who belong to him: he is the people's redeemer, related to them as a kinsman, and prepared to pay for their restoration.

In the New Testament Jesus is seen as the one who effects the deliverance and who has brought freedom to his people. The use of the words meaning 'redeem, redemption' (Greek *lutrousthai; apolutrosis*)[2] is not common in the gospels, though

Luke uses them in relation to Hebrew Scripture themes. So Luke describes Moses as the redeemer (Acts 7:35), since he rescued the Israelites from Egypt. The birth of John the Baptist is regarded as the assurance of the approach of God's redemption and salvation (Luke 1:68, 71), and the disciples on the road to Emmaus had hoped that Jesus was the one who would redeem Israel (Luke 24:21). Mark 10:45 (paralleling Matt. 20:28) provides the only use of the word 'ransom' (*lutron*) in the gospels to describe the work of Christ, though there are many examples in the Pauline letters of the description of Jesus' death as a payment or ransom (e.g. Rom. 3:24, 8:23; 1 Cor. 1:30, 6:20; Eph. 1:7).

The examples from the Pauline literature, though presumably often with an allusion to the Hebrew Scripture usage, all refer to the cost involved in effecting redemption or liberation. The value of God's act of redemption is inestimable, since the price paid was the death of Christ, God's son (Rom. 3:25; 1 Cor. 6:20). The terms which Paul used reflect the popular secular language adopted especially in buying freedom for slaves.[3] By payment of the ransom, slaves change their master. By God's act in Jesus Christ, believers find their true selves, as now belonging to Christ, their new master (*kurios*) (1 Cor. 6:19—20). The new status of believers is succinctly expressed in 2 Corinthians 5:17—19: 'If anyone is in Christ, there is a new creation: the old has past away: it has become new. Everything is due to God who reconciled us to himself through Christ and gave us the ministry of reconciliation, that God was in Christ reconciling the world to himself.'

Jesus is the image of God (2 Cor. 4:4), and therefore the perfect human being (Gen. 1:27). Human beings were now invited to share in the new relationship with God established by Jesus' death and resurrection. No longer were they alienated from God and from themselves, for they were no longer slaves to their own desires and passions, slaves to sin, but slaves of Christ, belonging to God as slaves belonged to their master (*kurios*), hardly able to call their souls their own. This is the theme of Paul's description of baptism in Romans 6:22: 'Now that you have been freed from sin and have become slaves of God you are as a result on the way to sanctification and to the goal of eternal life.' The language of freedom is turned upside down, so that Christian freedom, won by Christ, entails slavery to God. The popularity of this theme with Paul is perhaps shown by his preference for the title of Christ as *kurios*, the normal word to describe a slave's master. True freedom comes from serving the right master — a theme reflected in an ancient collect, where the phrase 'whose service is perfect freedom' renders the Latin original *cui servire regnare*, which literally means 'to be his slave is to be a king'.[4]

The writers of the New Testament use various models to describe the way by which this change of ownership was effected. Not unnaturally, the sacrificial imagery of the Hebrew Scriptures was often favoured, especially in the letter to the Hebrews. Jesus is seen as the expiation for the sins of human beings (Heb. 9:11—12; Rom. 3:21—26). Sacrifice, writes Ashby, 'is an ancient language through which relationship is established and maintained, and communication between the human and the divine carried on in material things.'[5] The offering of Christ became the once-for-all effective means of re-establishing the right relationship between God and human beings, because he is son of God, the true high priest (Heb. 5:5—10, 9:11—15). The person and the work of Jesus are inextricably linked. As the all-inclusive human being, the new Adam (Rom. 5:12—21), his death avails for all people. So the death of Jesus is described as being 'on behalf of' others, as in 2 Corinthians 5:14: 'We judged that one died on behalf of all: so all have died.' As the true human being, Jesus is the representative of all, who are invited to find new life by their unity with him.

But it is also as God that he offers himself in love to human beings. The love of God 'shed abroad in our hearts' (Rom. 5:5) would have no meaning if the one who died was other than God. Though Paul never actually calls Jesus God (except perhaps at Romans 9:5), he regularly ascribes to him the title *kurios* (Lord) which was used of YHWH in the Hebrew Scriptures (see Rom. 10:13). In Jesus, God himself was acting in a unique way to set right the relation between God and human beings. This is what is meant by the misleading term 'justification by faith'. The right relationship between God and human beings has been effected in the death and resurrection of Jesus Christ. The way is open to all people to enjoy the relationship with God for which they had been created. God's invitation offered in Christ is accepted by those who express their faith, their conviction, that Christ died for them and shares his life with them.

Just as the Word of God is regarded by the fourth gospel (John 1:3) as the agent of creation, so Jesus Christ, the incarnate Word, is the agent of re-creation. As the world was created by the word of God (Gen. 1:3ff.), so now in the person of Jesus the word of God became a human being (John 1:14). The first verse of the fourth gospel, like that of Matthew and of Mark, refers back to the opening verse of Genesis. The life of Christ effected a new creation, a new beginning, and in so doing gave meaning to human life. So the words of Jesus as presented in the fourth gospel describe the new relationship created by Christ: 'If you abide in my word you are truly my disciples, and you will know the truth, and the truth will liberate you' (John 8:31—32). Deliverance from meaninglessness, leading to true life as expressed in Jesus, was effected by the re-creating word of God. So the remarkable argument of Ephesians 1 describes the redemption (verse 7) effected by Christ as part of God's plan from the beginning (verse 4), whereby God took steps to overcome the alienation resulting from the misuse of human freedom. Creation and redemption are two parts of a single process by which human beings are able to enjoy freedom without frustrating God's plans by their abuse of it. By abusing their freedom they lose their freedom: by God's act in Christ they are invited to regain it.

Another widely used model is that which describes the obedience of Jesus, culminating in his death on the Cross and the resurrection, as a victory over the powers of evil and death (Col. 1:13; Rom. 8:38—39; Heb. 2:14). This theme is vividly reflected in the imagery of Revelation (12:7—12) with the account of the battle in heaven in which 'the great snake, the ancient serpent, called the devil and Satan, which leads the whole world into error, was cast down to the earth'.

In giving meaning to human life, and in his victory over evil and death through suffering, Jesus presented an example which his disciples were to follow — an example both of loving service and of patient endurance (John 13:14—15; 1 Peter 2:20—21). In his human life he showed what all human life was meant to be. This theme was expressed most vividly in Philippians 2:1—11, where the poetical description of Christ's humility is set out as a model for Christians to imitate.

To summarise the evidence of the New Testament, we might say that in Jesus Christ, the Redeemer, God's victory over human sin and the powers of evil is declared, and human beings are assured that they belong to God. In this way they were invited to find their true freedom and their true being by accepting their identification with the risen Lord and living his life in the power of the Spirit. The liturgical way of expressing such acceptance was baptism (Rom. 6:3–5), by which they were united with Christ and shared in the community of the redeemed.

## Later Developments

All the various models used by the writers of the New Testament were developed by later Christian writers as they attempted to explain in terms appropriate for their own day the mystery of God's love shown in Jesus.[6] All depended on the understanding that in Jesus the nature of God was fully revealed, and that by God's action in Jesus the relation between God and the world had been changed for ever. The work of liberation, of redemption, was possible only because Jesus Christ was both fully God and fully a human being, bridging the gap between the transcendent God and human creatures. As Athanasius put it in the fourth century, 'He was made a human being in order that we might be made divine.'[7]

So Irenaeus, bishop of Lyons, at the end of the second century, considered Jesus as the second Adam, representing ('recapitulating') in his person all human beings, and by his obedient offering of himself annulling and overcoming the harm caused by the first Adam. Just as the first Adam was defeated by the devil, so the second Adam defeated the devil through his obedient offering of himself to the Father. The victory availed for all human beings because of the person of Jesus, the all-inclusive human being, the true image of God, enabling human beings to enter into the victory won by Christ.[8] Later writers embroidered this story of Christ's victory over evil and sin in rather crude ways, often arguing from Mark 10:45, where the ransom (*lutron*) was interpreted literally and made to refer to the payment which had to be made by God to the devil to secure release for human beings. So Gregory of Nyssa, followed by other writers, thought of human beings as having sold themselves to the devil, from whom they needed to be ransomed in order to find their true being. The devil, in eagerness to overcome the person of Jesus Christ, took him like the bait on the end of the fisherman's line and was caught on the hook of his deity. Thus the devil was vanquished, and human beings had their freedom bought by the death of Jesus, the Son of God.

Whatever merits such a story had in times when the powers of evil were generally acknowledged, it gave the impression that somehow human beings belonged to the devil, from whom they had to be bought at a price. It was not therefore surprising that in the feudal society of the eleventh and twelfth centuries a new model was proposed by Anselm, archbishop of Canterbury. He argued in his *Cur Deus Homo*? [Why did God become a human?] that human beings, though conquered by the devil, never owed anything to the devil, who therefore could not expect to be paid for releasing them. Rather, human sin should be considered as a refusal to render to God the honour which is God's due, a refusal to pay the debt which human beings owed to God, the source of their life and being. Since human beings owed God everything, any act of disobedience to God meant that they were thereby in God's debt, without having any extra credit available on which they could draw to repay the debt. 'As long as he [man] does not repay what he took, he remains in fault; nor is it enough only to repay what was abstracted, but he ought for the insult done to return more than he took.'[9] The only way in which God's honour could be satisfied was by the offering of one who was a perfect human being. But no human being is able to make the satisfaction demanded; therefore God had to assume humanity, so that as one person, perfect God and a perfect human being, God might make satisfaction for the dishonour done to God by human beings. God required human beings to vanquish the devil, but only one who is truly God was able to do this. So the God–human Jesus Christ is alone able to effect the conquest of the devil which humans could never achieve by themselves.

Anselm's approach has the merit of explaining the seriousness of sin and the depth of God's love for those whom God made. Only one who was fully God could make an adequate offering. The intimate connection between the person and the work of Christ is essential if one is to avoid the suggestion that God demanded the sacrifice of someone other than Godself before redemption could be effected. This understanding of God's work of redemption was followed up by Calvin, who interpreted it in terms of the lawcourt, so that the death of Christ was seen as a sacrifice whereby Christ took upon himself the punishment, or penalty, due to human beings for their sin. This theory of penal substitution has been an important tenet of Reformed theology. It brings out the extent of God's love for God's people, but places the whole transaction in the context of the lawcourt, and, when combined with Calvin's doctrine of predestination, fails to give due allowance to the importance of human free will in the acceptance of redemption.

There were other ways of understanding the redemption effected by God in Christ. Athanasius, for example, in the fourth century recognised the victory won by Christ over the powers of evil, but stressed as a result the new creation of human beings. With his understanding of Jesus Christ as the incarnate *logos* (Word) of God, he held that just as the word of God was responsible for the original creation, so the Word of God alone could enable the creation to be renewed and re-created. The incarnation of the Word effected the re-creation, which was guaranteed by the resurrection. By God's act in Christ, the Word of God, human beings were re-created and enabled to share in the glory God intended them to have.

In the twelfth century Peter Abelard developed the idea of Jesus' life and death as an example of service which Christians were called upon to emulate (John 13:13–16). Jesus brought freedom to human beings by his own voluntary offering of himself in love, and by his resurrection he enabled others who believed in him to share in that same love. Abelard held that the life of Jesus was an example for all human life, but he saw it not simply as an impossibly high ideal to which human beings were to be encouraged to aspire. Rather, God in Christ empowered people freely to change their way of life. Since Abelard believed that human actions had to be genuinely free if they were to have any moral worth, he saw God's action in Jesus as the free expression of God's love, enabling believers to respond freely in love to God's demands. This is summed up in words which have been frequently quoted:

> It seems to us that we have been justified in the blood of Christ and reconciled to God through the unique act of grace displayed to us, by which his Son took upon himself our nature. By teaching us by word and by example he continued even to death and bound us more closely to himself in love. The purpose of this is that we may be set on fire by the extent of this divine grace... Our redemption is that supreme love in us which is due to the passion of Christ, which alone frees us from the slavery of sin and acquires for us the freedom of the sons of God, so that we may fulfil everything through love, rather than fear, of him who has shown us more grace than anything which can be imagined, as he himself said, 'Greater love has no-one than this that a person lay down his life for his friends' (John 15:13).[10]

Abelard's views take very seriously the twin concepts of the sovereignty of God and the free will of human beings. He rightly saw that a mark of true humanity was the ability to share in the freedom which God possesses in its fullness. Human actions have little moral value if they are not freely performed. Abelard's views therefore avoid the problems of predestination raised by Augustine, and later emphasised by Calvin.

All the different attempts to explain the mystery of God's love and the redemption of the world rely on ideas expressed in the New Testament, and all were attempts to explain in intelligible terms the meaning of the gospel, which asserted that freedom, redemption, had been brought to the world through God's act in Christ. They all depended on the right understanding of the person of Christ as the truly human being in whom God was revealed. They were conditioned, too, by the New Testament belief that redemption was concerned especially with the future destiny of the world and of individuals. Before attempting to formulate an acceptable understanding of redemption for today's world it is necessary to consider its reference to the future.

## Redemption and the Future Hope

There is no doubt that the New Testament writers saw the meaning of Jesus' teaching, life and especially his death and resurrection in eschatological terms. Redemption meant being saved from damnation and being assured of life after death. The future hope gave meaning to human life, which so often was nasty, brutish and short. Jesus himself seems to have thought along these lines. His teaching on the reign of God, which was certainly part of his original message, looked forward to the future, in whatever way he viewed his own ministry as the sign of the inauguration of God's reign. However differently his words were later understood, the evangelists and all the New Testament writers expected the return of the Lord and the consummation of God's purposes for the world (Matt. 24:32–42; Mark 13:14–27; 1 Cor. 15). One of the latest writings in the

New Testament (2 Peter), though attempting to explain the delay in the coming of the Lord, still regards it as certain (3:3—7). Luke too, in spite of his historicising approach, thought along these lines (Acts 1:11), though he recognised the need for the church to be organised for life in the world until the end should come. This understanding of redemption with reference to the future hope is expressed in the great hymn of Colossians 1:12—23, where God is described as the one who 'empowered you to share in the inheritance in light of God's people. He saved us from the power of darkness and transported us into the kingdom of his beloved Son.' The present status of Christians is not denied, but the present receives meaning from the future hope.

In a similar way the references to salvation in the New Testament are usually concerned with the future (for example, Rom. 5:9—10), though occasionally Christians are described as those on the way to salvation (Acts 2:47; 1 Cor. 1:18). So the church is called The Way (Acts 9:2), the community of those who are destined to share in the fullness of life after death. The act which guarantees redemption is in the past. So Paul can describe believers as those who *have been* put right with God (Rom. 5:1). But the fullness of their redemption is to be found in the future (Rom. 8:18—25). The theme of the future destiny of the world and of individuals is especially graphically depicted in Revelation, of which Rowland says, 'The belief that the present is all that matters . . . is shown to be the ultimate disaster for man.'[11]

It is this theme of future salvation which has been emphasised by the church throughout the centuries. Redemption has been seen as freedom from future punishment due to human sin. It was especially urged by Augustine, whose writings have had such a powerful influence on all Western theology. In *Civitas Dei* [The city of God] Augustine called the church 'the redeemed family of Christ the Lord and the journeying community [*civitas*] of Christ the king'.[12] The life of the Christian community is directed entirely towards the goal — 'What other end have we except to reach that kingdom which has no end?'[13] So the heavenly and the earthly form two communities, 'of which one is predestined to reign for ever with God, and the other to undergo eternal punishment with the devil'.[14] Christians were those who had been redeemed from the condemned lump (*massa damnata*) of humanity by the gracious act of God in Christ, signified and made effective in baptism, though Augustine was clear enough that more than the external rite was involved. He recognised that just as there were members of the church who would not share in the final destiny of the saints, so there were those who, though opposed to the church in this life, would be found to be members of the heavenly community.[15]

This conception of redemption became the hallmark of Christian preaching, so that the church claimed to be the only way to find redemption from the powers of evil and from everlasting damnation. The slogan *Extra ecclesiam nulla salus* (No salvation outside the church), used by Cyprian of Carthage in the third century in the controversy concerning heretical baptism, was given a wider and more absolute meaning.[16] The freedom of the children of God was to be found only through the ministry of the church, and in obedience to the clergy. Even the redemption of souls from the pains of purgatory was entrusted to the church. The gospel of God's love, creating a new relationship between God and human beings, became in the Middle Ages almost a formality, and was mediated in a somewhat mechanical way. It was this misuse of the privileges of the church which led to Luther's protest and his insistence on the personal response of faith if God's act in Christ was to be of benefit.

Luther argued that redemption was due not to the power of the church, but to acceptance of the grace of God by faith. Though he did not deny the importance of the church as the community of believers, his teaching led to an individual appropriation of the redemption through the faith of each believer. But the meaning of redemption was the same: the difference lay in the way to achieve it. Calvin on the other hand appealed to Cyprian's slogan to show that membership of the church was essential for salvation and departure from it meant destruction.[17] Calvin, however, defined the church as existing only 'where the word of God is purely and faithfully preached, heard and kept, and where the sacraments are duly administered'.[18] In all these cases redemption was viewed in terms of the future hope, and the church had the responsibility and duty of preparing people for their destiny.

## Redemption in South Africa Today

In the present century, attention has turned to a view of redemption as liberation in the present. The concern for social justice and for the overcoming of oppression, poverty and squalor is in the forefront of the church's agenda. This is not to deny the reality of the future hope, but the emphasis has shifted from the deliberate attempt to prepare oneself and others for entrance into heaven. It is the present with which we are concerned, but the significance of the present depends on the future hope. Eschatology is to be seen not as the doctrine of the last things after everything else, but rather as revealing the importance of the present as viewed in the light of the end. So Paul reminded his readers, 'Now is the propitious time [*kairos*], now is the day of salvation' (2 Cor. 6:2), thus encouraging them to act accordingly in the present. For the Christian, the *kairos* is always present, demanding a response here and now if freedom is to be made real. The myths of the end of the world, as of the beginning, describe our relation to God and the purpose of our creation. The gospel declares God's love for his creatures, and faith in God entails belief in God's purposes for his creation and release from a life without meaning. As F. W. Dillistone expresses it:

> The gospel gives meaning to an individual's life-span, to the corporate experience of God's people, and to the universal history of mankind. And at the heart of this story there is the witness to a great reversal when the death which symbolized the triumph of evil was negated by the resurrection which symbolized the victory of all that was good. For those who accept and live by this story the past stands constantly under judgement, the future is irradiated by hope.[19]

Human life is motivated by hope, by hope of achieving one's purpose, however limited that may be. So Aristotle started his *Nichomachean Ethics* with the statement, 'Every art and scientific enquiry, as well as every action and purpose, aims at some good: *the* good is therefore rightly defined as that at which everything aims.' The nature of this *summum bonum* has been very diversely understood. Christians are those who accept the truth of the gospel as defining the purpose of life. Redemption therefore can be described as freedom from a meaningless and purposeless existence where there is no choice, in which human beings are simply carried along by the tide of history. Where human actions are fully determined, there can be no hope, for there is no possibility of shaping the future, either personally or corporately.

Where there is a sense of meaning and purpose there is hope, and where there is hope there is the possibility for change. The Christian gospel gives the assurance of meaning and purpose in spite of all that seems to imply meaninglessness, and enables people to attain to fulfilment as true human beings. 'To hope in Christ is at the same time to believe in the adventure of history, which opens infinite vistas to the love and action of the Christian.'[20] Redemption from sin then means a rescue of people from alienation from themselves and from one another so that they might achieve authentic humanity by the exercise of their free choice. 'In the last analysis', writes Murphy-O'Connor, 'salvation consists in the gift of choice.'[21] Though it is true that one's choice is always limited by various external factors, it is still free enough to enable people to direct their course of action towards the end they desire. Having been set free by Christ, they attain to fuller freedom by bringing freedom to others.

The ability to choose enables people to participate in God's ongoing work of creation. As the redeemed people of God, Christians become at the same time the redeeming people of God, helping others to find the freedom which God intends them to have. They cannot add anything to the decisive work of God in Christ, but they can make this relevant and give others the hope to enable them to strive for the freedom which God wills for them. It is this theme which is embraced by liberation theologians, who regard faith and orthodoxy as empty words unless they are accompanied by orthopraxis – that is, caring and loving actions designed to bring liberation to the victims of violence, poverty and oppression.[22] Christians are called to express their faith, hope and love by their efforts to help shape the future in accordance with God's will. They are no longer simply the objects of the historical process, but are 'called to become subjects of their own history'.[23] They are to do this in solidarity with others, knowing that their own history is inevitably and intimately entwined with that of others. Though redemption includes the task of striving to liberate people from inhuman or oppressive political and social systems, it must not be confused with a purely social or political programme. The kingdom or reign of God is to be realised in the future. But this future hope inspires Christians to work for its achievement in this world. 'The political is grafted into the eternal,' as Gutiérrez puts it.[24]

The entering into the redemption won by Christ, from the human point of view, demands a personal choice, an act of will or expression of faith. It is a commitment to the truth of the story of Jesus, and a recognition of this story as the drama of God's liberating activity. In this sense redemption is personal and individual: only I can make my choice. But the making of the choice inevitably involves me with others. One cannot be saved by oneself: alone one perishes in alienation; salvation involves being with others. Redemption entails entrance into the *community* of the redeemed, who are now called to help others enjoy true human freedom. The attainment of freedom is due to the love of God shown in Jesus, who is now alive in those who belong to him, those who are (in Paul's favourite phrase) 'in Christ'. The 'struggle' for true freedom is therefore not primarily for one's own freedom, but for the freedom of others. To strive simply for one's own freedom is like striving to preserve one's own life at all costs, and this leads to death and loss of one's true life (Mark 8:35), for the life of each person is bound up with that of others.

In this work of redemption and liberation the church has an essential role, not in some mechanical way as the dispenser of grace, but as being 'the universal sacrament of salvation, simultaneously manifesting and exercising the mystery of God's love for man'.[25] By its own internal life, the church (which means all Christian people who recognise the claims of their common life) is called to display God's love both in the proclamation of the gospel and in working for the liberation of people from all that hinders them from attaining their true humanity. The mystery of God's redemption is set forth whenever the church meets together in the celebration of the eucharist. There the church rediscovers and expresses its identity as the body or person of Christ, deriving its life and behaviour from Christ its Lord who gave himself to redeem the world. Just as the Jewish Passover enables the participants to share in the redemption of God's people from slavery in Egypt, so at the eucharist communicants enter into the redemption won by Christ and thereby recognise their task in the world today. From its eucharistic worship the church is sent out, renewed by the sacrament of life, that it may carry on and make real in the life of the world the redemption and liberation which God has effected in the life, death and resurrection of Christ the Lord.

---

[1] Although *ga'al* originally meant 'to act as a kinsman' and *padah* 'to redeem by payment of money', the distinction in meaning is often far from clear, and both were usually translated by the same Greek word.

[2] A good brief discussion of the Greek words for redemption in the New Testament is found in B. F. Westcott, *The Epistle to the Hebrews,* 3rd edition (London: Macmillan, 1906), pp. 297–299.

[3] See especially G. H. R. Horsley (ed.), *New Documents Illustrating Early Christianity* (Australia: Macquarrie University, 1983), pp. 72–75.

[4] The second collect for Morning Prayer in the 1662 Prayer Book of the Church of England.

[5] *Sacrifice: Its Nature and Purpose* (London: SCM, 1988), p. 25.

[6] A good description of the different models, or parables, is to be found in F. W. Dillistone, *The Christian Understanding of Atonement* (London: Nisbet: 1968).

[7] *De Incarnatione* 54:3.

[8] The development of this 'classic' view of the atonement is described especially by G. Aulén, *Christus Victor* (London: SPCK, 1931).

[9] *Cur Deus Homo,* 1:11. English translation (Edinburgh: John Grant, 1909).

[10] *In Epistolam ad Romanos,* 3:28.

[11] C. Rowland, *The Open Heaven* (London: SPCK, 1982), p. 440.

[12] *Civ. Dei,* 1:35.

[13] Ibid., 22:30.

[14] Ibid., 15:1.

[15] Ibid., 1:35

[16] Cyprian argued that love (*caritas*) was an essential mark of the church. Where unity was broken through schism or heresy there was no true church.

[17] *Institutes of the Christian Religion*, 4:4.

[18] *Confession de la foi . . . de Genève* (1537), 18.

[19] Dillistone, *The Christian Understanding of Atonement*, p. 19.

[20] G. Gutiérrez, *A Theology of Liberation* (London: SCM, 1974), pp. 238–239.

[21] J. Murphy-O'Connor, *Becoming Human Together*, 2nd ed. (Dublin: Veritas, 1982), p. 143.

[22] See G. Baum, *Theology and Society* (New York: Paulist Press, 1987), p. 122.

[23] Ibid., p. 44; cf. p. 137.

[24] Gutiérrez, *A Theology of Liberation*, p. 232.

[25] The Pastoral Constitution on the Church in the Modern World (*Gaudium et Spes*) 45, in W. M. Abbott and J. Gallagher (eds.), *The Documents of Vatican II* (London: Chapman, 1966).

# 11

## Christian Community

## JOHN W. DE GRUCHY[1]

The word 'church' conjures up a variety of different and often conflicting images. For some people, 'church' has a very negative connotation: an authoritarian, patriarchal and conservative institution which cramps the Spirit of Christian freedom, joy and witness; an instrument of colonialism; or a legitimator of apartheid. For such reasons people have often expressed a preference for Christianity rather than 'churchianity', for Jesus of Nazareth but not the church of Christendom. There are other people, however, for whom the church is the indispensable womb within which their faith has been born and nurtured. For them, the church, despite its faults, is something essentially positive, a community of faith, hope and love without which Christianity would be inconceivable.

There are, of course, other responses which the word 'church' may evoke: a building, a priest or minister, a denomination, and so forth. But the really important issues lie at a deeper level. They have to do with the relationship between the church as a social institution and a theological reality, and the reason for the church's existence in the world.

Ecclesiology (the study of the church) is particularly concerned with this dialectical relationship between the church as a sociological and a theological reality. It recognises that the church is similar to many other human associations, but it also believes that the church is different, a mystery not fully intelligible to the human mind. From a Christian perspective the church is, in fact, an article of faith which is located, as the Apostles' Creed affirms, within the doctrine of the Holy Spirit: 'I believe in the Holy Spirit, the holy catholic church.' Many images expressing this conviction are to be found in the Bible, and others have been evoked in Christian tradition.

### Biblical Images

At least eighty images of the church are to be found in the Scriptures. These, Paul Minear reminds us, 'are modes of perceiving afresh that mystery of eternal life which God shares with his people, and as reminders of its neglected role as the body of Christ and the fellowship of the Holy Spirit'.[2] As such, images are precisely what the word indicates — products of the imagination of primitive

Christian communities as they sought to express their identity. The fact that Scripture contains so many images also suggests that no single image or model can capture the theological meaning or essence of the church in its fullness.

Christians trace the beginnings of the church to the origins of Israel — the call to Abraham to embark on his journey of faith as the first step in God's mission (*missio Dei*) to redeem the world, and the liberation of his descendants from bondage in Egypt, as the event which constituted Israel as the covenanted People of God, and revealed God's character (Yahweh) and the historical significance of God's mission.

'People of God' is a covenantal term, in which Israel's bond with Yahweh, and Yahweh's life as expressed in that community, are denoted (e.g. Isa. 63:8–9). The Hebrew term '*qahal* YHWH' was often translated in the Septuagint (the Greek version of the Hebrew Scriptures) as *ekklesia kuriou*, 'the church of the Lord' (e.g. 1 Chron. 28:8 and Mic. 2:5). Such language expressed Israel's sense of distinctiveness from the other nations as a 'called out' people. Many metaphors expressed this sense of distinctiveness, perhaps most notably the rich image of Yahweh being married to the people (for example, Hos. 2:16–20). This same image was picked up in the New Testament to refer to the relation between Christ and his 'bride', the church.

The church, as described in the New Testament, is in continuity with Israel (Rom. 9–11), and yet it is understood as being fundamentally reconstituted as a result of the life, death and resurrection of Jesus the Messiah and the outpouring of the Holy Spirit at Pentecost. Pentecost (Acts 2) marks a new beginning for the People of God, a new phase in their participation in God's mission to the 'whole inhabited universe' (*ecumene*), and a new empowering in order to fulfil that task. An important distinction between the Hebrew *qahal* and the Christian *ekklesia* (used to translate *qahal* in the Septuagint) is that the former is constituted ethnically, whereas the latter refers to a people bound not by national ties but by Jesus Christ. The New Testament church saw itself as commissioned to address the gospel to all people, and therefore to embrace all people within its fellowship (Acts 1:8).

All New Testament images for the church are centred on Christ. An early understanding of this relation is evidenced in the use of the term *ekklesia* in Matthew's gospel (16:18; 18:17), which indicates that the assembly of Yahweh is now to be found in those who gather around Jesus ('my church'). Likewise, parallels in the gospels to the Hebrew Scriptures indicate that the special relationship between Yahweh and Israel, through Jesus, has been transferred to the church. So in the fourth gospel, Jesus is described as the genuine vine (15:1), alluding to those passages that speak of Israel as God's vine (Isa. 5:1–7; Ps. 80:8–19). Where Israel failed, Jesus, the New Testament authors claim, has been successful. All those 'in him' are true Israel (see 1 Pet. 2:9–10; Gal. 6:16).

One of the key images for the church in the New Testament which describes this intimate relationship between Christ and the church is the 'Body of Christ'. Widely used by Paul, this image indicates that the church is not a collection of individuals but the historical manifestation of Christ in the world. In this image, the members of the church, like those of a human body, each have their part to play in the life of the whole (1 Cor. 12:12–13). Incorporation into this body through baptism represents, for Paul, the whole complex action by which the faithfulness of God is met by the faith and commitment of the believer.

While the church as the 'Body of Christ' is the presence of Christ in the world, the New Testament does not simply identify Christ and the church. Christ is the 'head' of 'the body' (Eph. 1:22 *et al.*) Or, recalling the analogy to the Hebrew *qahal*, the church is not its own master, but has been called into being to be a holy people in the service of Jesus Christ and the gospel (1 Pet. 2:9–10). The image of the church as the 'bride of Christ' (Eph. 5:22–32) shows both the intimate relation between Christ and the church and the distinction between them. This image is assumed by Paul in 1 Corinthians 11:2 and appears again in a different context in Revelation 19:7–9.

One of the fundamental images for the church in the Acts of the Apostles (2:42f.) is that of fellowship or community (*koinonia*). This image is rooted in the activity of the Holy Spirit as the action of God bringing unity and giving life to the body. The first Christians regarded themselves essentially as a fellowship of believers 'in Christ', who worshipped God together 'in the fellowship of the Holy Spirit' (2 Cor. 13:13), a phrase which refers both to sharing *in* the Holy Spirit and to the community which is its result. In other words, the church was experienced as participation through the Spirit in the life of the triune God. For this reason, Eastern Orthodox theologians continually remind us that the essence of the church is communion – it exists in the interrelatedness of human beings, God and society.[3]

On this understanding, *koinonia* is not to be regarded as something 'spiritual', separate from daily concerns and life. Rather, as in Acts, it was exemplified in the sharing of possessions: 'they had all things in common (*koine*)' (2:44–45). It was this life as a community, in which all members participated equally, that characterised the first Christian churches. The Christian community was called to be a counter-culture (Rom. 12:1–2) in which the normal divisions of society were overcome (Gal. 3:26–29); a 'new creation', which was the beginning and sign of God's reconciled humanity (2 Cor. 5:17f.; Eph. 2–3). All of this is well expressed in the World Council of Churches' statement on 'The Unity of the Church as Koinonia: Gift and Calling':

> The grace of our Lord Jesus Christ, the love of God, and the communion of the Holy Spirit enable the one church to live as sign of the reign of God and servant of reconciliation with God, promised and provided for the whole creation. The purpose of the church is to unite people with Christ in the power of the Spirit, to manifest communion in prayer and action and thus point to the fullness of communion with God, humanity and the whole creation in the glory of the kingdom.[4]

There is no stress on the church as an institution in the biblical images. But some form of organisation was both inevitable and necessary. The first Christians, so Acts informs us (2:43–47), met together, worshipped publicly as well as in private, and elected various officers to take care of their affairs. They exhibited, in other words, signs of an emerging social institution, a development which became more pronounced as the first century blended into the second and third, and then exponentially so as the centuries came and went. But already in the apostolic period, the unity of the church was expressed by adherence to common teaching (Acts 2:42; 1 Cor. 11:2; 2 Thess. 2:15), common forms of admission to membership (baptism), and the regular celebration of the eucharist, and in the appointment of special ministers, presbyters, bishops (if they are to be differentiated from presbyters) and deacons. How this affected ecclesiology can be seen by looking at some of the models for the church which developed over the centuries.

## Historical Models

In his important study *Models of the Church*, Catholic theologian Avery Dulles delineates five such models: the institutional, the mystical–communal, the sacramental, the proclamatory or kerygmatic, and diaconal or servant model. Each model marks off a distinctive understanding of the nature and mission of the church.

The first model, which dominated the thinking of the Middle Ages and is reflected in much Catholic theology, stresses continuity of structures but at the expense of making the maintenance of these structures more important than mission. The institutional church is always the church, the spiritual and the social structure being undialectically related. Dulles claims that this model is the most problematic of the five because it is far too static. It fails to acknowledge that the church is fallible and subject to judgement. An alternative strand in Catholic tradition suggests a second model (mystical–communal), held by Thomas Aquinas in the Middle Ages and Yves Congar more recently. Stressing the interiority of the church's union with God and others, this model is in strong continuity with the New Testament images but risks making the structural aspect of the church 'appear superfluous'.[5] Not taking sufficient account of this can so easily lead, as we shall see, to an unbiblical dualism.

The third model (sacramental) tries to synthesise the emphasis on visibility in the first and on interiority in the second. Exemplified in the reflection of such theologians as Karl Rahner, this sacramental view claims that the church 'signifies what it contains and contains what it signifies'.[6] The church is the sacrament of Christ in the world. That is, in its structures and activities, the church is 'a sign of the continuing vitality of the grace of Christ and the hope for redemption that he promises'.[7] The major problem with this model is that it can fall prey to 'an almost narcissistic self-contemplation' which is 'not easily reconcilable with a full Christian commitment to social and ethical values'.[8]

While the first three models have appealed to Roman Catholic theologians, the last two (proclamatory or kerygmatic, and the diaconal or servant models) have been expressed more within Protestant ecclesiology and practice. The fourth model, espoused in this century especially by theologians such as Karl Barth, but also by Catholics such as Hans Küng, stresses the church as herald of the gospel, pointing not to itself (as the sacramental model might tend), but to Jesus Christ. This model, however, tends to reduce witness to preaching and, therefore, may fail to allow for proclamation in deed as well as word. Hence, in his critique of

Barth's kerygmatic theology, Dietrich Bonhoeffer claimed that the church, rather than standing over against secular life, must find itself 'in the midst' of the struggles of the world. 'The church', Bonhoeffer wrote, 'is the church only when it exists for others.'[9] This diaconal or servanthood model sees the church as only authentically being the church when it is engaged in serving the needs of the world. The danger of this model is, of course, that of 'secularisation', whereby the church loses its distinctive character in the world. With this in mind, Bonhoeffer also spoke of the necessary 'secret discipline' (prayer, worship, sacraments) which was required to enable the church to retain its identity and truly be 'for others'.[10]

Since each model affirms a side of the truth of the church, yet none grasps it entirely, Dulles argues that a plurality of models is needed in developing a contemporary ecclesiology. More precisely, the emphases of each of the other four models can be used to deepen the particular one opted for. No model may be taken in isolation from the others without reductionism. For instance, one weakness of the servant model – its tendency to blur the distinction between church and world – can be addressed by borrowing from the kerygmatic model the emphasis that the word of God is sovereign and therefore cannot be domesticated. The tendency of the kerygmatic model to reduce the church to 'a series of totally disconnected happenings' can also be helped by critically retrieving features of the institutional model, which stresses continuity and tradition. Yet, as James Cochrane has pointed out, these options are not to be regarded simply as a matter of preference or choice.[11] The task of ecclesiology is that of continually reflecting on what it means for the church to be faithful to Jesus Christ in the world, and to enable it to structure its common life (*koinonia*) accordingly.

We will not discuss in this chapter the various traditional forms of church structure (congregational, presbyterian, episcopal) or other aspects of church order, canon law or discipline. These are all important, but would take us away from our main concern. What is significant, however, is to recognise that the word *ekklesia* is used in the New Testament to describe both the church as a local community or congregation of God's People, and the universal church as embracing all Christians on earth and in heaven. Both understandings are important.[12] In contemporary ecclesiology much stress has been rightly placed on the 'local church', whether understood as a single congregation, a 'base community', or, within the Catholic tradition, as a diocese. The local church is the presence of Christ within the community of Christians in each particular context. This has widespread implications for the development of ecclesiologies which are contextually appropriate and which, none the less, are ecumenical – relating all churches and Christians together in the universal church.

## The Church and the Reign of God

As we have now seen, most images for the church point to its character as a spiritual fellowship which transcends what we normally expect of a social institution. Yet we have noted that the church is also an institution, or set of institutions, which embodies similar characteristics to other social organisations and often has the same kind of problems and flaws. The church is, for example, often socially stratified and segregated by race, class and culture, and sometimes even wedded to particular nationalisms. So much of this seems to be at variance with what we read about in the New Testament that it is difficult to reconcile the biblical images with these expressions of the social reality of the church in the modern world.

As we have seen from our examination of the various historical models of the church, much ecclesiology has to do with relating the theological and the social dimensions of the church to each other. One temptation is to keep them separate and to argue that the church is to be understood as the kingdom of God on earth or the mystical body of Christ (Dulles's models one and two), and therefore beyond sociological inquiry and critique. A variation of this position would be to regard the church as essentially invisible and spiritual, and therefore not to be equated in any way with the social structures normally called by that name, a danger which is often found in Protestant ecclesiology. But any ecclesiology 'abstracted from the actual life of the church in society, any theory therefore seeing only some idealized church, is a mere dogmatic assertion, the perpetuation of an illusion'.[13]

An opposite tendency is to regard the church only as a social institution, one of several players within the public and political arena, which may or may not fulfil a useful role. This functionalist reduction of the church is a common one. Many people who reject the truth claims of Christianity none the less accept the importance or value of the church within society. But the problem with this understanding of the church is that it really undermines the reason for the church's existence. Why should the church not simply declare itself to be a social welfare organisation or a political party? By the same token, it takes away the motivation of Christians to be engaged in the life of the world, ignores the source of their empowerment, and downgrades the unique contribution which the church can make to society as pointing beyond itself to the reign of God in Jesus Christ.

As we have noted, one danger of the institutional model is that of equating the church with the kingdom, or reign, of God. The biblical teaching on the 'reign of God' has been dealt with in several other chapters of this book and needs no repeating here. But what is of fundamental importance for ecclesiology is the recognition that the church is not the kingdom of God, but exists to bear witness to God's reign in Jesus Christ. In Küng's words, 'The Church is not the kingdom of God, but looks towards the kingdom of God, waits for it, or rather makes a pilgrimage towards it and is its herald, proclaiming it to the world.'[14] The church, through its life and praxis, is called, to put it slightly differently, to be the sign and anticipation of the coming of God's reign.

One important consequence of this relationship between the church and the kingdom is that the church is always to be evaluated in the light of God's reign in Christ. Other social institutions may be judged in terms of the contribution which they make to society, but because the church claims to be something qualitatively different, it has to be judged in terms of the message which it proclaims and claims to live by. Hence the insistence in the New Testament that 'judgment begins with the household of faith' (1 Pet. 4:17). Sociological critique is necessary and helpful; theological critique is fundamental and essential to the well-being of the church. There is, thus, the continual need for prophetic critique of the church in the light of the gospel of God's reign, and the need to recognise that the church is only truly the church when it is constantly in the process of being reformed according to that gospel (*ecclesia est semper reformanda*).

The relevance of the church derives from its faithful praxis, not the other way round. This does not imply that the church should not seek to relate to the issues facing the world, and to do so in ways which enable it to communicate the gospel more effectively. But the criterion must always remain the gospel of God's reign in Christ. While the struggle for faithfulness in the church often involves unseemly power conflicts ('church politics'!), it should really be about the nature and demands of the gospel, witness and discipleship. In other words, the ongoing ecclesiological task is bound up with hermeneutics, with the attempt to understand the truth of the gospel in relation to the challenges and issues presented by the specific contexts within which the church is called to bear witness to the reign of God.

## The Marks of the True Church

The problem of determining whether the church is truly being faithful as the church of Jesus Christ has long concerned Christian theologians. In the first few centuries, the question focused around the distinction between orthodoxy and heresy, the true church as against the false church. As a result several 'marks' or 'notes'—unity, holiness, catholicity and apostolicity—were expressed in the ecumenical creeds. The true church, it was argued, was not divided into several sects, but was united in faith, doctrine and ministry; it was instituted and set apart by God to be God's instrument in the world; it was universal, embracing local communities of faith throughout the inhabited world (*ecumene*) and comprised of people of every nation and language; and it could trace its historical origins and development back to the Apostles and their successors.

While the Roman Catholic Church has traditionally claimed to be the one and only true church that gives evidence of these classical marks, the Protestant Reformers in confessing the creed interpreted the notes in a less formal or static sense. This was captured in the Reformation description of the true church as that community of faith 'in which the Word of God is faithfully proclaimed and the sacraments duly administered'. In other words, the church was regarded less as an institution which could claim to be in direct continuity with the Apostles through the succession of its bishops, with the Pope as the successor of Peter, and more as a fellowship of believers gathered together around the Word and sacraments. This did not mean that the Protestant churches did not begin to develop their own institutional forms, nor did it mean that the Word and sacraments were absent from the Catholic Church. It was really a different way of claiming to be in continuity with the apostolic church, for that was, of course, the basic issue.

Christians still confess the church as one, holy, catholic and apostolic. But this is essentially a confession of faith, not a description of social reality. The reality is that the church is tragically divided into countless and often competing denominations, and is far too compromised in its existence and witness to claim to be 'holy'. How, then, are we to understand these marks of the church when we confess them in the classical ecumenical creeds?[15] Like the biblical images for the church, they are statements of faith rather than descriptions of social reality, pointers to the divine mystery of the church which at the same time summon the church to become what it is meant to be. They express the meaning of the Lordship of Jesus Christ as head of the church, and therefore continually stand in judgement over the church as it exists, challenging it to reformation and conversion. Thus, if we take the confession of unity as an example, what it is expressing is a given reality which all Christians have in Christ, yet one which has to be continually expressed. That is the essence of ecumenism.

If the classical marks of the church are expressed in the creeds, contemporary marks of the church have emerged in relation to the church's witness and mission in the world. During the church struggle against Nazism in Germany, it became clear that the 'true church', as distinct from the false, had to do as much with ethics as it had to do with doctrine. This has also become obvious within the church struggle in South Africa where 'orthodoxy' has sometimes given support to apartheid. The faithful praxis (orthopraxis) of the church, in other words, is now recognised, as it was in the New Testament, as an essential mark of the true church.

This emphasis on faithful praxis as a mark of the true church has been articulated strongly within liberation, Black, feminist and prophetic theologies, and we refer the reader to those chapters in this volume for a fuller discussion. But it is of considerable importance to recognise here that the description of the church as the 'church of the poor' has become fundamental for contemporary ecclesiology. Its roots can, of course, be traced back to the Bible itself, and there are many examples in church history of more radical Christian communities and religious orders which have sought to express it. The church is not a community of the powerful, but of the powerless; not of the rich, but of the poor. It is not the church aligned to the state, but the church which provides an alternative society 'in but not of the world'; a church in solidarity with those who are the victims of society.

The description of the church as the 'church of the poor', like the other more classical marks, is not simply a description of the church, for in that regard it too is not an accurate account, but a summons to the church to become what it is meant to be. This is a reminder that the reformation or renewal of the church invariably takes the form of a struggle within its life. To use contemporary jargon, the church is always a 'site of struggle', a place of conflict between 'true' and 'false' church, between the church captured by norms which are contrary to the gospel and the church seeking to be faithful to the mission of God into which it has been summonsed by Jesus Christ. In the South African context, the *Kairos Document* is a powerful challenge to the church to locate itself more fully within the transformative mission of God, to 'quite simply participate in the struggle for liberation and for a just society... Church activities must be reappropriated to serve the real religious needs of the people and to further the liberating message of God and the Church in the world.'[16]

This contemporary imaging of the church is not unrelated to the classical marks; on the contrary, it breathes new life into them, rescuing them from the staleness of meaningless repetition. In Moltmann's reformulation, we may say that the 'church's unity is its *unity in freedom*. The church's holiness is *its holiness in poverty*. The church's apostolicity bears *the sign of the cross*, and its catholicity is linked with its *partisan support for the oppressed.*'[17] All of which brings us to recognise that the nature of the church cannot be discerned apart from its task in the world.

## Participation in the Missio Dei

We have consistently recognised that the church is more than just a human institution, in that its very origin, existence and significance lie in something beyond itself, namely the presence and power of the Holy Spirit. While this gives the church a sense of divine mystery, it may also create the impression that the Spirit belongs to the church, moves within its confines, and serves its interests. That this is not the case lies in the fact that the very nature of the church has to do with its participation in the *missio Dei*. It was Karl Barth who first drew attention to the fact that mission is not in the first place something that the church does, but rather something that God does.[18] The triune God is a missionary God, in whose very heart lies a sending activity in which the Father sends the Son and the Spirit into the world because of redemptive love. The proclamation of the gospel involves an invitation for people to participate in this mission: the Son sends the disciples out in the presence and power of the Spirit (John 20:21, 22).

Recognising that the theme of mission belongs to the doctrine of God and only then to ecclesiology may seem strange to us, for the very existence of the church in South Africa has depended upon overseas churches sending missionaries to these shores as part of *their* work. But if the ecumenical consensus about the *missio Dei* is correct, then this understanding of mission is severely limited and limiting. Rather, mission begins with God, and is God's mission in and to the world. The church does not initiate: the church participates in it. Mission is the total task which God has set the church for the salvation of the world because mission arises from God's love and concern for the entire world in all its dimensions. By locating the church within the divine sending activity of the triune God, we are therefore also making clear that mission is not just something that the church does as one activity amongst others, but the very ground for its existence.

Quoting a number of sources, the South African theologian and missiologist David Bosch in his magisterial work, *Transforming Mission*, draws out the implications of this understanding of mission for ecclesiology:

> Mission is not a 'fringe activity of a strongly established Church, a pious cause that may be attended to when the home fires are first brightly burning ... Missionary activity is not so much the work of the Church as simply the Church at work'. It is a duty 'which pertains to the *whole* Church'. Since God is a missionary God, God's people are a missionary people. The question, 'Why still mission?' evokes a further question, 'Why still church?' It has become impossible to talk about the Church without at the same time talking about mission. One can no longer talk about Church *and* mission, only about the mission *of* the Church.[19]

From this perspective, then, a contemporary ecclesiology needs to be grounded in the fact that the church exists by virtue of its participation in the *missio Dei*. Where the church fails to participate in God's mission, it ceases to be the church.

Participation in the *missio Dei* gives to the church its particular character in the world, for the testimony of the Scriptures is that since the dawn of time God has been at work transforming chaos into creation and confusion into community. The church itself is a sign of this new community which God is seeking to create. Thus it was that the Christians of the early church were accused of 'turning the world upside down' because of the way that they transformed the society around them (Acts 17:6). The mission of God, as proclaimed by Jesus (e.g. Luke 4:18ff.), is holistic. God's redemptive concern for the world has to do with every aspect of life, whether personal, social, or environmental. The struggle for justice and liberation, the need for forgiveness and reconciliation, the healing of mind and body, the search for meaning and the awakening and sustaining of faith, hope, and love, and the renewal of the earth, are all part of the *missio Dei* and therefore the mission of the church.

Throughout this chapter we have noted how difficult it is to define the church undialectically or from one viewpoint only. We have seen that it is both a sociological and theological reality, relating to the human and the divine; it is both a mystical and a diaconal community with both a kerygmatic and a sacramental task; it is both an institution, sometimes quite powerful, and a fragile gathering of repentant sinners; and it has both an unbroken heritage which goes back to Pentecost and beyond, and a broken ability to serve its Lord faithfully. In our reflections on the church's participation in the *missio Dei*, we have once again stressed one significant side, namely the church as agent in the transformative work of God in the world. But this can lead to a misunderstanding of the church if we do not see its participation as linked to its very being as a community, its life of communion as expressed in prayer and worship.

Paradoxically, the church cannot become a channel and instrument in the world unless it has a creative life of its own in the 'fellowship of the Spirit'. If the church has anything to offer the world, it is because the church is different from the world at precisely this point. As Berkhof puts it, the church can only participate in the *missio Dei* 'if her being-in-the-world is a being-different-to-the-world'.[20] And this means that the internal life of the church is of fundamental concern, for it is this which constitutes its witness to and participation in the mission of God. Through the reality of its covenantal and sacramental life, the church becomes a sign of what the missionary triune God is doing in the world. The church becomes the 'firstfruits' of God's purposes, or, in Berkhof's wonderful phrase, 'the experimental garden of a new humanity'.[21]

## Baptism, Eucharist, and Ministry

Baptism and the eucharist are central aspects of the life of the Christian community. Traditionally referred to as sacraments, they need to be understood not on their own, nor in an individualistic sense, but as integral to the life and mission of the church as a whole. Indeed, the sacraments, together with prayer and preaching of the Word, give the church its unique character and, through the agency of the Spirit, empower believers for mission in the world.

The word 'sacrament' is derived from a Latin word, *sacramentum*, referring to something being consecrated to God. This was used to translate the Greek word *mysterion* used in the New Testament to indicate God's hidden plan of salvation revealed in Jesus Christ. A sacrament is therefore more than a ceremony; it is a sign which points to God's loving and transforming presence in the world and our lives. Some signs only point to something else; they do not communicate that to which they refer. A sign pointing to Cape Town does not put us in immediate touch with the city, but our bodies are signs of who we really are. A sacrament is this sort of sign. It communicates and makes real to us that which it signifies. For just as one's body is filled with one's presence, so too is a sacrament filled with the presence of Christ through his Spirit.

Traditionally a sacrament has been described not only as a sign but also a cause of grace. However, the word 'cause' led to many misunderstandings, suggesting that the sacraments worked almost magically, as if by some power possessed by the words, the gestures, the things used. Hence the Protestant Reformers rejected this idea and stressed that the sacraments have no inner power of their own. Whatever good is communicated through them comes as a result of God's Spirit acting in those whose faith is awoken through the sacraments. Today ecumenical discussions have made it clear that there is no unbridgeable gap between Protestants and Catholics on this issue. For all would agree that rituals have no power of their own. The sacraments are not signs of some absent reality but rather the celebration of the transforming presence of God in our midst.

Traditionally, both Western and Eastern Christendom recognised seven sacraments: baptism, confirmation, eucharist, penance, anointing of the sick, orders and matrimony. However, at the time of the Reformation, Protestants reduced the number to the only two for which they believed there was sufficient scriptural warrant, namely baptism and eucharist, though Martin Luther also regarded penance as a sacrament. In what follows we will focus only on baptism and the eucharist.

Christians have always laid great stress on the importance of baptism. It marks the beginning of a person's sharing in the life of the Christian community – not only the invisible life that is the transforming presence of Father, Son and Spirit, but also the visible life that involves confessing one's faith in Christ and all that Christ taught and achieved for humanity. Baptism is therefore the primary bond binding all Christians to each other. In the World Council of Churches' document *Baptism, Eucharist and Ministry*, which reflects a 'significant theological convergence'[22] on the sacraments, baptism is seen as 'a rite of commitment to the Lord' and 'a sign of new life' which is manifest in various images: 'participation in Christ's death and resurrection', 'confession of sin and conversion of heart', the bestowal of the Spirit, 'a sign and seal of our common discipleship', and 'a sign of the Kingdom of God and of the life of the world to come'. Baptism does not negate the necessity of faith, or responsible discipleship, but is both 'God's gift' and 'our response'. Whether baptism is of infants or believing adults, it embodies God's initiative and entails the same mandate to respond.

The eucharist is variously described in the New Testament and Christian tradition (Lord's Supper, Holy Communion, Mass), but the word 'eucharist' is now widely used ecumenically because it expresses the central theme of gratitude (*eucharisteo*, to give thanks) rather than focusing on one element within the celebration. It also expresses what the church is meant to be as a community living in the 'fellowship of the Holy Spirit', and seeking to express its life as the 'Body of Christ'.

The origin of the eucharist is Christ's last meal with his disciples. In the Scriptures this meal is associated with the Jewish Passover ceremony (Matt. 26:17ff.; Mark 14:12ff.; Luke 22:7ff.; cf. John 13:1ff.), celebrating those events that led to the establishment of Israel as God's chosen people: the Exodus and the Covenant. In the same way, the eucharist is a 'memorial' (*anamnesis*) which recalls in the present what God has done in Christ for our redemption, and it is a celebration of Christian hope, an anticipation of the redemption of the whole universe in the 'second advent' of Christ (1 Cor. 11:25f.). As *Baptism, Eucharist and Ministry* indicates, the eucharist invokes, and is dependent upon, the Spirit, whose presence is a foretaste of the kingdom of God. As a foretaste of the kingdom, the eucharist embodies reconciliation, and moves the church to be actively pursuing just relations, not only within itself, but also in the world. The eucharist is, in fact, an 'instance of the Church's participation in God's mission to the world'.[23]

The issue of ministry is a vexed one in today's church. Some churches ordain leaders as priests, bishops or deacons, others as pastors or ministers. Some churches do not ordain leaders at all, claiming that all Christians, as members of the body, are 'priests'. Some churches ordain women, others do not. The view of ministry is dependent, largely, on the model of the church embraced. For example, those who see the church as institution, or 'perfect society', see leadership as hierarchical, analogous to that of the state. A communitarian model, on the other hand, sees leadership as mainly 'fostering fellowship'.[24] The sacramental model stresses the priest as mediator. Those who embrace a kerygmatic model see leadership primarily in terms of preaching. Finally, a servant model involves the leader as turned outward, 'to help the world move toward its true goal in Christ'.[25]

Ministry can only be truly understood, however, in the light of 'the calling of the whole people of God'.[26] Ordained ministers have a special calling within the task of the church 'to assemble and build up the body of Christ by proclaiming and teaching the Word of God, by celebrating the sacraments, and by guiding the life of the community in its worship, its mission and its caring ministry'.[27] But this ministry is to equip the whole People of God (*laos*) to fulfil its task in the world (Eph. 4:11f.). Ministry is a means of enabling mission. There is, in fact, widespread ecumenical recognition that there are many different ways ministry may be structured, but as *Baptism, Eucharist and Ministry* indicates, all ministry should be exercised in a 'personal, collegial and communal way'.[28]

Much more could be said about ecclesiology, and related themes and issues will be found in many chapters within this volume. What is clear, however, is that the church is in many ways the focal point for doing theology. For whatever else theology is about, one of its primary tasks is to enable the church to reflect critically on its life and witness in the world. In this sense, all theology in some way or another impinges upon the church. 'Community, ministry, and theology', Edward Schillebeeckx reminds us, are dependent upon each other, and 'fundamentally dependent — in a process in which they are relativised — on the living God, who brings his creation in Jesus Christ, through our history, to a final consummation after history'.[29]

[1] In drafting this chapter I gratefully acknowledge the ecumenical input of John Suggit, Brian Gaybba, Malusi Mpumlwana, Barney Pityana, Steve de Gruchy and Steve Martin.

[2] Paul Minear, *Images of the Church in the New Testament* (Philadelphia: Westminster, 1960), p. 26.

[3] John D. Zizioulas, *Being as Communion* (New York: St. Vladimir's Press), 1985.

[4] Michael Kinnamon, ed., *Signs of the Spirit*, Official Report of the Seventh Assembly (Geneva: World Council of Churches, 1991), p. 172.

[5] Avery Dulles, *Models of the Church* (Garden City: Doubleday, 1974), p. 63.

[6] Ibid., p. 74.

[7] Ibid., p. 201.

[8] Ibid., pp. 202, 79.

[9] Dietrich Bonhoeffer, *Letters and Papers from Prison* (London: SCM, 1971), p. 382.

[10] Ibid., p. 286.

[11] James Cochrane, *Servants of Power: The Role of English-speaking Churches 1903–1930* (Johannesburg: Ravan, 1987), p. 227.

[12] See the discussion in Hans Küng, *The Church* (London: Burns and Oates, 1968), pp. 84ff.

[13] Cochrane, *Servants of Power*, p. 219.

[14] Küng, *The Church*, p. 95. On the relationship between the church and the reign of God, see the whole of the discussion on pages 43–104.

[15] For an extended discussion, see Küng, *The Church*, pp. 263ff.; Jürgen Moltmann, *The Church in the Power of the Spirit* (London: SCM, 1977), pp. 337ff.

[16] *The Kairos Document*, revised second edition (Braamfontein: Skotaville, 1986), pp. 28f.

[17] Moltmann, *The Church in the Power of the Spirit*, p. 341.

[18] See for example the evaluation by Hendrikus Berkhof, *Christian Faith* (Grand Rapids: Eerdmans, 1979), p. 413; and David Bosch, *Transforming Mission: Paradigm Shifts in the Theology of Mission* (Maryknoll, N.Y.: Orbis, 1991), pp. 373, 389.

[19] Bosch, *Transforming Mission*, p. 372.

[20] Berkhof, *Christian Faith*, p. 414.

[21] Ibid., p. 415.

[22] *Baptism, Eucharist and Ministry*, Faith and Order Paper no. 111 (Geneva: World Council of Churches, 1982), p. ix.

[23] Ibid., p. 15.

[24] Dulles, *Models of the Church*, p. 171.

[25] Ibid., p. 179.

[26] *Baptism, Eucharist and Ministry*, p. 20.

[27] Ibid., p. 22.

[28] Ibid., p. 26.

[29] Edward Schillebeeckx, *The Church with a Human Face* (London: SCM, 1985), p. 228.

## Select Bibliography

*Baptism, Eucharist and Ministry*. Faith and Order Paper no. 111. Geneva: World Council of Churches, 1982

Baillie, D. M. *The Theology of the Sacraments*. London: Faber, 1957

Boff, Leonardo. *Church, Charism and Power: Liberation Theology and the Institutional Church*. London: SCM, 1985

Boff, Leonardo. *Ecclesio-genesis*. London: Collins, 1986

Bosch, David. *Transforming Mission*. Maryknoll: Orbis, 1991

Dulles, Avery. *Models of the Church*. Garden City: Doubleday, 1974

Küng, Hans. *The Church*. London: Burns and Oates, 1968

Minear, Paul. *Images of the Church in the New Testament*. Philadelphia: Westminster, 1960

Moltmann, Jürgen. *The Church in the Power of the Spirit*. London: SCM, 1977

Ruether, Rosemary Radford. *Women Church: Theology and Practice*. New York: Harper and Row, 1988

Schillebeeckx, Edward. *The Church with a Human Face: A New and Expanded Theology of Ministry*. London: SCM, 1985

Schillebeeckx, Edward. *Church: The Human Story of God*. New York: Crossroad, 1991

# 12

# Towards a New Heaven and a New Earth

## KLAUS NÜRNBERGER

> Then I saw a new heaven and a new earth... There will be no more death
> or mourning or crying or pain, for the old order of things has passed away.
> He who was seated on the throne said: Behold, I am making everything
> new! (Rev. 21:1–5)

Generation after generation of believers, afflicted by injustices, suffering, death
and despair, have been consoled by these promises. That is the good news. The
bad news is that many people have been lured into wild speculations and
misleading illusions, often with devastating consequences. How much truth – and
what kind of truth – is lodged in these expectations?

Eschatology is a reflection on the 'last things' – that is, things which the
Christian faith expects to happen 'at the end of time'. This chapter will explore
the inner logic which has led to the evolution of eschatological statements in the
history of biblical faith. This inner logic may be stated thus: At the root of
eschatology lies the common human awareness that what reality is does not
correspond with what reality ought to be. Such an awareness emerges and grows
in times of suffering and need. Indeed, biblical faith evolved as the result of a series
of redemptive experiences in which God was believed to have intervened, or
promised to intervene, in concrete predicaments with the intention of
transforming the situation of need into a situation of well-being, thus changing
what is into what ought to be.

Although redemptive experiences are always partial and provisional, through
faith they point to things more comprehensive and more definite. Concepts such
as creation 'in the beginning of time' and transformation 'at the end of time' are
examples of this. The concept of creation indicates that reality is 'very good', at
least as far as present reality corresponds with what it ought to be. Eschatology, in
contrast, articulates the conviction that reality shall be transformed, at least as far as
it does not correspond with what it ought to be. In other words, reality shall be
very good.

## God's Future in the Biblical Traditions

At the root of biblical faith, including its eschatological hope, lies the experience of the redemptive acts of God in history. Redemptive experiences happen under conditions of time and space. Therefore they are by necessity limited and provisional, never comprehensive and final. A redemptive act of God in history is always the promise of something greater. And the promise and the expectation always go beyond their fulfilment. Because faith is trust, it is expectant. It is oriented towards the future by definition.

Whenever in trouble, Israel remembered what Yahweh had done in times of old and expected Yahweh to act again. Deutero-Isaiah, for instance, maintained that God had defeated the chaos monster when the universe was created, that Yahweh led Israel through the Reed Sea when they were liberated from Egyptian slavery; so, then, Yahweh will also deliver the Jews from Babylonian exile (Isa. 51:9–11). The expectations of an intervention of Yahweh came to a head through the national catastrophes of 720 and 586 BC. The prophets declared that Israel had broken the covenant, and announced doom. This was a very radical statement. It pulled the rug from underneath the feet of the old Israelite faith. The crisis was immeasurable. But the prophets also affirmed God's faithfulness. Yahweh would indeed act again. The 'day of the Lord' would come.

This orientation of faith towards the future was instigated by an unacceptable present. There was oppression by kings and elites within the country and aggression at the hand of foreign powers. There was economic misery. There was religious apostasy and moral decadence. In condemning various dimensions of evil, the prophets transcended the present, pointing towards a new situation which their God would bring about: a wise and righteous king, the subjugation of the enemies under his benevolent rule, overall peace and prosperity, a new set of motivations within each individual and the people as a whole. So when the people of God were afflicted by suffering, the prophets combined judgement with promise and thus turned biblical faith from an orientation towards the past (stability) to an orientation towards the future (change).

But the promises of the prophets did not materialise – at least not to the expected extent. As suffering deepened and the obstacles to a new dispensation seemed ever more insurmountable, biblical hope became more radical. In defiance it proclaimed the present agonies to be the birth pains of a new age. What was humanly impossible to achieve, God would bring about. A cataclysmic transformation was at hand which would lead not only to the restoration of the kingdom of Israel to its Davidic and Solomonic glory but to a giant reconstruction of the universe as a whole.

While this radical eschatological thinking would flower in the apocalypses such as Daniel, its roots are in pre-exilic prophecy. Not only Israel but other nations, not only the social order but the human heart, not only human reality but nature is expected to change. During the Exile, contact with the Persian religion helped the Jews to develop a vision of reality in its historical evolution. In Persia it was believed that history moved through different stages. The last stage would culminate in a cataclysmic showdown between the forces of good (personalised in the god Ahuramazda) and the forces of evil (personalised in the god Angramainyu). The victory of good over evil would lead to ultimate salvation.

The Jews adopted the cosmic dimensions of this religion, although they never accepted the existence of two competing gods. Whereas in earlier times the people of God expected the intervention of God to help Israel in concrete needs such as foreign invasions, droughts or disease, the expectation was now radicalised. Reality as a whole would be reconstructed. A new human heart, a new social order, even a new natural order would ensue, because evil in all its forms would be overcome.

The universalisation of faith went hand in hand with its individualisation. If all people are important, then each person is important. The thrust of this eschatology in universal and individual terms was threefold. First, it is God's intention to bring about complete, comprehensive and universal redemption. Israel was to be the privileged instrument of God after the reconstruction of the world as a whole under the reign of Yahweh. The negative implication of this conviction was that evil would be eradicated totally through judgement, condemnation and the 'second death'.

Second, God's intention cannot be frustrated by inner-worldly obstacles, be they superhuman powers, political systems, the hearts of evil men or the given structures of the natural world. Not even death can thwart God's justice. The implication is that those who died will rise to be judged and be either justified or condemned.

Third, the initiative to bring about ultimate and total redemption is God's, yet we anticipate it in faith. The apparent shift away from human responsibility to God's exclusive initiative in bringing about the expected turn of events was due in part to the powerlessness of the Jews as an oppressed group. In part it was due to their desire to glorify the majesty of their God in the face of the seemingly overwhelming power of the gods of the imperial authorities. But in the apocalypses human initiative was only dormant temporarily. Again and again it burst into political action when circumstances allowed and when the believers thought that God's time had come.

Roughly at the same time another theology reaffirmed the validity of the cosmic order as intended by God: chaos was constrained by means of a cosmic structure (Gen. 1); the sanctuary on Mount Zion, where Yahweh was accessible by name, functioned as the centre of the universe; time was structured around the Sabbath; and the Torah, the law of God, was the foundation of human well-being. This is the message of the so-called priestly writer whose task it was to provide the religious foundations for a re-established community in Jerusalem after the Exile. It is in this context that the creation narrative of Genesis 1 is located.

The concept of creation in the beginning indicates God's original intentions for reality, while the concept of eschatological reconstruction says that these intentions will materialise in the end. Both concepts declare that God's intention is to achieve the comprehensive well-being of God's creatures. Both say that this intention materialises through God's creative power. How, then, do these develop in early Christianity?

Both John the Baptist and Jesus of Nazareth shared apocalyptic expectations. They proclaimed that the reign of God was imminent and that it was time to gear one's life to its approach. However, Jesus not only announced the approach of the Kingdom, he enacted its redemptive thrust. He communed with the outcasts, healed the sick, comforted the downtrodden. But he also castigated the self-sufficient and the self-righteous, the rich and the powerful. Evil was seen to be challenged, if not overcome, wherever he went.

On the basis of his teaching and his behaviour the disciples expected Jesus to be the Messiah or, to be more precise, the expected Prince of Peace (Isa. 9, 11). Their expectations were crushed when Jesus' bold entry into Jerusalem, the expected capital of a reorganised world, ended with his capture, condemnation and execution as an impostor and revolutionary. Their hope was shattered. But then they had experiences which convinced them that God had legitimised Jesus, the crucified, by raising him from the dead. This reaffirmed their conviction that the eschatological future had dawned. Biblical passages such as Isaiah 53 enabled them to understand the crucifixion as part of the redemptive purposes of God. As the 'suffering Servant', Jesus was in fact the Messiah. His resurrection was the beginning of the general resurrection of the dead. He would soon return to judge humankind and reconstruct the world. And if Christ was the Judge and the criterion of the last judgement, then those who followed Christ would go free because they fulfilled the ultimate criterion of authenticity.

Paul was not so optimistic about the possibilities of fulfilling God's will. All people were sinners and unlikely to survive the last judgement. In fact the Christ-event constituted God's new initiative to save humanity. He suspended the law as a condition of acceptance. If God was willing to go to the extreme of letting God's representative lose his life and honour on the Cross, then God's love had to be unconditional. God was willing to accept the unacceptable and suffer the consequences in anticipation of an eschatological transformation. God's grace granted both forgiveness of sins and participation in the life of the risen Christ through the power of the Spirit.

The suspension of the law as condition of acceptance led to two fundamental changes in eschatology. First, the new dispensation was no longer focused on Israel but included the 'nations'. That is, biblical faith became universal and non-discriminatory. Second, the purpose of resurrection changed: while in apocalyptic literature resurrection was to make the last judgement possible, after which there would be a 'second death' for the condemned, Paul argues that all people are sinners, all are eternally lost and receive their punishment in death, while resurrection is the gift of a new life, already now mediated to us by the risen Christ in the power of the Spirit.

The apocalyptic expectation, too, was disappointed. After a few decades of waiting, disillusionment set in and new interpretations had to be found. Some saw the interim as a period of testing (1 Pet. 1:3–12). Some attributed the delayed return of Christ to God's patience with the wicked (2 Pet. 3:9). Some believed that all of humanity had to be reached by the gospel first, and that the missionary task had not been completed (cf. Matt. 14:14). Luke, the author of the book of Acts, concluded that Christ did not appear at the end of times, as had been believed till then, but in the middle of times. Between the time of Christ and the end there was the time of the church and its mission (Acts 1:6—8).

But in the long run all these explanations proved unsatisfactory. As apocalyptic hope lost its plausibility, faith turned from a forward to an upward direction. Increasingly the theological expression of the discrepancy between what is and what ought to be was translated from the apocalyptic model of a conflict between 'this age' and the 'age to come', to the Hellenistic model of a contrast between appearance and truth.

This change can best be observed in the evolution of the Pauline school. While Paul's early letters are steeped in the apocalyptic tradition (see 1 Thess. 4:13—5:11; 1 Cor. 15:20—28), the Deutero-Pauline letters (Colossians and Ephesians) are no longer geared to the eschatological future. Instead they emphasise the validity of a truth claim. Instead of saying 'What ought to be, shall be!', they say 'What ought to be, is already there, though hidden.' God's intentions have been a mystery hidden from all generations in all ages but have now been revealed in Christ, mediated by the apostles and other teachers to his 'saints', so that the latter enlighten each and every human being (Col. 1:25—29; Eph. 3:2—10).

There are a number of consequences arising from this shift. First, hope is no longer directed towards a new earth in the eschatological future but towards God's glory in heaven (Col. 1:5). Second, Christ is not expected to subdue all his enemies when he comes, but is already enthroned above all the powers which determine the universe (Eph. 1:20—23; cf Col. 1:15—20). These powers only have to be informed by the church of God's intentions (Eph. 3:10), namely to reconcile the entire cosmos in Christ (Col. 1:19—20; Eph. 1:9—10). Third, while according to Paul we believe that we shall live with Christ (Rom. 6:8), the Deutero-Paulines inform that we have already been raised and enthroned with Christ in heavenly glory (Eph. 2:6; Col. 2:13). Fourth, the new humanity has already been established in the church, which encompasses old enemies, namely Jews and Greeks (Eph. 2:11—22). Fifth, the true life of the members of the new community is already lived 'in heaven', though the fact still has to be made manifest (Col. 3:1—4). What matters now is that the community grows (Col. 2:19), or is built up, as Christ's 'Body', by gaining greater insight, living a new life (Eph. 4:1—16) and resisting and overpowering the forces of darkness which are antagonistic to the rule of Christ (Eph. 6:10ff.). While the effect on ethics seems to be the same, what ought to be has been translocated from the eschatological future to what already is 'in essence' but not yet fully revealed.

The letter to the Ephesians also emphasises the church as an institution. Believers are built up into a new humanity, the church, which represents a new social structure. For this purpose Christ has granted the gifts of spiritual leadership (4:7ff.). By its very existence the church is to be a witness to the cosmic powers (3:10). Believers must subject themselves to accepted moral precepts. This again involves a spiritual battle against the cosmic powers which are not yet subject to the heavenly king (6:10ff.). The motif of the cosmic order has again established itself.

The point in these writings is that everything of importance has already happened; the only question is how we realise the potentials opened by God for us and the universe. 'Building up the body' by means of institutionalised offices became important. Though in the pastoral letters (1 & 2 Tim.; Titus) apocalyptic expectations still figure here and there, the focus is on authority in the church and on questions of appropriate behaviour. This trend ushered in the understanding of the church as an institution of salvation whose authorities dispense God's gifts and judgements.

## Modern Facets of Eschatology

Despite the presence of apocalytic literature (such as the book of Revelation) in the late first and early second centuries, by the time the pastoral letters were written questions of office, order and morality had become the major preoccupation of the church. This tendency continued right into the Middle Ages and beyond. Leaping across vast stretches of church history, we can only mention a few facets.

To begin with, the cosmic expectations of apocalyptics became 'last things', which would probably happen one day, but which had no real significance. Instead one's personal prospects before the judgement seat of God became the paramount concern. In other words, the cosmic comprehensiveness of apocalyptics was lost. The Greek idea of an immortal soul destined for eternal life was combined with the Jewish idea of the last judgement. God's acceptance was again perceived to be conditional on the fulfilment of the law as administered by the authorities of the church. The fear of hell became a moral whip and was manipulated by religious demagogues and oppressors alike.

Hence during this time the kingdom of God was believed to have incarnated itself in the church as an institution of salvation. One could not really expect much more than to be under the strict but benevolent guidance of an ecclesiastical leadership which represented Christ on earth. Time and again the apocalyptic spirit of change surfaced in heretical groups, religious orders and enthusiastic movements, and was often severely persecuted. Excitement concerning the imminent end of the world led to all sorts of enthusiastic and not always wholesome expectations and actions.

During the time of the Enlightenment and Romanticism the kingdom was seen in terms of the religious, moral and cultural upliftment of the human race. Western imperialism was regarded as the instrument which carried progress, reason and morality to the ends of the earth. This cultural optimism reached its peak during the nineteenth century. The horrors of the First World War brought about a complete change in direction. The 'dialectical theology' of the early twentieth century saw eschatology as the crisis of human self-understanding and achievement, brought about by a 'Word' which came 'directly from above', from a God who was perceived to be the 'wholly Other'.

New scientific discoveries and the encounter with other cultures and religions brought about a complete relativisation of the cosmic frame of reference in Western thought. What is above? What is below? What is a beginning and an end? What is religious truth? To regain some sort of foundation Western thought began to concentrate on the subjective experience of the individual. This also implied a clear distinction between subject and object. Conviction was reduced to the inner realm of the individual soul, and the outer world was left to science, technology and politics. The philosophical father of this trend was Descartes. Its theological version began to emerge in the Reformation, but it really came into its own in Pietism. It was spread by revival and missionary movements all over the world. Under its spell Christian theology was not able to sustain the cosmic comprehensiveness of the apocalyptic approach, but concentrated more and more on the relation of the individual to his or her own authentic self in relation to God. Existentialism is also an extreme modern version of this trend.

Existentialism has powerful antecedents in the 'present eschatology' of Paul and especially the gospel of John. For existentialism, the decisive events in life are located where they are actually experienced: not in a distant past and not in a distant future, but in the immediacy of the present moment. The present moment is the *kairos*, the crucial time which calls for a decision. In making decisions between alternative attitudes and actions we define ourselves as righteous or sinful or, to use existentialist terminology, as authentic or unauthentic.

What is authentic and what is not? There is a formal criterion of authenticity: an authentic life is determined neither by what others say — that is, by social conditioning, conventions, fads, collective interests, ideologies or traditions — nor by our own superficial whims and desires, but by conscious, reflected and responsible self-determination. To gain authenticity I have to take control of my own life and assume my own responsibility. I cannot hide behind the collective attitudes and actions of others or of some higher authority.

There is also a material criterion of authenticity: we are willing to receive life as a gift from the Source of reality, and do not try to gain it by our own achievements. This is Rudolph Bultmann's version of the dialectic between grace and law. A receptive attitude implies that we never have authentic life at our disposal; it is ever only accessible in our response to a challenge. It never arrives, it is always arriving; it is never present, let alone past, but always 'future'. This is what makes it 'eschatological'. The eschatological future is present as potentiality in every moment of life.

There is a further implication of this approach: the criterion of an authentic life is not a set of rules and regulations, but involvement in God's life-giving, redeeming, healing, upbuilding love. According to John, the Jewish Torah is superseded by 'grace and truth' in Christ (John 1:17); the Greek impersonal *logos* is redefined as God's personal self-communication in Christ (John 1:1,14). God is defined as love (1 John 4:17f); this means that God is only real for us as the power of a creative and redemptive movement, which is manifest in Christ and in which we are involved.

For eschatology, the ultimate showdown between what is and what ought to be does not take place in a future drama. According to John, the last judgement takes place whenever we encounter the living Christ (1:12; 3:18, 36; 5:24). The judge presiding over the last judgement is the risen Christ. The risen Christ, however, is not a mythological figure seated at the right hand of God in heaven, but the 'Spirit' who is present with his disciples (John 14:17f.; cf. 2 Cor. 3:17). That is, the risen Christ is God's way of opening up the possibility of authentic life for you and me, here and now. The determining factor is one's response to the challenge of one's potential authenticity 'in Christ'. Those who let themselves in for it already have 'eternal life', those who reject or neglect the offer are already condemned (John 3:16—21; 5:24). What may or may not happen beyond the grave, or beyond the end of universal history for that matter, is existentially irrelevant.

Existential theologians claim that future eschatology is only a projection of what happens now towards an envisaged reality beyond the limits of time. But the argument can also be reversed. Paul, for one, retained the traditional apocalyptic framework of eschatology (1 Cor. 15:21—28) and believed it to be the precondition for its existential impact. Until our 'flesh' decays in the grave we are constantly faced with the choice between 'walking according to the flesh' or 'according to the Spirit'. Authenticity is defined by Paul as being 'in the Spirit', or 'in Christ', or 'Christ in us'. The Spirit gives anticipatory access to the eschatological fulfilment which is still to come. If Christ had not risen into the eschatological future, our faith would have no basis and would be entirely futile (1 Cor. 15:13—18). We would have nothing to identify with, except our own sinful selves. The decision we have to take again and again is to appropriate what has happened in Christ, who died to sin and rose to righteousness (Rom. 6:10; 2 Cor. 5:21), by 'considering ourselves dead to sin but alive to God in Christ Jesus' (Rom. 5:11). This conscious identification with what happened in Christ is symbolically enacted in our baptism (Rom. 6:3ff.).

We have seen how eschatology became ever more concentrated on the individual and his or her personal authenticity. Ironically, a neo-marxist philosopher, Ernst Bloch, played a major role in bringing about a renewed appreciation of the more comprehensive understanding of eschatology found in apocalyptics among modern theologians such as Jürgen Moltmann, Johann Baptist Metz, Wolfhart Pannenberg and various kinds of liberation theologians. Political theology, as initiated by Moltmann, shared the existentialist concern for the unity of reality, which excludes another world and another 'age' beyond history, for the critical importance of personal commitment and involvement, which excludes 'objective truth' based on mere speculation or dogmatic tradition, and for the futuricity of salvation. The gospel is promise, and faith is hope — and obedience.

But political theology translated the vision of what ought to be from personal authenticity to the authenticity of the social order. It also translated the location of authenticity from the continuing process of individual human existence to the historical future of society. According to political theology, eschatological hope grants the freedom from an ostensibly static universe, and the inspiration to join a dynamic movement into an open future.

Political theology appropriates the biblical vision of the eschatological 'kingdom of God' and defines it as a situation of freedom from oppression and social justice. As a real utopia, the kingdom is always ahead of us in the form of a shifting horizon, and functions as a continuous challenge for us to transcend and overcome the oppressive structures of the present order. The pattern is similar in liberation theology, Black theology and feminist theology.

Political theology presented a critical corrective to existentialism. The existentialist concentration on personal authenticity obtained through momentary decision-making blurred the vision of believers as regards the importance of the wider social contexts which are subject to great movements in historical time. Thus it severely truncated the horizons of human responsibility. Recently the horizons have been widened even further to include the authenticity of the natural environment. Yet the existentialists' insistence on personal authenticity, the political insistence on social authenticity and the ecological insistence on the dignity of creation do not exclude but complement each other.

But even the inclusion of nature into theological reflections is not yet sufficient. The natural sciences have opened new vistas on cosmic reality. We now discover that, according to the second thermodynamic law (or the law of entropy), the universe is engaged in a process which moves from an absolute concentration to an absolute dissipation of energy. This process is characterised by waves which lead to temporal and localised energy concentrations in the form of ever more complex constructs — a process which is described as evolution.

Some thinkers believe that evolution opened up the possibility of an 'eschatological' perfection, the most influential of these thinkers being Teilhard de Chardin. But this optimistic picture is thwarted by the fact that evolution must be seen in the context of entropy: each construct is not only short-lived, but it also comes into existence at the expense of other such constructs. Each achievement has its cost in terms of suffering. Humans, for instance, are not only mortal themselves, they also cannot live without the death of other creatures. And because the overall process moves from concentration to dissipation, the balance sheet is always negative.

These new insights revitalise the 'utopian' character of eschatology. Today existential, political and ecological concerns must once again be embedded in the context of a cosmic vision. As we have seen, the ancient prophetic tradition ended up with the apocalyptic realisation that the world, as it is constructed at present, cannot usher in comprehensive well-being. Authenticity is evasive, whether in terms of a sinless heart, a just social order or a natural environment which is neither hostile nor vulnerable.

Apocalyptic literature teaches us that eschatology is a protest against experienced reality as a whole. The hope of faith does not only transcend the given towards potentials which may be realised in the future, but it also transcends all thinkable possibilities of this world. Ultimate fulfilment can only be achieved by the transformative intervention of a benevolent and omnipotent God. Apocalyptic eschatology is the defiant reaction of faith to the iron laws and inevitabilities of 'this world' — whether during the time of ancient Near Eastern empires or during the age of the scientific discovery of cosmic processes. It is the postulate of the approach of a giant miracle which puts all inner-worldly causality out of action. Faced with impenetrable walls and immutable laws, humans become vulnerable to despair, cynicism, fatalism and lethargy. Where should the necessary reassurance come from if not from the 'great nevertheless', the defiant protest of faith against reality?

Hope does not only serve to conquer our destructive desires and challenge our human initiative to move forward constructively, to conquer social evil and mobilise for social reconstruction, to arrest the deterioration of the environment and conscientise us for ecological responsibility — in short, to utilise our human capabilities to their full extent; it also serves to conquer our desperation where human capacities and earthly possibilities are finally and totally exhausted. It reassures those who have stared into the abyss of death and destruction that the power centre of reality is located beyond this reality, namely in its divine Source.

The most immediate and the most radical experience of powerlessness and futility on the personal level is the realisation of the inexorable and inescapable advent of death. Eschatological hope transcends death in the form of the vision of resurrection, understood not as the continuation of human potentials (for instance in the form of an immortal soul), but as a new creation of God. But there are also more intermediate forms of despair which need this type of transcendence. The frustrations stemming from physical handicaps, intellectual limitations, professional failures, irredeemable family conflicts, unsuccessful revolutions or disillusionments experienced after great social transformations, all heavily weigh down the human psyche. And hopelessness is the greatest killer — of joy, of initiative, of loving concern, of social and ecological responsibility, even of physical life.

## Prerequisites of an Eschatology for Today

The first prerequisite of an eschatology for today is clarity concerning its purpose. The rationale of a Christian eschatology is to reassure, liberate and motivate people in situations of need. This is how eschatological hope emerged in biblical times, and this is where it plays its constructive role today. Venerable doctrine or speculative curiosity alone cannot sustain a viable eschatology. Modern humanity is torn apart between the 'progressive' fervour of technological optimism and revolutionary enthusiasm, on the one hand, and fear of rapid deterioration and catastrophe on the other. Population growth, environmental pollution, breakdown of moral values and social cohesion, the growth of violence and brutality, the emergence of new diseases, the threat of a nuclear holocaust — these are the spectres of our time. Modern humanity needs a powerful message of hope to weather the storms of the future, especially in South Africa.

Because human need occurs in all dimensions of reality, an eschatology for today must be comprehensive or holistic. The personal core of one's being (the soul) must be seen in the context of its physical existence, the individual in the context of the community, the community in the context of society, society in the context of the natural world, and earthly nature within the vast dimensions of the universe. The hope for the reunion of a disembodied soul with a personal Saviour in heavenly bliss is as inadequate as the hope for a transition from the class struggle to the classless society. According to biblical faith, God's ultimate intention is the comprehensive well-being of creation as a whole. It encompasses the personal, communal, social-structural and ecological dimensions of life.

An appropriate eschatology must express the singular contribution of the Christian faith: our relation to God and to one another will be determined not by human achievement but by God's gift of grace. There will be no law which we have to fulfil to become acceptable. This has immediate existential repercussions. Eschatology grants freedom when it transcends the prison of a stagnant traditionalism which fetters our initiatives and cripples the unfolding of our potentials. It grants freedom when it transcends the slave masters of ambition and competition in the modern technological rat race, which whip us into action and leave us in frustration. It grants freedom when it transcends the dead weight of static conservatism or the disillusionment of a failed revolution. It grants freedom when it transcends our personal failures and limitations. It involves us in the creative authority, the redemptive love and the comprehensive vision of God, who is the Source, Lord and Judge of reality as a whole. All these are instances in which the demands of a law are superseded by God's gift.

Finally, there will be no death in God's eschatological future. Or expressed in cosmic terms, the process of entropy will be superseded by a new creation. That is the hardest nut to crack for a modern scientifically informed consciousness. What can it mean? It simply means that the human being has to transcend reality and all its limitations or become its victim. We are supposed to be free from reality and depend on God. That is the core of the eschatological message.

For human beings death is the ultimate evil. It terminates life and destroys all relationships: to oneself, to others, to the world, to God. When you die, the world has come to an end for you. Faith in resurrection is, like faith in a new heaven and a new earth, not based on empirical evidence and rational argument. Personal life after death is by no means more plausible than the apocalyptic transformation of the world and the advent of the kingdom of God. Both are based on the human capacity to transcend the given.

While faith can be extremely realistic about the nature of existing reality and its limitations, precisely because it has this capacity to transcend it refuses to accept that experienced reality is absolute or final. The proclamation of the resurrection of the dead and of a new heaven and a new earth is a protest statement, an act of defiance, directed against the inevitabilities of reality on behalf of human dignity, freedom and authenticity, made in the name of a God who is irrevocably committed to the comprehensive well-being of his creatures and who is the Master of reality.

## Select Bibliography

Brunner, E. *Eternal Hope*. London: Lutterworth, 1954

Ewert, H. and E. Cousins (eds.) *Hope and the Future of Man*. London: Garnstone Press, 1973

Gutiérrez, G. *A Theology of Liberation*. London: SCM, 1974

Hanson, P. D. *The Dawn of Apocalyptic*. Philadelphia: Fortress, 1979

König, A. *New and Greater Things*. Pretoria: Unisa, 1988

Kümmel, W. G. *The Theology of the New Testament*. London: SCM, 1974

Levenson, Jon D. *Creation and the Persistence of Evil: The Jewish Drama of Divine Omnipotence*. San Francisco: Harper and Row, 1988

Moltmann, J. *Theology of Hope: On the Ground and the Implications of a Christian Eschatology*. London: SCM, 1967

Neuner, J. and J. Dupuis. *The Christian Faith in the Doctrinal Documents of the Catholic Church*. London: Collins, 1983

Schmid, H. *The Doctrinal Theology of the Evangelical Lutheran Church*. Minneapolis: Augsburg, 1889

Schmithals, W. *An Introduction to the Theology of Rudolf Bultmann*. London: SCM, 1968

Schwarz, H. 'Eschatology' in C. E. Braaten and R. W. Jenson (eds.), *Christian Dogmatics*, Vol. 2. Philadelphia: Fortress, 1984

Tillich, P. *Systematic Theology*, Vol. 3. Chicago: University of Chicago Press, 1951

PART FOUR
# Theologies in South Africa

# 13

# African Theologies

## LUKE LUNGILE PATO

There are, for purposes of this discussion, at least four noteworthy facts which must be recorded in respect of Christianity and Christian theology on the African continent. The first is the antiquity of Christianity in Africa. The New Testament contains indications that suggests that places like Ethiopia, Egypt and Cyrene had been penetrated by Christianity during the first century.[1] But many 'recognised' biblical exegetes have not allowed the Bible to tell the stories of the people of Africa. Experiences in the New Testament which are distinctively African have been trivialised, presumably for the purpose of maintaining Eurocentrism. Recently, some Bible scholars have reacted to this challenge and have begun to re-examine the ways in which the African aspects of the Bible have been traditionally interpreted within the mainstream academic curriculum and the churches.[2]

The second fact is related to the first and has to do with the antiquity of Christian theology in Africa. During the second and third centuries, the African church could boast of such great leaders and theological thinkers as Clement of Alexandria, Origen, Tertullian and Cyprian; and a century later of the highly influential Augustine of Hippo. The influence of these theologians extended well beyond Africa. In short, Christian theology, like Christianity, is not a newcomer to the African continent.

The third fact is the absence of historical records about Christianity and theological activity on the African continent from the seventh century onwards, with the exception of Egypt and Ethiopia. It is only in the fifteenth and sixteenth centuries that African Christianity in respect of North, West and Central Africa becomes prominent in the historical record, and in the nineteenth century with regards to Southern Africa. It appears that Christianity experienced a variety of problems that affected its existence down the centuries. This observation raises the questions: What were the reasons that led to the virtual extinction of Christianity in some places? Even more important, what is the church in Africa and particularly South Africa doing to avoid a similar occurrence?

The fourth fact about Christian theology in Africa, particularly when viewed in the light of its antiquity, is its non-Africanness. Until very recently, the experience and world-view of the people of Africa have been ignored. As Robert Schreiter has observed in his *Faces of Jesus in Africa*, 'For too long, embracing Christ and his message meant rejection of African cultural values. Africans were taught that their ancient ways were deficient or even evil and had to be set aside if they hoped to be Christians.'[3]

Missionary theologies made African Christians invisible and inaudible. This is, of course, a specific manifestation of the wider problem of Christianity's reluctance or, in some instances, refusal or inability to incarnate itself in new cultural forms. This was true of Jewish Christianity in relation to Graeco–Roman culture, of Graeco–Roman Christianity in relation to Arabian and Persian and African cultures, and more recently of Western Christianity in relation to African and other non-Western cultures.[4] Indeed, Christianity in Africa is at present burdened by European structures and European mind-sets.[5] It is worth putting on record though that this incapability of Western Christianity to incarnate itself in African cultures goes hand in hand with the dominant position of European culture as the starting point of theological reflection and activity.

Now, this non-Africanness, this foreignness, this assumption that the ethos of European culture is the starting point of Christian theology on the African continent, has been recognised for what it is and challenged by African Christians. The myth that theology could not be anything but Western in form and character has been unmasked,[6] as has the assumption, even by Africans, that the place to study theology was Europe or North America. This changing perception of Christianity and theology in Africa has been prompted by the realisation that questions, assumptions and agendas of theology in Africa have not been set and fixed by the African church and society, and that there *is* such a thing as an African or black perspective, which is distinct from a European or white perspective.

And so, in the following pages, we examine the development of African theologies and their concerns, with special reference to the South African context. We discuss also the significance of theological reflection and activity, and the use of the Bible, in African theologies developed on the African continent in general and in South Africa in particular. The discussion not only represents a review of theological positions and concerns but also highlights certain serious misconceptions and prospects of African theologies.

## The Use of the Term 'African Theology'

Until fairly recently, one seldom heard of theology being 'African' or even the doing of theology in an African style. Yet African Christians, priests, pastors, ministers, evangelists and teachers have been active for a number of centuries. While it is difficult to say precisely who was the first to come up with the term 'African theology', it is not difficult to identify the reasons for its late appearance in the history of Christianity in Africa. Gabriel Setiloane observes that the term 'African theology' was used for the first time in 1965 by the All Africa Conference of Churches (AACC), and that even then it was understood to be more of a nationalistic slogan.[7] According to Gwinyai Muzorewa, the first assembly of AACC in 1958 laid the foundation on which African scholars began to construct African theology.[8] However, one can argue that the beginnings of African theology in South Africa are to be traced back to the nineteenth-century Xhosa prophets Ntsikana and Nxele.[9]

Conservative African voices on the subject of African theology have also been heard. Byang Kato is a good example. Whilst he recognises the need for a Christian theology that addresses itself to the African situation, he is very suspicious of the legitimacy and genuineness of African theology. He seems to see recognition of African theology as something of a threat to Christian theology. According to Kato, 'African Theology seems to be heading for syncretism and universalism.'[10] And so he concludes, 'it is more appropriate to talk of Christian Theology.'[11] Kato's basic concern is not so much the legitimacy of African theology as the authority of the Bible in relation to African religion and tradition. He writes: 'the Bible must remain the absolute source... It is only as the Bible is taken as the absolute Word of God that it can have an authoritative and relevant message for Africa.'[12] Kato's downright opposition to syncretism is, ironically, a real enemy of and threat to the evolution of a meaningful African theology. I shall return to this point when I discuss key features, concerns and sources of African theology.

It is important to note that there is a plurality or diversity in African theology. While it is entirely correct to speak about African theology in the singular (as I have been doing), the notion of African theology, although it has its value, can cause tension and misleading generalisations if it is stretched too far. There are as many forms or concrete manifestations of African theology as there are African peoples, varying in perspective and symbolism one from the other. Denial of the plurality of African theology only serves hegemonic domination and erodes the diversity of African ethnicity and culture.

## Factors Leading to the Development of African Theologies

A number of factors, some of which were not essentially theological, helped to produce the climate within which African theologies could evolve. One was the movement towards political independence in many former British colonies in Africa. As John Parrat puts it, it seemed incongruous to African Christians that while African nations were becoming independent politically, the church in Africa should remain essentially controlled by European missionaries.[13] With the end of colonialism the church was left with a creative opportunity and challenge to develop a new vision, a new theology and strategy for action that would deal with not only the legacy of colonialism but also the implications of its end.

Secondly, there was increasing disillusionment with traditional Western theology, and a realisation that these traditional approaches to theology did not really make sense within African cultural patterns and thought forms. African Christians found classic Western approaches to theology alien and alienating. They did not, for instance, provide motivation for opposing the evils of racism, capitalism, colonialism and sexism. European theology failed to understand the indigenous cultures, religions and traditions of Africa, and to relate to them in a respectful way, or to enter into a creative dialogue with them. Such theology was too statement-oriented and speculative: it did not get involved in the real drama of African people's lives, or speak in the religious and cultural idioms and expressions of the Africans in a meaningful way. It remained academic, elitist and individualistic.

A further factor in the evolution of African theology was the rediscovery of the value of traditional African culture. In South Africa the emergence of the Black Consciousness Movement in the late 1960s and early 1970s with its stress on 'blackness' gave great impetus to a new respect for things African and black. This self-discovery led to the conviction that the African heritage is not and never was 'of the devil', but needed to be taken seriously and related to Christian faith. As a result of the impact of Black Consciousness, black people began to wake up to the fact that the colonial mentality did not necessarily convey the full truth. They began to realise that there are values in their cultures that are just as good as, if not better than, those of their colonisers. Once this was realised, black people began to have confidence in their ability to work things out for themselves, on their own terms and in their own way. Certainly, the rise of Black theology in South Africa in the early 1970s was a sequel to this development.

Further impetus for the development of African theologies was given by an increasing realisation that even locally constructed theologies were too wedded to Western assumptions and ideologies. Even after the departure of European colonialists, Western theological perspectives continued to dominate the popular and ecclesiastical thinking of African people. They continued to use symbols, stories, metaphors and motifs that were in fact negative and oppressive to themselves. The colonialists and missionaries had succeeded in producing a form of people whom the Portuguese colonisers used to call *assimilados*. They posed a real threat to the evolution of an authentically African theology. For example, the continued insistence on celibacy for African clergy conflicts with the fact that in many African societies a man's place is determined by his proven ability to have children. Such culturally insensitive and oppressive attitudes are being unmasked by African Christians themselves. And so African theology emerged also out of a movement that made theology and church practice more critical of what is really destructive in them.

A further factor in the evolution of African theology was the rise of the African indigenous churches from the early 1900s.[14] The AICs emerged out a socio-cultural and political conflict posed by the dominance of colonial power and European Christendom. Black people had assumed subordinate positions not only in society but also in the church. They had been uprooted and were no longer secure in their own land and culture. This situation precipitated the need for black people to take control of the shaping of their lives, their destiny and their faith. Hence the emergence of the AIC movement.

The AICs have become fully aware of the need to give their heritage theological articulation. Paul Makhubu of Khanya Institute and his colleagues, through encouragement given by the Institute for Contextual Theology, are beginning to produce literature reflecting their ethos.[15]

As has been pointed out already, the AICs represent efforts by black Christians to break free from European socio-cultural dominance. From its inception the missionary enterprise, as an integral part of European colonisation, posed a threat to African culture and its religious world-view. This threat to the

Xhosa people in South Africa reached its climax in the 1860s when the political and economic independence of Xhosa society was severely compromised. Xhosa traditional custom, and political and economic independence were not the only targets of missionary ideology; the institution and authority of the African chiefs was equally earmarked. The attacks on African traditional rituals and customs, and the institution and authority of chiefs, threatened the whole fabric of society.

Therefore, the emergence of the AICs may be seen as representing the protest of black people against socio-cultural, political and economic domination. The AIC movement symbolises the black revolt against all forms of European exploitation. African theology evolved as an attempt by Africans to give theological articulation to their spiritual, political and economic struggles.

### African and Black Theologies

Since the beginning of the Black theology movement in the 1970s, there has been an ongoing debate about its relationship with African theology.[16] The debate has been more heated especially in South Africa as a result of the urgent challenge presented by the ideology of apartheid. Because of its direct engagement with the socio-political situation, Black theology in South Africa has tended to be seen as more relevant. No-one can deny that the quest for socio-political and economic liberation continues to represent the desperate concern among black people in South Africa. And indeed, Black theology has had more impact in this regard in its theological articulation of the concerns of black people. In contrast to Black theology, African theology has been regarded as reactionary because of its past tendency to focus on tradition and culture.[17] Ironically, Byang Kato has argued quite passionately in his response to Steve Biko that Black theology is reactionary and racist.[18] However, some understanding has developed between these two experiences of God at work among the people of South Africa. African theology is increasingly seen as complementary to Black theology. Similarly, Black theologians have become more aware of their African heritage than before. Black theologians are, as it were, spiritual descendants of African theologians. The process of identifying integral connections between political struggle and culture holds prospects for the development of a more liberating theological reflection and activity in South Africa.

### Some Key Questions and Concerns of African Theologies

The major concerns of African theologies have always been twofold: a theological reflection on the relationship of Christian theology to African cultures, on the one hand, and to social, economic and political realities, on the other.

Some earlier African theologians such as John Mbiti from Kenya, Charles Nyamiti from Tanzania, Kwesi Dickson from Ghana and Gabriel Setiloane of South Africa focused their theological endeavours on cultural issues, such as the African symbols and images of God, as well as the African concepts of community, *ubuntu-botho* (human solidarity), family and rites of passage. African culture, religion and *ubuntu* were singled out as formative expressions of the life and experience of African people. These expressions represented also the sources and interpretative instruments at the disposal of the African theologian for understanding African people. In turn, these categories were interfaced with the Christian faith as embodied in the Hebrew and Christian Scriptures.

The identification of the category of culture as an interpretative instrument for understanding Africans has been criticised. Itumeleng Mosala and John Pobee in particular have argued that these approaches have viewed Africanness and culture in some static, ahistorical form, and that the experiences of the African people are depicted in relation to a mythical, monolithic, timeless African tradition.[19] On the contrary, Mosala and Pobee affirm that African culture and Africanness should not be regarded as purely a matter of the pre-colonial past. African culture, they argue, embodies what is happening here and now and is, therefore, a living and contemporary experience. Mosala goes further to say that 'culture is ultimately not ethnic. It is not African, Indian, coloured, white, English or Afrikaans. It is historical and class-based.'[20] Indeed, African theologies need to realise that culture is a valuable weapon against foreign domination, and a basis for liberating theological reflection and activity. Therefore, they must move away from oppressive perceptions of culture that regard it as merely a thing of the pre-colonial past. Culture must be seen also in terms of what is happening here and now in the struggles of African communities for health, wholeness, *ubuntu* and being truly human. Such a shift in the perception of African culture should constitute a more creative basis for liberating theological reflection and activity in African theology.

Similarly, other African theologians like T. Tshibangu from Zaire, Kofi Appiah-Kubi from Ghana and Desmond Tutu and Manas Buthelezi from South Africa have adopted a distinctively synthetic approach in their theological reflection and activity. They believe that cultural, socio-political and economic considerations must be interwoven if African theologies are to deal adequately with the problems facing Africans. In other words, unless African theologies are practical, dynamic and based on real life experiences of the people of Africa, they will remain alien and alienating.

I want to give prominence to this point in order to highlight the challenge of African theology in South Africa. Since the beginning of missionary activity, Christian faith in South Africa has been in bondage to the cultural, ideological, political and economic interests of white colonial settlers. Thus even when the Christian faith had been accepted by Africans, it continued to play an ambivalent role. This ambivalent role of missionary Christianity is illustrated by the fact that the clash between Africans and Europeans in the late nineteenth and early twentieth centuries was never simply a clash between Christianity and 'heathenism'. The clash was in essence a clash between cultures: an indigenous one and an imperialist one. The destruction of the African cultural systems and social structures made Africans considerably vulnerable not only to conversion but also to starvation. Not only were they without land, houses, crops, and grainpits, in short homeless, but were forced to seek work and engage their services to strange masters in distant lands.

Without a theology whose questions, agendas and programmes arose out of an engagement with the ongoing cultural, political, ideological and economic struggles of the African people, African theology in South Africa could never be liberated and liberating. Put differently, African theology is not a possibility for Africans until and unless Africans free it from Western Christianity, which presupposes European economic and political systems. African theology needs to be remade in the light of the realities of the people of South Africa, such as unemployment, poverty, cultural alienation, sexism, drought, disease, conflict, injustice and racism. Such a theology would represent not only the voice of Africa but also the voice of the voiceless.

## Use of the Bible in African Theology

In what follows I will attempt to outline the positive role that the Bible can play in African theology and, at the same time, show the disadvantages of tying African theology too closely to the Bible.

Virtually all African theologians have argued independently, and at various times, that the Bible is normative for African theology and that it should be seen and used as the direct source of African theology. John Pobee, for example, says about African theology and the Bible: 'since it is the Christian faith that we wish to communicate in African terms, our starting point should be the source of the church's faith. We refer to the Bible, the foundation document of the church. African theology has to be rooted in the Bible.'[21] Similarly, Byang Kato put his case for the use of the Bible as the direct source of African theology in these words: 'In our effort to express Christianity in the context of the African, the Bible must remain the absolute source. It is God's Word addressing Africans and everyone else within their cultural background.'[22]

This recognition gave rise to a consultation of African theologians held in Ibadan, Nigeria, in 1966, under the auspices of the All Africa Conference of Churches. Papers presented at the consultation were subsequently published in a book, edited by Kwesi A. Dickson and Paul Ellingworth, entitled *Biblical Revelation and African Beliefs*. Similar consultations and workshops took place in South Africa during the 1960s and early 1970s at the Lutheran Missiological Institute at Mapumulo in Natal and led to the publication *Relevant Theology for Africa*.[23]

The fundamental concern in the use of Scripture by African theologians is not so much to recapture the original meaning of texts but to ensure and demonstrate that African theology regards the Bible as its direct source and that it has a sure biblical foundation. The Bible is used as a yardstick to evaluate African world-views and practices. The Bible is, as it were, used to purify the ancient ways of Africans rather than to transform African values and symbols. African theologians assume that it is only appropriate to appeal to biblical texts to authorise their theological constructs. In other words, they seek to convince themselves and their opponents about biblical-rootedness and therefore the legitimacy of their African theologies.[24] No special attention is paid to how this is to be realised.

And so, attempts to use the Bible as a direct source of African theology have so far yielded meagre results. The major theoretical weakness of this position is that it does not as yet take the African context seriously. Even the tools of exegesis which are used are not different from those which gave rise to traditional Western theology.

With regards to the assumption that the Bible serves as a direct source for theological proposals, African theologians would be well advised to read David Kelsey's perceptive analysis of the uses of Scripture in theology.[25] Kelsey demonstrates that the Bible has never provided (and can never serve as) the direct source of theological proposals. The basic reason, he argues, is that all theological positions are human constructs and are influenced by the time and place in which they were written. Therefore, to view different theologies as having the Bible as their direct source is naïve.

This observation is not meant to suggest that African theologians should ignore the Bible in their theological reflection. African theologians are part of the Christian community for whom the Bible occupies an important place. They have to use the Bible. The appeal to the Bible identifies African theology not only with the Bible but also with Christianity. By referring to the Bible, African theology identifies itself with Christianity. However, as David Kelsey has rightly warned, it must be borne in mind that the Bible does not establish the truth of the claims of theologies. This is also true of African theology.

African theologians could learn from the development of theologies in other parts of the world as well. Asia is a good example. Besides using the Bible, Asian Christians are involved in using other resources that are common to the people of Asia. The Taiwanese theologian C. S. Song pioneered the method of creatively juxtaposing myths, stories and legends with biblical narratives and constantly going beyond the written word to the symbolic meaning. In *The Tears of Lady Meng*, he used a well-known Chinese folk-tale and blended it with the biblical theme of Jesus' death and resurrection.[26]

African theologians must also go beyond the Bible and Christian documents, not with a view to undermining Christian faith, but so as to rediscover the integral connections which can hold African tradition and its world-view together with the Christian faith. Rather than dismissing African folk-tales and myths as pagan and evil, seeking to purify them, African theologians must place them alongside the biblical stories. Such theological reflection will ground African theology in the experience of being African, as encapsulated and expressed in the stories. Even more important, a creative use of Africa's own cultural heritage to complement the biblical narratives will illustrate at least two things.

Firstly, it will indicate the respect and pride of African Christians for their religious and cultural inheritance. An identification of integral connections between the biblical narratives and African myths and legends may help to remove prevailing suspicions and tensions which Christianity has caused among Africans. African Christians are torn apart and seek wholeness. They have an identity crisis. They are torn apart by loyalty to the Christian faith on the one hand, and loyalty to African culture and history, on the other. A change of perception about the Bible and African cultural expressions could make a significant contribution to African Christian identity.

Secondly, it re-opens the question of the limitations of the closed Christian canon. More recently, African American, feminist, womanist and Black theologians have been exposing the restrictions of working with a fixed canon. They claim, and rightly so, that it fails to include their struggle and pain, which are as hallowed as the biblical narratives. Biblical scholars tend to operate with the notion that there is no salvation outside the canonical text — which is comparable to the outdated Roman Catholic view that there is no salvation outside the Christian church. African theologians should ground African theologies in the African experience, just as theologians of liberation have grounded their theologies in the experience of liberation.

What I suggest here is not a novel idea. Gabriel Setiloane in his book *The Image of God among the Sotho–Tswana* came to the same conclusion when he argued that myths purporting to explain the 'origin of things', including people on earth, abound in Africa. But, regrettably, he says, Robert Moffat, the first missionary of the London Missionary Society among the Batswana, discounted them because they were parochial. The Western view of Adam and Eve has been accepted as superior, and accepted generally by people of a 'dominant' culture.[27] When placed alongside biblical creation accounts, these myths illuminate biblical narratives and make them alive.

## Conclusion

This, I think, should be the goal of African theologies. If the church has any future in Africa, that future lies with black people. Hence the need to make them feel that they belong, that the church takes them and their traditional way of life seriously, and that they have responsibility for the life and well-being of the church and its credibility in the world.

[1] See Acts 8:26–40; 11:20; 18:24; Mark 15:21.

[2] See, for example, Cain Hope Felder, *Troubling Biblical Waters: Race, Class and Family* (Maryknoll: Orbis Books, 1989); Itumeleng Mosala, *Biblical Hermeneutics and Black Theology in South Africa* (Grand Rapids: Eerdmans, 1989); R. S. Sugitharajah (ed.), *Voices from the Margin: Interpreting the Bible in the Third World* (London: SPCK, 1991); Cain Hope Felder (ed.), *Stony The Road We Trod: African American Biblical Interpretation* (Minneapolis: Fortress Press, 1991); Gerald West, *Biblical Hermeneutics of Liberation: Models of Reading the Bible in the South African Context* (Pietermaritzburg: Cluster Publications, 1991).

[3] R. J. Schreiter (ed.), *Faces of Jesus in Africa* (Maryknoll: Orbis Books, 1991), p. viii.

[4] This idea is also clearly articulated by E. K. Mosothoane, 'John William Colenso: Pioneer in the Quest for an Authentic African Christianity', in L. Kretzschmar (ed.), *Christian Faith and African Culture* (Umtata: Unitra, 1988), p. 44.

[5] This point is fully developed in respect of the Anglican Church in Southern Africa in Luke Pato, 'Becoming an African Church', in Frank England and Torquil Paterson (eds.), *Bounty in Bondage* (Johannesburg: Ravan Press, 1989).

[6] It would be ungracious to ignore the role of a number of Europeans in the development of African theology. In 1947 Fr Tempels had published his *Bantu Philosophy*; a little later Geoffrey Parrinder began his sympathetic study of African religions; Bishop Sundkler in 1960 wrote his *The Christian Ministry in Africa*; Dr Harold Turner and others began to examine the indigenous churches; and more recently John Parrat, formerly of the University of Botswana, published a standard book entitled *A Reader in African Christian Theology*.

[7] G. M. Setiloane, *African Theology: An Introduction* (Johannesburg, Skotaville, 1986), p. 30.

[8] Gwinyai H. Muzorewa, 'African Liberation Theology', *Journal of Black Theology*, 3:2 (Nov. 1989), p. 57.

<sup></sup>9 Cf. Janet Hodgson, *Ntsikana's Great Hymn: A Xhosa Expression of Christianity in the Early 19th Century Eastern Cape* (Cape Town: University of Cape Town, 1980); 'A Study of the Xhosa Prophet Nxele', in *Religion in Southern Africa*, 6:2 and 7:1 (1985—86).

[10] Byang H. Kato, 'Black Theology and African Theology', *Evangelical Review of Theology*, 1 (Oct. 1977), p. 47.

[11] Ibid.

[12] Ibid.

[13] John Parratt (ed.), *A Reader in African Christian Theology* (London: SPCK, 1987), p. 2.

[14] In South Africa, the work of the Research Unit for New Religious Movements and Independent Churches directed by G. C. Oosthuizen is a valuable theological resource and research centre. For more information see my article, 'The African Independent Churches: A Socio-Cultural Approach', *JTSA*, 72 (Sept. 1990), pp. 24—35.

[15] Their standard work at the moment is *African Independent Churches: Speaking for Ourselves* (Johannesburg: Institute for Contextual Theology, 1985).

[16] To mention only a few, see, for example, Desmond Tutu, 'Black Theology/African Theology: Soul Mates or Antagonists?', *Journal of Religious Thought*, 33 (1975); E. E. Mshana, 'The Challenge of Black Theology and African Theology', *African Theological Journal*, 5 (Dec. 1972); Setiloane, *African Theology*, pp. 43—45; Kato, 'Black Theology and African Theology', pp. 35—47.

[17] See also John de Gruchy, 'South African Theology Comes of Age', *Religious Studies Review*, 17:3 (July 1991), p. 220.

[18] Kato, 'Black Theology and African Theology', pp. 39ff.

[19] See especially Itumeleng Mosala, 'African Independent Churches: A Study in Socio-Theological Protest', in Charles Villa-Vicencio and John de Gruchy, *Resistance and Hope* (Cape Town: David Philip, 1985), p. 110; and John Pobee, *Toward an African Theology* (Nashville: Abingdon Press, 1979), p. 19.

[20] Mosala, 'African Independent Churches', p. 111.

[21] Pobee, *Toward An African Theology*, p. 20.

[22] Kato, 'Black Theology and African Theology', p. 47.

[23] Hans Jürgen-Becken (ed.), *Relevant Theology for Africa* (Durban: Lutheran Publishing House, 1974).

[24] See especially John Mbiti, *New Testament Eschatology in an African Background* (London: Oxford University Press, 1971).

[25] David H. Kelsey, *The Uses of Scripture in Recent Theology* (Philadelphia: Fortress Press, 1975).

[26] C. S. Song, *The Tears of Lady Meng* (Geneva: World Council of Churches, 1981).

[27] Gabriel Setiloane, *The Image of God Among the Sotho–Tswana* (Rotterdam: Balkema, 1979).

# 14

# Confessing Theology

## JOHN W. DE GRUCHY

One understands the confession of the Reformation very badly if one imagines that those churches *had* something in and with their confessions of faith. One understands them only when one sees that in their confessions they had been faced with certain historical tasks, and *did* something.

— Karl Barth[1]

### Confessing or Confessionalism?

In Germany it is customary to refer to the Protestant and Catholic churches not as denominations (which is a word that has its origins in the United States) but as confessions. The word is derived from the Reformation and post-Reformation period when the Lutheran and Reformed churches produced confessions of faith (for example, the Lutheran 'Augsburg' or the Reformed 'Helvetica' or 'Westminster'), by which they declared what they believed and how the church should be ordered. These confessions of faith became subordinate standards alongside of Scripture which were used to guide these Protestant churches in their interpretation of the gospel and to distinguish them from the Roman Catholic Church and its teaching.

The idea of a confession of faith has its roots in the New Testament and the post-Apostolic period in church history. When people were converted to faith in Jesus Christ and were baptised, they had to confess their faith publicly. This is already evident in the writings of Paul (cf. Rom. 10:9). The declaration that 'Jesus is Lord' is regarded as the earliest confession of Christian faith. As the church developed, so this confession was expanded to interpret what it meant to confess Jesus as Lord in response to various challenges to what became orthodox faith over against heresy. This led to the formulation of what was referred to as the 'rule of faith' in the second century, and then later to the drafting of the various creeds (for example, the Nicene and Apostles' creeds). But behind these creeds, as behind the Reformation confessions of faith, lay the primary act of confessing Jesus as Lord — an act that sometimes led to conflict between the church and state, and thus became the main reason for martyrdom (a word which literally means 'witness', which is precisely what confessing Jesus as Lord is about).

The Reformation confessions of faith, like the ecumenical creeds before, soon became propositional means whereby the churches could test orthodoxy rather than expressions of a dynamic confession of Jesus as Lord. Confessionalism took the place of confessing Christ. It is important, then, to make a distinction between confessional theologies and what we have called Confessing theology. Confessional theologies express the orthodoxy of particular church traditions as these are to be found in confessions of faith. As such, they have value in providing a means whereby that tradition can determine its faithfulness in continuity with the past. The danger is that adherence to the letter of such confessions can become a substitute for listening to what the Spirit may be saying to the churches today through Scripture, and thus prevent a genuine confessing of Jesus Christ in relation to particular contexts and historical moments. To remain faithful to the literal statements of a confession of faith does not necessarily mean that the church is faithfully confessing Jesus Christ in such situations; it may well be a means of escape from that task and challenge.

Confessing theology is concerned with the faith and obedience which lie behind the historic creeds and confessions, and which are expressed in particular situations. Of course, we are not suggesting that doing Confessing theology is the same as engaging in the act of confessing Jesus as Lord, for like all theology, Confessing theology is a second-stage operation, a reflection on the witness of the church, in this instance on confessing Jesus as Lord within particular contexts. At the same time Confessing theology also prepares the way for the church to confess its faith in new situations, both by reminding it of its obligation to do so and by helping it to understand what such a confession may mean within new historical moments.

In this chapter we are referring to that Confessing theology which arose in South Africa in response to the heresy of apartheid. This theology has been profoundly influenced by the Swiss theologian Karl Barth, as well as by Dietrich Bonhoeffer, the German theologian and martyr.[2] Of course, they have not been the only voices of importance even though they have been the dominant ones. Reference to Barth in this connection is a salutary reminder that Confessing theology, like all the types of South African theology discussed in this section, is not only a reflection on Christian witness, but also an attempt to provide a systematic and coherent basis for this primary task of the church. Confessing theology, for example, assumes the trinitarian character of Christian faith and would, therefore, in any attempt to develop a systematic account of confessing Jesus Christ, locate that confession within the broader and more systematic framework of dogmatic theology. At the same time, it seeks to retrieve the *loci* (the traditional word which refers to the various parts of dogmatics) of Christian belief from the perspective of what it means to confess Jesus as Lord in particular contexts.[3]

In so far as contemporary expressions of Confessing theology, not least in South Africa, trace their lineage to Barth and Bonhoeffer and the Confessing Church struggle against Nazism in the German Third Reich, we need to begin our reflection by considering what confessing Jesus Christ meant in that context and how it later influenced South African theology and witness.

## Confessing Christ against Apartheid

Shortly after the rise to power of Adolf Hitler in Germany, Barth and his younger colleague Bonhoeffer came to the conclusion that a *status confessionis* had arrived in Germany, the first since the time of the Reformation in the sixteenth century.[4] By this they meant that a situation had arisen which demanded that the church confess its faith anew against an ideology which was subverting the gospel and its proclamation.[5] Suddenly matters which under other circumstances might have been indifferent or of secondary importance in the life of the church, such as its form and structure in the world, became issues which were fundamental to its life and witness. The church was forced to take a stand for the truth if it wanted to remain the church of Jesus Christ. This led to the formulation of the Barmen Declaration at the founding synod of the Confessing Church, the first article of which is a classic statement in the confessing tradition:

> Jesus Christ, as he is attested to us in Holy Scripture, is the one Word of God whom we have to hear, and whom we have to trust and obey in life and in death. We reject the false doctrine that the church could and should recognise as a source of its proclamation, beyond and besides this one Word of God, yet other events, powers, historic figures, and truths as God's revelation.[6]

The Barmen Declaration, which was largely the handiwork of Karl Barth, clearly reflects the influence of neo-orthodox theology at the time in Germany. This can be seen most strikingly in its Christocentric character, with its rejection of any claim, whether Nazi or liberal, that revelation can be found outside of Jesus Christ as the 'Word of God'.

Although the Barmen Declaration in hindsight can be seen as defective in certain respects, notably in not mentioning the persecution of the Jews, it was nonetheless a courageous confession of Jesus Christ as Lord over against the claims of Hitler and the Nazis. The issue was no longer that which divided the churches of the Reformation from Rome, but a struggle for the very life of the Protestant church in Germany, and thus a struggle also for the soul of the nation. To confess Jesus Christ as Lord meant rejecting the false claims of Hitler and Nazi ideology, just as it had meant, for earlier Christians, rejecting Caesar's claim to divinity. Confessing Christ was in unequivocal opposition to totalitarianism. Thus although most of those at Barmen were concerned about maintaining the integrity of the church, the political consequences of their confession were clearly apparent, not least to Hitler and his cohorts who soon unleashed their fury against the Confessing Church.

Since the Second World War several attempts have been made by churches, especially within the Reformed tradition, to restate and confess their faith anew. There has also been considerable ecumenical discussion in recent years as to whether or not the church is faced with a *status confessionis* in a variety of contexts.[7] But nowhere has this been more true than in South Africa in relation to apartheid.

The Sharpeville massacre in March 1960, and the events which followed, plunged South Africa into a new era of growing conflict and polarisation. Recognising the signs of the times, the South African member churches of the World Council of Churches convened a consultation at Cottesloe in Johannesburg to debate the issues and formulate a plan of action.[8] Despite the fact that the delegates of the white Dutch Reformed Church (NGK) agreed to the statement adopted at Cottesloe, this was later rejected by their synods, largely through political pressure. Tragically, a *kairos* moment of opportunity for confessing the claims of Jesus Christ over against racism was tragically lost, so that what might have changed the course of South African history for the better became a symbol of judgement condemning our nation to decades of growing oppression, suffering and violence.

One of those who did recognise the *kairos* and who responded to it was Beyers Naudé, a moderator of the Transvaal synod of the NGK, who had been at Cottesloe. Deeply influenced by the example of the Confessing Church struggle in Nazi Germany, Naudé recognised that a *status confessionis* had arrived. In 1963 he launched the Christian Institute as a step towards the possible formation of a confessing church movement in South Africa in the struggle against apartheid. In doing so he laid the foundations for many of the confessing and prophetic initiatives which were later undertaken by South African Christians, even though some of the initiatives moved in different theological directions.[9]

Of particular importance for the development of Confessing theology was the publication of *The Message to the People of South Africa* in 1968 by the South African Council of Churches. The *Message* rejected apartheid as a 'false gospel', and was widely regarded as the South African equivalent of the Barmen Declaration.[10] It declared:

There are alarming signs that this doctrine of separation has become for many, a false faith, a novel gospel which offers happiness and peace for the community and for the individual. It holds out to men security built not on Christ but on the theory of separation and the preservation of racial identity. It presents separate development of our race groups as a way for the people of South Africa to save themselves. Such a claim inevitably conflicts with the Christian gospel, which offers salvation, both social and individual, through faith in Christ alone.

Shortly after the publication of the *Message*, certain other theological developments took place, notably the emergence of Black theology in South Africa, and the debates that centred around the World Council of Churches' controversial Programme to Combat Racism. As a result the theological focus of the *Message*, as well as the work of the Christian Institute, began to change. Confessing Christ as Lord over against apartheid was no longer the main focus, though it remained an important aspect of Christian witness.

In the light of continuing oppression and a resurgence in the black-led struggle against apartheid, what was now required was Christian solidarity with those who were oppressed, and participation in the struggle. This development paralleled in some ways what had happened in Germany, particularly in the life and thought of

Bonhoeffer, who became increasingly disillusioned with the Confessing Church because it was far too concerned about its own well-being. Bonhoeffer saw the need to become personally involved in helping Jews escape from persecution and death, and he also became part of the conspiracy against Hitler. In this way Bonhoeffer's witness has provided an internal critique of Confessing theology, affirming its prophetic core yet questioning the way in which it has been used in some ways even to reinforce what the *Kairos Document* later called 'Church Theology'.

## Connecting Confessing and Liberation Theology

The Soweto student uprising in 1976, which culminated in the following year in the murder by the security police of the Black Consciousness leader Steve Biko, produced the next *kairos* situation in South Africa. That same year the Lutheran World Federation meeting in Dar es Salaam declared that a *status confessionis* existed in South Africa, and challenged the white Lutherans in the country to reject apartheid. But it was not until five years later, at the Ottawa meeting of the World Alliance of Reformed Churches (WARC), to which the Dutch Reformed Church and several other South African churches belonged, that this theme was taken up in a way which had a significant impact on the South African situation. In the words of Allan Boesak, who was then its moderator, the WARC recognised 'that apartheid is a heresy, contrary to the Gospel and inconsistent with the Reformed tradition'.[11] This led to the suspension of the membership of the white NGK.

Confessing theology had returned to the centre of the theological debate and church witness, but it had done so now in a new key. Not only was it a black-led initiative, but it was focused on the question of the moral legitimacy of the state, a legitimacy which was dependent to a great extent on the support of the white NGK. Of particular importance was the fact that the Dutch Reformed Mission Church (*NG Sendingkerk*) drafted a new confession, the Belhar Confession of Faith, later adopted by the church in 1986, in which the rejection of apartheid was made an article of faith.

The adoption of the Belhar Confession by the NG Mission Church was an historic event because it was the first time in the history of the Dutch Reformed family of churches since the seventeenth century that a new confession had been adopted by one of its member churches as an authoritative standard of faith and practice.[12] This is a excellent example of the way in which the confessing of Jesus Christ within a given context sometimes leads to the formulation of a confession of faith which in turn seeks to give that confessing act the support of the church as a whole, and thus ensure that the confession has continuity in the life of the church. Thus the acceptance of the Belhar Confession became necessary for ordination, and formed a basis for discussions pertaining to the uniting of black and white Dutch Reformed churches. Its significance can be appreciated especially when it is seen in relation to the segregationist origins of the church in the nineteenth century. For the Belhar Confession categorically rejected the synodical decision of 1857 to allow segregation in the church; it equally rejected apartheid as a heresy; and it affirmed the true nature of the church's unity and

# Key contacts in Information Learning Services

## Service Desk
# 01904 876696
E: ils@yorksj.ac.uk

## Academic Services
**Academic Liaison Librarians**
*for help with referencing/finding books and resources etc.*
www.yorksj.ac.uk/ils/all/

**Digital Trainers**
*for help with Word/Powerpoint/file management/Mahara etc.*
E: digitaltraining@yorksj.ac.uk
T:  01904 876391/876151

## Print Services
T: 01904 876025
E: printservices@yorksj.ac.uk

## Media Services
T: 01904 876706
E: mediaservices@yorksj.ac.uk

## Quiet study being disturbed?
Text **HUSH**, followed by your message, to **81025**

York St John University

information
learning
services

key
contacts

mission. In doing so, it declared that confessing Jesus as Lord was more than the rejection of an ideology: it was also making a commitment to the struggle for God's justice in the world. In this way Belhar went a significant step beyond Barmen and made the connection between confessing Christ and the liberation of the poor and oppressed.

In this we see a creative response to the challenge of liberation theology from the perspective of a Confessing theology, thus taking the latter an important step beyond Barmen. This is also a reminder that a genuine Confessing theology is not closed to new theological developments, but is always seeking to discern what a faithful confession of Jesus as Lord should mean in new contexts. Faithfulness to Jesus Christ has to relate not only to the struggle against apartheid, but also to the way in which the God who is revealed in Jesus Christ is 'in a special way the God of the destitute, the poor and the wronged' and who therefore 'calls his Church to follow him in this'. Thus the Belhar Confession stated that the church must

> stand by people in any form of suffering and need, which implies, among other things, that the Church must witness against and strive against any form of injustice...
> that the Church as the possession of God must stand where he stands, namely against injustice and with the wronged; that in following Christ the Church must witness against all the powerful and privileged who selfishly seek their own interests and thus control and harm others.

In its conclusion the Belhar Confession went beyond simply confessing by word and called for resistance against apartheid and other forms of oppression. 'Therefore, we reject any ideology which would legitimate forms of injustice and any doctrine which is unwilling to resist such an ideology in the name of the gospel.'[13]

## Confessing Theology in a Time of Reconstruction

After the end of the Second World War, the witness of the Confessing Church had a diverse and even contradictory influence upon the Protestant churches in East and West Germany. In the German Democratic Republic (East Germany) it inspired the church in its witness against the communist regime, especially during the early years when it was subject to constant persecution. But the example of Bonhoeffer also enabled the church to go beyond simply the rejection of socialist totalitarianism, and to discern within socialism something which resonated with the gospel's concern for the poor. Thus the 'church in socialism' was able to relate in critical solidarity to the state, rejecting its atheism and totalitarianism, yet affirming those aspects of socialism which were for the common good. In more recent times, elements within the Protestant church in the former East Germany drew on the legacy of the Confessing Church and especially the insights of Bonhoeffer to provide space for the emergence of the democratic movement and thus for the overthrow of the discredited regime.

In West Germany the situation was quite different. On the one hand, the Barmen Declaration was interpreted by some in a fundamentalist way. Thus Barmen was used to oppose any attempt by the church to participate in political struggles for liberation on the ground that this meant compromise with marxist ideology. But on the other hand those who sought to be faithful to the Confessing Church legacy saw the need to go beyond its mere repetition and ask what it now meant to confess Jesus Christ in a new historical moment, when the issues had to do with Jewish—Christians relations in the light of the Holocaust, nuclear disarmament and world peace, and the growing gap between rich and poor in the world. In other words, to confess Christ concretely was not a matter of repeating the formulae of Barmen in defence of reactionary political, ecclesiastical and theological positions, but doing in a new context what the confessors at Barmen had done in theirs.

The question which the church in South Africa has to ask at this present period of transition and in the years of reconstruction and nation-building which lie ahead is yet again what does it mean to confess Jesus Christ as Lord. But two interrelated challenges have to be faced now which were largely ignored in the struggle against apartheid. The first is the question of the Lordship of Jesus Christ in relation to people of other faiths or no religious faith at all. The second challenge comes from feminist theology in particular and radically questions the use of Lordship language as patriarchal, hierarchical and domineering, leading to social attitudes and actions which are destructive of genuine community and, some would argue, even of the environment.

Several comments need to be made in response to these very important challenges to Confessing theology, the first being that they have to be taken with the utmost seriousness and not shrugged off as though they were of no validity or consequence. The second response is the need to recognise the danger of a Christian triumphalism which often lurks behind the confession of Jesus as Lord, but which actually undermines what it is about. To proclaim Jesus as Lord does not give the church any right to dominate and control the shaping of the new society in a way which is insensitive to the faith and convictions of others. The third response is to recognise that because Jesus may be confessed as Lord, this does not legitimate the male domination of women, something which is equally contrary to the example which Jesus set in the gospels.

The question to be faced, then, is whether we should not do away with this fundamental confession which was the earliest expression of faith in Jesus, and which through the centuries has enabled Christians to oppose the absolute and totalitarian claims of one regime after another. An immediate answer would be that the denial of the Lordship of Jesus Christ would empty the New Testament of one of its most central themes. After all, the New Testament was written from the perspective of faith in Jesus as the risen Lord and therefore the Christ. If we are to take the Scriptures with any seriousness, and Confessing theology insists that we do, we dare not jettison this fundamental aspect of Christian faith. What is required rather is that we ask again what the Lordship of Jesus really means in our contemporary context.

*Confessing Jesus as Lord*

One of the major debates in twentieth-century biblical studies and theology has to do with the relationship between the 'Jesus of history' and the 'Christ of faith'. While it is true that the Jesus portrayed in the gospels is the Christ proclaimed as

Lord, it is also true that if the 'Christ of faith' loses its connection with Jesus of Nazareth it surrenders the substance of the New Testament witness to the truth of God's revelation. The failure of the Barmen confessors to speak out on the Jewish question stemmed from a failure to recognise the implications of the fact that the Christ they confessed was in fact Jesus the Jew. Bonhoeffer was one of the very few theologians to recognise this connection and to make it explicit.

The proclamation that Jesus is *Lord* derives from the conviction that God 'raised Jesus from the dead', thus vindicating him as Messiah. But we have to recognise that it is *Jesus* who is proclaimed as Lord — that is, the one who came to serve, the one who showed solidarity with the victims of society, the one who was crucified by religious and political authorities. This Jesus is Lord. Or, to put it the other way round, while the confession of Jesus as Lord derives from belief in the resurrection, its substance derives from the crucifixion. Jesus' Lordship can only be understood from the perspective of the Cross — that is, through solidarity with a suffering world in need of redemption and hope.[14] Thus to confess Jesus Christ as Lord can never mean that the church has some kind of right to dominate society; it can only mean that it exists to be in solidarity with the victims of society and to serve those in need in a redemptive way. The role of the church in the transformation of society and its democratic reconstruction does not derive from any political power which it may have, but from the redemptive power of the Cross, the message of repentance, forgiveness, reparation and reconciliation.

## Confessing Guilt

Another important dimension to Confessing theology is the growing recognition that the confession that Jesus is Lord should arise out of repentance for past failure. Although the Confessing Church in Germany courageously opposed Nazism, it failed to speak out on behalf of the victims of Nazism: Jews, communists, gypsies and other persecuted minorities. Thus the confession of Jesus as Lord was severely compromised. Bonhoeffer was, yet again, one of the few theologians to recognise this failure and to call the Confessing Church to acknowledge its guilt. Only in doing so could it witness faithfully to the gospel in a post-war context.

In like manner, the confession of Jesus as Lord in a time of reconstruction in South Africa has to be born out of a confession of sin and guilt for complicity in apartheid.[15] However much some Christians and churches may have contributed to the ending of apartheid, others have given it legitimacy, or remained silent when they should have spoken and acted. Thus it is only with humility and a sense of sorrow for the past that the church today dare confess Jesus as Lord and participate in the reconstruction of society. In fact, it has to learn to listen more to the victims of injustice and act in solidarity with them, and therefore learn to speak less. Hence the need to discover the *praxis* of confessing Jesus as Lord.

## Self-Interpreting Praxis

One of the dangers of Confessing theology is the illusion that if the church speaks the right word in a given context it has therefore done all that is necessary. This is not to deny the importance of preaching, or the publication of documents which speak out against injustice and stand up for the truth. That often takes a great deal of courage, and it also has a certain transformative power. Indeed, Confessing theology recognises that faithful proclamation is of critical importance for the witness of the church. But it also recognises that confessing faith is far more than a matter of words.

There is a time to speak, but there is also a time to remain silent and simply do what is right. Yet again the model is Jesus himself, in whom word and deed became one. Writing in 1932, long before his own decision to join the resistance against Hitler, Bonhoeffer argued that confessing Jesus Christ has to do as much with Christian praxis as it has to do with proclamation by words. He wrote: 'the first confession is the deed which interprets itself.'[16] If the church acts more faithfully, then it may not have to speak as much as it sometimes does. Its praxis will interpret the meaning of its confession.

This leads us to recognise that heresy is not only a matter of false or one-sided belief, it can also be a matter of ethics. Hence the agreement with liberation theologies that orthopraxis is as important as orthodoxy. As we have stressed, faith and obedience belong together in confessing Jesus Christ as Lord, the one informing and interpreting the other. The rejection of apartheid as a heresy is a good illustration of this connection, because at one level apartheid has to do with political ethics and racism, and yet at another it is a reflection of a false anthropoplogy, soteriology and ecclesiology. Christian praxis should provide testimony to the gospel and not undermine its claims.

## De-absolutising Principalities and Powers

The dangers which originally gave rise to Confessing theology are always with us. National Socialism may be defeated, but neo-Nazism, fascism and other dehumanising ideologies remain potent forces in the modern world. Apartheid legislation may go, but racism will remain and even take on new forms. A new non-racial and non-sexist democratic order may be born, but the danger of totalitarianism will be beneath the surface of any society. In other words, the Christian church will always have to remain vigilant to the dangers of political power, its tendency to corrupt, its desire for absolute control, its ability to serve its own interests rather than the common good. Whatever the dangers inherent in the confession of Jesus Christ as Lord, Christians dare not surrender their commitment to challenge the legitimacy of all governments or political movements which oppress people, especially when they also claim absolute authority. It is the task of Confessing theology to assist in the unmasking or de-absolutising of dehumanising 'principalities and powers', whether in the state or even in the church.

One way of describing the relationship between the church and those in power in this transitional era and in a future South Africa is in terms of critical solidarity. The critical or prophetic dimension implies continued resistance to what is unjust and false, and continued protest on behalf of what is just and true. The prophetic struggle against injustice must continue; standing for the truth never comes to an end. But being in critical solidarity also means giving support to those initiatives which may lead to the establishment of a new, just social order. It means that the church remains prophetic in its stance towards the emergent nation, but now on the basis of a shared commitment to the realisation of that new nation. In other words, while Confessing theology accepts the need for the church to be of help in the reconstruction of the nation, it insists that one of the most important elements in that task is to bear witness to values that are transcendent and that are critical of any misuse of power or patriotism.

In conclusion, it must be emphasised that Confessing theology today recognises the legitimacy of a plurality of theological approaches, and of the need to be in critical correlation with them. It also recognises the dangers of rhetoric against heresy. There are many theological and ethical issues which are complex and open to a variety of interpretation, and there is always the danger of theological arrogance and presumption. At the same time, Confessing theology insists that there are parameters and boundaries to what Christians believe and confess, and that time and again it is necessary to recognise the arrival of a *status confessionis* or *kairos* and therefore of heresy. Hence Confessing theology continues to insist that it is always necessary that the church stand for the truth of the gospel in a way which is clear and uncompromising, and that at some moments this requires a recognition of heresy and a corresponding confession of Jesus as Lord.

[1] Karl Barth, 'Das Bekenntnis der Reformation und Unserer Bekennen', *Theologische Existenz heute*, 29, pp. 6f., quoted by A. C. Cochrane in 'The Act of Confession-Confessing', *The Sixteenth Century Journal*, 8:4 (1977), p. 63.

[2] See John W. de Gruchy, *Bonhoeffer and South Africa* (Grand Rapids: Eerdmans, 1984); Charles Villa-Vicencio (ed.), *Reading Karl Barth in South Africa* (Grand Rapids: Eerdmans, 1988).

[3] As an example, see John W. de Gruchy, *Liberating Reformed Theology* (Grand Rapids: Eerdmans, Cape Town: David Philip, 1992).

[4] See the correspondence in Dietrich Bonhoeffer, *No Rusty Swords* (London: Collins, 1965), pp. 226f.

[5] D. J. Smit, 'What Does *Status Confessionis* Mean?', *JTSA*, 47 (June 1984).

[6] Translation by Douglas Bax in *JTSA*, 47 (June 1984)

[7] Eugene TeSelle, 'How Do We Recognise a *Status Confessionis?*', *Theology Today*, xlv: 1 (April 1988), pp. 71f.

[8] See John W. de Gruchy, *The Church Struggle in South Africa* (Cape Town: David Philip, 1986), pp. 62f.

[9] See John W. de Gruchy, 'A Short History of the Christian Institute' in Charles Villa-Vicencio and John W. de Gruchy, *Resistance and Hope* (Cape Town: David Philip, 1985), pp. 14ff.

[10] De Gruchy, *The Church Struggle in South Africa*, pp. 115f.

[11] Quoted in De Gruchy and Villa-Vicencio, *Apartheid Is a Heresy*, p. 88. See also the Foreword by Allan Boesak.

[12] On the background to the Belhar Confession and the issues which its raises, see D. J. Cloete and D. J. Smit, *A Moment of Truth* (Grand Rapids: Eerdmans, 1984).

[13] The Belhar Confession, article 4.

[14] See the discussion in John W. de Gruchy, 'Barmen: Symbol of Contemporary Liberation?', *JTSA*, 47 (June 1984).

[15] See John W. de Gruchy, 'Confessing Guilt in South Africa Today in Dialogue with Dietrich Bonhoeffer', *JTSA*, 67 (June 1989); De Gruchy, 'Guilt, Amnesty, and National Reconstruction', *JTSA*, 83 (June 1993).

[16] Dietrich Bonhoeffer, *Das Wesen der Kirche* (Munich: Chr. Kaiser Verlag, 1971), p. 58.

## Select Bibliography

Bethge, Eberhard. *Bonhoeffer: Exile and Martyr*. London: Collins, 1975

Boesak, Allan A. *Black and Reformed: Apartheid, Liberation and the Calvinist Tradition*. New York: Orbis, 1984

Cloete, D. J. and D. J. Smit. *A Moment of Truth*. Grand Rapids: Eerdmans, 1984

Cochrane, A. C. *The Church's Confessions under Hitler*. Philadelphia: Westminster, 1962

De Gruchy, John W. and Charles Villa-Vicencio. *Apartheid Is a Heresy*. Grand Rapids: Eerdmans; Cape Town: David Philip, 1983

De Gruchy, John W. *Liberating Reformed Theology*. Grand Rapids: Eerdmans; Cape Town: David Philip, 1992

Villa-Vicencio, Charles and John W. de Gruchy *Resistance and Hope: South African Essays in Honour of Beyers Naudé*. Grand Rapids: Eerdmans; Cape Town: David Philip, 1985

# 15

# Black Theology[1]

## BARNEY PITYANA

Black theology broke into the public realm in South Africa with the publication of *Essays in Black Theology* in 1972. But the publication was preceded by the banning of one of its original editors, Sabelo Ntwasa, and the subsequent banning and exile of its remaining editor, Dr Basil Moore.[2]

Long before these events, Black theology was being developed through workshops and seminars throughout South Africa. The University Christian Movement took the initiative in organising and encouraging a movement of Black theology in South Africa. In doing so, it was largely inspired by the Black Consciousness Movement. The target audience was ministers and pastors as well as theological colleges and seminaries. In 1968 a delegation from the UCM (South Africa) participated in the national conference of the University Christian Movement in the United States. Upon their return, Basil Moore published a discussion essay entitled 'Towards Black Theology'. The essay provoked heated debate about the direction of theological discourse in South Africa at the time. In the formal sense, therefore, South African Black theology can be dated from about 1968.

If a white liberal theologian and a multiracial Christian students' organisation could be said to be the progenitors of the Black theology movement in South Africa, in the United States that honour must be bestowed upon a young black university professor, Dr James H. Cone. In March 1969 James Cone published his *Black Theology and Black Power*. The origins of Black theology can be found in the civil rights movement, Black Power (especially Stokely Carmichael and the Student Non-Violent Co-ordinating Committee), and the Black Panthers with their militant call for black liberation. For it was out of this manifestation of black anger and impatience that the National Committee of Negro Churchmen was formed in 1966. The Student Non-Violent Co-ordinating Committee issued the challenge for black pastors to become 'relevant', and to examine the implications for faith of the slogan and politics of Black Power. More pointedly, black Christians were challenged to examine what these new developments could mean for their faith, nurtured in the predominantly white ecclesiastical power structures.

## Black Theology and the Black Context

Although Black theology had different beginnings in the United States from those of South Africa, a common feature of both settings was the fact that the social and political condition of the black population raised fundamental questions about the meaning of the Christian faith. The Christian faith became part of the problematic for reflective and sensitive black Christians. Questions were raised about God and justice, Christian doctrine, especially the nature of God, Christian witness, the role of the oppressive and dominant culture in determining the parameters of belief, and the role of those same religious beliefs in ensuring subjugation and conformity. Under close scrutiny, it could not be denied that the Christian faith was an instrument of continuing white racism in the same way that it was the handmaid of colonialism and the spirit behind the slave trade. James Cone resolved this dilemma for black Christians when he said that 'when the murderers of humanity seize control of the public meaning of the Christian faith, it [was] time to seek new ways of expressing the truth of the gospel'.[3] Black people had to take charge of their own faith; its content and its meaning had to be expressed and developed by them and them alone.

This 'new way' of expressing the faith of the black folk within the universal faith, which had become appropriated by the forces of colonisation and domination, was itself a practice of liberation. Allan Boesak called this 'a new way of theologising; a new way of believing'.[4] To free theology from its Babylonian captivity to the Euro-American cultural and political elite was the task of Black theology.

Black theology, however, could not be a viable option for such 'new' or 'liberated' black Christians while they accepted uncritically the norms and values of traditional Christian doctrine and practice. While they utilised a white interpretation of the Christ-event, Christianity would remain remote and detached from the life situation of the oppressed. But when blacks utilised a hermeneutic of suspicion, they would discover a new vehicle for expressing what they felt deeply. Black theology, therefore, arises as a critique both of the social conditions of the black folk and of the inadequacies of traditional religion. But such a critique in itself is not new to Black theology. James Cone argues that theology is the critical side of faith and that without it faith loses its distinctive identity.[5] Once black people arose in revolutionary action under the slogans of Black Power (in the USA) and Black Consciousness (in South Africa), Black theology became the necessary adjunct to this rising tide of consciousness and revolutionary thought and activity. Black theology, therefore, arises out of reflection and action from the black situation.

It is for that reason that Black theology has been called a 'situational theology': situational, because it takes seriously the circumstances of the black people and reflects on the meaning and significance of faith in such conditions. The condition of black people has been one of oppression and injustice; of nothingness and insignificance; in a word, of 'non-personhood'. The task of Black theology is to restore the full humanity of black people and to imbue them with the confidence that they are creatures of God. That sense of value and worth finds its highest expression when the oppressed and the poor rise up against injustice and oppression.

It is, accordingly, not without significance that the context of the struggles against racism in the US and South Africa was so determinative. James Cone, commenting on the Black Power movement in the United States, says: 'If Christ was not to be found in black people's struggle for freedom, if he were not found in the ghettos with rat-bitten black children, if he were in rich white churches and their seminaries, then I want no part in him.'[6]

But Cone did not leave it at that. He went on to argue that Black Power was part of the re-humanisation of black people. They were exercising their right to say no to racism and asserting their right to human dignity. So essential was this exercise of right in Cone's theology that he believed that this power was derived from Christ.[7] To call Christ the Black Messiah was not to claim any exclusive identification with the person and redemptive activity of Christ. It was to state that in Christ there is a full, total identification with the suffering and struggles of the oppressed. Christ, however, cannot be reduced to 'the Black Messiah' since his reality is multi-dimensional. Therefore, while it is impossible to identify Christ with unjust and oppressive activities, all people in their goodness and in their humanity have something of Christ in them. It was on these grounds that Cone identified the project of Christ with the struggle for liberation of black people.

South African Black theology was much more circumspect than Cone. Identification of the struggle for liberation with the purposes of Christ had not reached maturity. In any event, the language of Black Power in South Africa was much more muted, given the more oppressive conditions prevailing then. What Black theology in South Africa sought to do was to reflect on and interpret the faith in the light of the black condition. The major concerns and methods of South African Black theology included analysis of the political situation, the denunciation of racism, especially racism in the structures of the church, and a reinterpretation of aspects of Christian doctrine, especially the role of culture, concepts of God and Christology. Black theology saw itself as a movement for the mobilisation of black people within and outside the churches. Many blacks were steeped in the conservative and authoritarian traditions of the church; many were too afraid to challenge the teachings of the church in fear of being excluded from the mainstream of the church; others could not risk the consequences of political action through Black theology. The task of Black theology, therefore, continued to be directed at building a mass movement, and yet without alienating the mass of the opinion-formers in the black church and by finding allies among the white radical Christians.

## Sources of Black Theology

### The Bible

Black theology is steeped in the black church and in the faith and life of black people. In these communities the Bible has become normative. Scripture is closely identified with the being of the Christian. The Bible is also very accessible to many people and it is, in the faith consciousness, understood to be 'the Word of God'. The Bible breathed new life in the darkest moments of despair and suffering. It pointed the oppressed to 'another way'. Through the Bible and its interpretation, black Christians could belong to the one universal church even if their interpretation differed from that of the dominant church.

There is a very strong stream in black religion of belonging. Black Christians need to belong and not be isolated or marginalised. James Cone testifies that the Bible, for the black church, is the 'primary source for knowledge about Jesus and God'.[8] He seems to say that one cannot do Black theology without reference to the Bible. Itumeleng Mosala claims that 'for black South Africans, [the Bible] is a weapon of struggle'.[9] Allan Boesak also emphasises the centrality of the Bible in Black theology as 'critical reflection *in the light of the Word of God,* which means that all action and all reflection is finally judged by the liberating gospel of Jesus Christ'.[10] When Black theologians who are biblical scholars are challenged about this captivity to the ancient Scriptures, they argue that the Bible has been for too long an instrument of oppression. But black people have always relied on the Bible for their liberating activity. It would therefore, they argue, be irresponsible to abandon scholarly investigation of the Bible.[11]

Earlier Black theologians, however, did not argue from the fact that the Bible itself was a problem for black liberation. They utilised biblical material but relied on exegesis to illustrate their points. James Cone uses the Bultmannian demythologising method of exegesis and appropriates a Barthian biblical radicalism. For him, the Bible is the written Word of God which, faithfully interpreted and correctly understood, affirms the liberation of the oppressed. As in Karl Barth, Jesus occupies the centre-stage in Cone's theology. Like Barth, Cone wished to stand traditional theology on its head, to be provocative. 'No longer would I allow an appeal to divine revelation to camouflage God's identification with the human fight for justice,'[12] he averred. Cone's process of demythologising took the form of asserting that traditional Christianity was already ideologically loaded against the interests of the oppressed. Dominant religion was racist. The Bible had to be 'demythologised' in order to free it from the political bias in the dominant mythology of the church. Allan Boesak, on the other hand, states that the task is to 'proclaim the gospel in its authentic perspective, namely, that of liberation ... to proclaim the gospel according to its original intention: as the gospel of the poor.'[13]

This reliance upon biblical interpretation and exegesis was the preferred method of early South African Black theologians. Allan Boesak, as we have demonstrated, relied upon the normative character of the Bible as the Word of God. Desmond Tutu drew deeply from the fountain of liberal European biblical scholarship and Catholic spirituality to exegete biblical passages. Even Manas Buthelezi's Christian anthropology and his Christology were essentially drawn from liberal Lutheran theology. Criticism at this stage was not focused on the content of the Bible but on the distortions or alleged distortions of the Bible for reasons of racial bigotry. All these early scholars seemed to guard their orthodoxy jealously. The questioning and interrogation of the biblical text is a later development.

The advent of Itumeleng Mosala's *Biblical Hermeneutics and Black Theology in South Africa*[14] signalled a radical departure from traditional exegesis. Mosala utilises the social scientific and critical approaches to the Bible pioneered in the United States by Norman Gottwald and others. He digs into the social structure of the biblical communities and the circumstances of the writings, uncovering class biases and racist contents and designs. Mosala claims that failure to recognise the presence of such ideologies in the Bible has led to a superficial and selective reliance on a few texts in order to dramatise the claims of Black theology. South African Black theology in recent times has devoted much attention to biblical hermeneutics along the lines of Cain Hope Felder and Randall Bailey, both of the Interdenominational Theological Center in Atlanta, Georgia.

What this historical-materialist trend in biblical hermeneutics has done is to move Black theology very strongly in the direction of a class analysis and to diminish the attention paid to race and culture. While this approach has maintained the integrity of the biblical material and avoided the selectivity which earlier Black theology's exegesis was rightly criticised for,[15] it has unfortunately also marginalised the claims of indigenous Christianity and the African traditional religions.[16]

*Liberation*

It cannot be overemphasised that Black theology arises out of reflection upon black experience: of slavery and subjugation, of racial and class oppression, and of social domination. Even though in the United States slavery has been abolished for more than a hundred years, the effects of enslavement are etched into the consciousness of African Americans. Slavery is part of the psycho-social make-up of African Americans. Besides slavery, African Americans have had to struggle for equality and self-determination, for civil rights and justice. While constitutionally all Americans are equal, black Americans find themselves in an alienating environment which denies their humanity.

In South Africa, where the African population is the indigenous majority, blacks have laboured under the oppression of apartheid, having been denied access to power and decision-making processes. The state machinery of apartheid South Africa repressed dissent and routinely violated human rights. Like Black Power in the United States, Black Consciousness sought to bring an end to colonialism and challenge the oppressed people to struggle for liberation.

So central has been this understanding of liberation in Black theology that James Cone stated that the definition and understanding of freedom had to be determined by the oppressed people themselves:

> The only option we blacks have is to fight in every way possible, so that
> we can begin to create a definition of freedom based on our own history
> and culture. We must not expect white people to give us freedom.
> Freedom is not a gift, but a responsibility, and thus must be taken against
> the will of those who hold us bondage.[17]

For Allan Boesak too, Black theology is a theology of liberation. But Boesak cautions against Cone's formulation of Black theology as reflection 'in the light of the black situation'. He argues that Cone may be attaching too much theological import to black experience as if, he says, 'these realities within themselves have revelatory value on par with scripture'. For Boesak, 'the black experience provides the framework within which blacks understand the revelation of God in Jesus Christ. No more. No less.'[18] Dorothee Soelle, writing from the perspective of feminist liberation theology, explains that the original meaning of the Greek word *soteria* is 'to be rescued from life-threatening danger'. Christ the liberator inspires people to struggle for freedom. 'In his spirit and with his strength to aid them, they [the oppressed] have entered into the process of liberation.'[19] Nduna Mpunzi, writing on the South African situation, says that liberation has two aspects, both of which are of the essence of Black theology. One is the freedom of the individual to assert the fullness of his or her humanity. The other is that Black theology 'is a powerful call for the freedom of black people'.[20] This statement is typical of Black Consciousness at an early stage, when political and structural liberation was not fully developed. Blackness has less to do with the colour of the skin than with the fact that it is a means of identifying an inherent condition of subjugation and alienation. Blackness accompanies a specific social experience, which Black theology captures and renders normative for its reflection.

The question remains: What is the import of the conditionality and contextuality of Black theology? If Black theology is a theology of liberation, how is 'liberation' understood? As the politics of South Africa change, or as civil rights in the United States are extended to black people, what, in these circumstances, is the meaning of 'liberation' in Black theology? At one level, surely, Black theology addresses the stultifying effects of years of oppressive theology. It challenges black Christians not only to challenge the dominant theological discourse but also to devise different ways of talking about God and witnessing to their faith. To that extent it is a call to vigilance and the continual reformation of all theology. But such theological activity cannot and should never be an end in itself. It becomes the basis of the faithful coming to a deep and effectual understanding of the love of God in Jesus Christ, the God of liberation.

Secondly, the call to liberation should have less to do with the simple desire to be 'like' the dominant religion, where 'like' means identical or similar to. What true liberation should aspire to is the freedom of the soul, which liberates one to search, investigate, advance new ways of understanding God and thus make an original contribution to the theological enterprise. If the exercise is simply about power, then it will replicate the inexorable cycles of control and domination. Dorothee Soelle says that the goal of the feminist movement is not to aspire to men's power as such but to change the discourse which makes it possible only for men to be in positions of power. Responding recently to the charge that Black theology has been preoccupied for too long with the analysis and criticism of dominant theology, Dr Jacquelyn Grant, also of ITC, Atlanta, noted that as the reality of oppression is not simply a legislative matter but one of structural change, Black theology would have difficulty moving beyond this. There is no evidence as yet that such a change is on the horizon. Black theology, she insists, must not yield to the pressure to move on to 'positive' engagement and making proposals for change.[21] The question remains: What is the relationship in changing circumstances between this understanding of 'liberation' and the political liberation which gave birth to Black theology?

*Culture*

Black theology arises precisely because black people have experienced alienation within the church. Both what the church teaches and the sources for that teaching are unrelated to the thought-forms, values, history and experience of black people. Black culture is hardly represented – and then certainly not in a positive light – in the construction of theology. As a result many black people have lived for very long in two worlds: their own world and the white world in which Christianity is represented to them. This is alienating because that same world is the one which constitutes the foundation of the oppressive and dominant system. Black people, therefore, are having to embrace that which is alienating and life-denying for them.

And yet black people have their own culture, which sustains them in life, provides a means for understanding reality and shapes their religious consciousness. Much of that culture has been suppressed in favour of the European culture in which Christianity has been packaged. In the United States, Black theology from its infancy realised the potency in the theological expression of the cultural tradition of the black church. This tradition has unique forms of spirituality and worship, involving dance and movement, as well as an emphasis on preaching the Word with conviction. Indeed there has been a growing realisation that the religion of black Americans bears features of its African roots. Gayraud Wilmore, quoting Charles H. Long, asserts that Black theology demonstrates the 'total otherness' of African America, representing the 'other' identity of the United States.[22] Cultural awareness in Black theology is a journey of discovery, a key to unlocking the gates of the promised land.

In South Africa, however, the debate about culture has been clouded by a political environment in which black culture was viewed as 'backward' or 'mute' in political matters. Furthermore, there was the danger of acceding to the apartheid regime's imposition of what Steve Biko called 'an arrested view of culture'. Culture had become an instrument of domination. Against this background one can understand Allan Boesak's caution when he says: 'A contextual theology must not yield to uncritical accommodation, becoming a "cultural theology" or a religion of culture. An authentic contextual theology is a prophetic one; it is not merely an exhumation of the corpses of tradition as African theology was sometimes understood to be.'[23]

This is at the heart of the debate between Black theology and African theology. Black theologians like Bishop Manas Buthelezi charge that African theology is simply a christianisation of the anthropologists' conception of African traditions and culture. John Mbiti counters that Black theology is an unAfrican politicisation of theology. At the heart of this is the soul of Africa – culture and religion expressing the identity of who Africans are.[24]

Despite these reservations, Black theology has had to engage the issue of culture and in the process lift culture from the clutches of an oppressive discourse. To this end, theologians such as Bonganjalo Goba[25] and Sigqibo Dwane[26] have sought to make the links between Black theology and African traditional cultures.

Itumeleng Mosala has developed perhaps the most politicised understanding of the liberatory character of culture. Dwight N. Hopkins also sees culture as 'an element of resistance'. Making reference to liberation fighter Amilcar Cabral, Hopkins describes culture as a means of resistance for liberation which 'judges, critiques and thus normalises the effectiveness and radicality of culture (manifested in the ideological plane) and politics (manifested in a physical and historical reality and a people's history)'.[27] Liberation begins by reclaiming a discourse of affirmation and asserting those values around which one's identity is shaped and world-view understood. The power to think creatively is necessary for black people if they are to be truly liberated. Hopkins concludes that in 'a black theology of liberation the culture of politics and the politics of culture go hand-in-hand'.[28]

## The Future of Black Theology

An appraisal and evaluation of Black theology has to be undertaken in the light of the upheavals that have beset the world in recent times. At the same time that Black theology took root in North America during the era of Reagan, when the social and political condition of the poor deteriorated sharply, there were also great political upheavals in the South. The overthrow of military dictatorships in Latin America, the dangerous and rapid escalation of the Cold War, the collapse of the Soviet Union and the disintegration of the Warsaw Pact states have marked this period. Southern Africa saw the independence of Namibia in March 1990. The process towards change began in South Africa almost simultaneously.

South Africa went through the most intense form of struggle in the mid-1980s. While black leadership was visible in the church during that time, the theological focus appeared to shift from Black theology to contextual theology. This reflected the political shift in the country as the ascendancy of the non-racial United Democratic Front and the Congress movement manifested itself. In addition to the prevailing political mood, it could be argued that the shift took place because Black theology had become moribund. It had failed to make the impact which its earlier incarnation as a movement of the people had promised. What appears to be now the case, and this is perfectly understandable, is that Black theology proponents in South Africa are organically associated with AZAPO and other Black Consciousness formations. Commendable work has been done by a few scholars, especially in the Faculty of Theology at the University of South Africa. But publication has been limited. Mosala's *Black Hermeneutics* has not been followed by any other substantial work.

During this period, however, the strength of Black theology has been in the development of international networks. Black theologians have made a major impact in EATWOT and have strengthened bonds with Black theologians in the USA. On the other hand, American Black theologians have developed links with the budding Afro-Brazilian Black theology movement. Within South Africa, however, Black theology appears to be isolated in academic institutions, engaged in an abstruse academic discourse. Perhaps this is due to the fact that the leading Black theologians are no longer pastors, parish ministers or even seminary lecturers, and have therefore not been able to impact on the life of the church at the base ecclesial level. Some may well ask: Has Black theology outlived its usefulness?

On the one hand, it could be that Black theology no longer captures the imagination of the oppressed because political strategies have now multiplied and opportunities have extended. On the other hand, because Black theology does not seem to have advanced its argument much further over the past 25 years, it has lost the attention of the faithful.

These criticisms were highlighted in a recent report by Basil Moore. He interviewed a large number of people to discover where Black theology had gone since the publication and banning of *Essays in Black Theology* in 1972.[29] The essential criticisms highlighted are that Black theology is set in an oppositional mould, that it has become disconnected with the ongoing struggles of the people today, that it has lost its anchor in the grassroots. While I do not wish to address, justify or refute any of the criticisms, I want to use them as pointers to the future for Black theology.

Can Black theology make a contribution to the changing circumstances of South Africa? While the domination of South African society by racist values and the denial of the value and dignity of black people will continue in church and society, there are different forms which common action and strategies take to counter the effects of such injustice and alienation. The question is whether a polarised and conflictual theology will help society discover those common values upon which a good society may be built. Can Black theology become the vehicle for reaching out to the common humanity and values which may bind the diverse cultures and communities in South Africa together?

The question must be asked whether Black theology has been able to make a lasting and radical paradigm shift in theological discourse. Simon Maimela touches on an aspect of this when he says that the burden of Black theologians is their 'naïve, if not unsophisticated belief that the Bible is normative for Christian theology'. Moreover, he charges, Black theologians continue to operate within the traditional modes of theological method, which presuppose that there are fixed truths that the Bible reveals. This is a trap, a tomb out of which Black theologians cannot escape. Maimela challenges Black theologians to 'candidly admit that they have found it morally necessary to take upon themselves the responsibility of searching for new ways of talking about God's presence in the world, hoping to construct a theology which will lead to black liberation, self-realisation and fuller humanisation'.[30]

Failure to make this break with traditional theological methods can be detected in the failure of Black theology, especially in South Africa, to accommodate feminist or womanist theology. Sister Bernard Ncube of the Institute for Contextual Theology says that there is a need for a Black theology 'which is also a feminist theology'.[31] Another aspect of this failure has been the inability to challenge not just the patriarchalism but also the authoritarianism which prevails in the formal structures of the church. A theology that makes it possible for former Black theologians to have been co-opted successfully into the structures of the institutional church without managing to effect change in that institution is seriously flawed. Black theology needs to address the question of theological method once again; not in such a manner as to mark a critical distance for its own sake but in order to develop a new consciousness out of which the liberation ethic could become a permanent feature of theological discourse and critical and strategic action.

[1] See also Molefe Tsele, 'Ethics in Black Theology', in the second volume of *Theology and Praxis* (Cape Town: David Philip, 1994).

[2] These circumstances account for the confusing variety of editors for the different editions of the volume. The first was published in South Africa under the imprint of Ravan Press as *Essays in Black Theology* edited by Mokgethi Motlhabi. Dr Motlhabi joined the Black Theology Project of the University Christian Movement, the original sponsors of Black theology in South Africa, to replace Ntwasa. Once overseas, Basil Moore published the essays as *Black Theology: The South African Voice* under the imprint of C. Hurst in London in 1973.

[3] *My Soul Looks Back* (Nashville: Abingdon, 1982), p. 43.

[4] Black Theology, *Black Power* (London and Oxford: Mowbrays, 1978), p. 10.

[5] *My Soul Looks Back*, p. 43.

[6] Ibid., p. 44.

[7] Alistair Kee, *A Reader in Political Theology* (London: SCM, 1974), p. 121.

[8] *My Soul Looks Back*, p. 81.

[9] 'Why Apartheid Was Right about the Unliberated Bible', unpublished paper given at the EATWOT seminar in Johannesburg, 17–22 August 1993.

[10] *Black Theology, Black Power*, p. 12.

[11] At a seminar organised by the Ecumenical Association of Third World Theologians (EATWOT) in Johannesburg on 17–21 August 1993, Professor S. S. Maimela put this position to Itumeleng Mosala (University of Cape Town) and Randall Bailey (Interdenominational Theological Center, Atlanta). Neither were convinced about the irrelevance of the Bible for Black theology. See Maimela's article, 'Black Theology and the Quest for a God of Liberation', *JTSA*, 82 (March 1993), pp. 54–66.

[12] *My Soul Looks Back*, p. 45.

[13] *Black Theology, Black Power*, p. 10.

[14] I. Mosala, *Biblical Hermeneutics and Black Theology in South Africa* (Grand Rapids: Eerdmans, 1989).

[15] See Boesak, *Black Theology, Black Power*, p. 122

[16] See Itumeleng Mosala, 'African Independent Churches: A Study in Socio-Theological Protest' in Charles Villa-Vicencio and John De Gruchy (eds.), *Resistance and Hope: Essays in Honour of Beyers Naudé* (Grand Rapids: Eerdmans, 1985).

[17] *My Soul Looks Back*, p. 47.

[18] *Black Theology, Black Power*, p. 12.

[19] *The Window of Vulnerability* (Minneapolis: Fortress, 1990), p. 63.

[20] In Moore, *Black Theology*, p. 138.

[21] From a discussion at the EATWOT seminar, Johannesburg, 17–22 August 1993.

[22] In Kee, *A Reader in Political Theology*, p. 126.

[23] *Black Theology, Black Power*, p. 14.

[24] On this debate see essays by Desmond Tutu, Manas Buthelezi, John Mbiti, Gabriel Setiloane, James Cone and Gayraud Willmore in K. Appiah-Kubi and S. Torres (eds.), *African Theology en Route* (Maryknoll: Orbis, 1981) and in John Parrat (ed.), *Readings in African Christian Theology* (London: SPCK, 1987).

[25] See 'Corporate Personality: Ancient Israel and Africa' in Moore, *Black Theology*, pp. 65–73.

[26] See 'Gospel and Culture', *Journal of Black Theology in South Africa*, 1 (1987).

[27] *Black Theology: USA and South Africa* (Maryknoll: Orbis, 1989), p. 179; compare with Takatso Mofokeng, 'A Black Christology: A New Beginning', *Journal of Black Theology in South Africa*, 1 (1987).

[28] Ibid., p. 180. For an interesting socialist understanding and interpretation of the culture of liberation, see Karen Press, 'Towards a Revolutionary Artistic Practice in South Africa' in *Popular and Political Culture for South Africa* (Cape Town: Centre for African Studies, University of Cape Town, 1990).

[29] *Lord, Help Thou Our Unbelief: Black Theology Revisited* (unpublished manuscript, March 1993).

[30] 'Black Theology and the Quest for a God of Liberation', p. 65.

[31] Quoted in Moore, *Lord, Help Thou Our Unbelief*, p. 24.

## Select Bibliography

Boesak, Allan A. *Black Theology, Black Power*. London and Oxford: Mowbrays, 1978

Cone, James H. *My Soul Looks Back*. Nashville: Abingdon, 1982

Hopkins, Dwight N. *Black Theology: USA and South Africa: Politics, Culture and Liberation*. Maryknoll: Orbis Books, 1989.

Kee, Alistair (ed.) *A Reader in Political Theology*. London: SCM, 1974

Moore, Basil (ed.) *Black Theology: The South African Voice*. London: C. Hurst, 1973

Soelle, Dorothee: *The Window of Vulnerability: A Political Spirituality*. Minneapolis: Fortress Press, 1990

Villa-Vicencio, Charles and John W. de Gruchy (eds.) *Resistance and Hope: South African Essays in Honour of Beyers Naudé*. Cape Town: David Philip, 1985.

Villa-Vicencio, Charles. *Between Christ and Caesar: Classical and Contemporary Texts on Church and State*. Cape Town: David Philip, 1986

# 16

# Liberation Theology[1]

## CHARLES VILLA-VICENCIO

Liberation theology has emerged as one of the most exciting and far-reaching developments in the theology of the second half of the twentieth century, signalling the coming of age of the third-world church. It has taken theology out of the academic ivory tower of Europe into the streets and shantytowns of Latin America. In so doing it has shifted the focus of theological discussion from the intellectual discourse of Western philosophy to the life and death struggles of poor and oppressed communities. The outcome has been more than a call for new subjects and issues to be added to the theological agenda. It has been a call for a fundamental reorientation of theology itself, providing a radically new perspective on the theological task.

This call needs to be understood in relation to the dominant role played by the Roman Catholic Church in the Portuguese and Spanish colonisation of Latin America. The Catholic Church provided a religious legitimation of colonial exploitation and oppression of the native people. While there were some missionaries who sided with the indigenous people in their fight against colonialism, the church, as an institution, was held in captivity to the colonial powers. Likewise, when Protestantism was established in Latin America in the nineteenth century it became aligned with the emerging middle classes and their growing economic interests. Ideologically bound by the political interests of the United States, they also supported the existing political order and regarded the revolutionary poor as victims of communist agitators.

The contours of Roman Catholic theology between the colonisation of Latin America and the present time have been outlined in a number of publications.[1] The decisive shift away from a European-dominated theology to a contextual focus did not occur until the time of the Second Vatican Council, which first met in October 1962. It has often been pointed out that even then Latin American and third-world delegates were significantly outnumbered by European and first-world delegates to the Council. Yet, for a variety of reasons, the Council marked the beginning of a shift in theological perception away from an exclusively European orientation.

The Latin American church had in the meantime been undergoing a process of renewal since the beginning of the twentieth century. This renewal was precipitated by the need to deal pastorally with the socio-economic conditions and political structures imposed on the region by the colonial powers. At the same time there was an emerging ecclesial renewal and a sense of collegiality among bishops and clergy, who had made a conscious decision to identify with the needs of the poor. This culminated in the first meeting of the General Conference of the Latin American Episcopacy (CELAM) in 1955. Other regular meetings were held over the next decade to give expression to the emerging 'new Christianity' of the Latin American church. With the end of the Second Vatican Council behind them, bishops from Latin America and other third-world countries met at Mar del Plata, where they issued a statement entitled 'Theological Reflection on Development'.[2] The document affirmed that the conversion demanded by the gospel 'affects the whole man, his physical and social as well as his spiritual and personal being'. From this theological basis they systematically affirmed their 'independence in the face of political, social and economic systems', which they judged to be responsible for their oppression.[3] This document marked a shift in the emphasis of Latin American theology away from dependency (defined at the time as 'development', of the kind associated with neo-colonial reliance) to 'liberation' and self-determination.

In 1968 the Second General Conference of the Latin American episcopacy met in Medellin, with Pope Paul VI delivering the opening address, in which he urged the delegates to promote social justice and to love the poor. He exhorted the poor 'not to put their confidence in violence or revolution'. In a second speech he went further, saying: 'Some conclude that the basic problem of Latin America cannot be resolved without violence', but stressed that 'violence is neither evangelical nor Christian'.[4] The Medellin Conference was not ready to leave matters there. It argued that in some situations violence may be legitimate, although warning that this violence could lead to new injustices. Donal Dorr summarises the shift in emphasis between the Pope's statement on violence and that of the Medellin Conference.[5] He suggests that the Pope recognised that there might be certain exceptional situations in which violence is required (even though it is not Christian). The Medellin document takes a less critical position on the issue. It reverses the order of the Pope's concern, arguing that revolutionary insurrection is sometimes legitimate, while allowing that such action can give rise to new injustices. The shift in emphasis marked the beginning of a new age in the Latin American church. Gutiérrez makes the point:

> Vatican II speaks of the underdevelopment of peoples, of the developed countries and what they can and should do about this underdevelopment; Medellin tries to deal with the problem from the standpoint of the poor countries, characterising them as subjected to a new kind of colonialism. Vatican II talks about a Church in the world and describes the relationship in a way which tends to neutralise the conflicts; Medellin demonstrates that the world in which the Latin American Church ought to be present is in full revolution. Vatican II sketches a general outline for Church

renewal; Medellin provides guidelines for a transformation of the Church in terms of its presence on a continent of misery and injustice.[6]

In effect, Medellin extended the ideas of Vatican II and the thought of popes John XXIII and Paul VI to give expression to what would become the basis of Latin American liberation theology. Emphasising the importance of the social context and analysis (something highlighted in Vatican II documents), the bishops proposed that the oppression of the poor was a consequence of economic exploitation, the arms race and nationalism. In other words, they regarded it as a consequence of the existing international order. They insisted that theology address these realities, not with a view merely to reflect on the nature of these events, but rather with a sense of compulsion to change them.

The Medellin document is, at the same time, clear that the basis for the liberation of the poor is to be found in the gospel of Jesus Christ. It is Christ who came to liberate humanity from all the slavery to which sin has subjected it. This slavery includes socio-economic and political injustice and oppression. Of equal importance is the insistence that these issues can only be addressed in solidarity with the poor. Such a theology involves more than theorising about issues. It involves active engagement with the poor in their struggle for liberation.

Different liberation theologians have developed their distinctive approaches to theology by drawing in different ways on the Medellin themes: the preferential option for the poor, socio-economic liberation as integral to salvation, and a shift from theory to praxis. To understand this development, it is important to understand the context of this theology, namely dehumanising poverty amidst the wealth of a minority. The authorities that benefited from this situation tolerated no opposition. Many who protested disappeared mysteriously, were imprisoned, tortured or killed. This context of Latin American theology has, of course, given it an appeal in similar situations of exploitation well beyond the confines of its own border — not least in South Africa.

The church often did little to oppose the oppressive regimes in Latin America, and in some cases supported them. This left individual Christians who were prepared to oppose these regimes isolated from their own churches. The story of Archbishop Romero in El Salvador is enough to indicate that the church in Latin and Central America was in many ways divided against itself, leaving its most faithful leaders and adherents vulnerable to attack. In many ways the struggle for liberation is located as much within the Latin American church as it is between first and third world churches. That the struggle for theological freedom from Vatican control by Latin American theologians has become a major point of contention can be seen in the recent action taken against the Franciscan theologian Leonardo Boff. Having been censured by the Vatican for his writings, he eventually resigned from the priesthood in order to be able to exercise a critical theological role without hierarchical restriction.

## A New Way of Doing Theology

The point has already been made that liberation theology views itself not just as another chapter or theme to be added to a textbook on systematic theology or ethics, but as a new way of doing theology. Leonardo and Clodovis Boff describe their understanding of liberation theology in this way: 'Reflecting on the basis of practice, within the ambit of the vast efforts made by the poor and their allies, seeking inspiration of faith and the gospel for the commitment to fight against poverty and for the integral liberation of all persons and the whole person – that is what liberation theology means.'[7]

This new way of doing theology involves two choices: the first is to show a preferential option for the poor, and the second is to turn theology into a critical reflection on praxis.

## The Preferential Option for the Poor

In a society characterised by injustice, oppression and conflict, neutrality is impossible. The church (like any other institution) sides either with the victims or with the perpetrators of injustice. Indeed, to make 'no choice' is to allow the *status quo* to continue. The basis of liberation theology is a self-conscious choice to side with victims. This is a choice grounded theologically in the affirmation that the God of the Bible is a God of justice who, while loving all people, sides with the oppressed against the oppressors.

This option for the poor has two methodological consequences. The first is based on the realisation that all ideas, including religious ideas, are part of the conscious or subconscious struggle for domination between the oppressed and the oppressor. Ideas, it is argued, are inevitably used to support the interests of one group or another – and to the extent that the dominant theology is the work of persons and a church essentially supportive of the *status quo*, it is likely to support the interests of the *status quo*. If theology is to reflect the interests of the majority of the world's population, who are poor, it must be consciously done from the perspective of the poor and marginalised.

This, of course, places an extra burden on the theologian. Miguez Bonino, a Protestant liberation theologian, suggests that it requires the theologian to occupy what he calls a 'double location' in his or her work: 'On the one hand there is the theologian's location within a theological discipline with its particular epistemological conditions and demands; on the other hand the theologian is also a social agent within a particular social formation.'[8] His argument is that theologians, despite their social location, are required to seek to see things from the perspective of the poor, and do theology from this perspective. This is not to suggest that the spiritual or moral insight of the poor is superior to that of others. It is rather that they see reality from a different perspective.[9] They provide a perspective from the 'underside' of society which theologians (given their biblical mandate to serve the cause of the poor) cannot afford to ignore.

A second methodological implication follows. It is that dominant theology answers the dominant questions and issues raised within the first world. Until the time of the Reformation, theology dialogued with Greek and Roman thinkers, notably Plato and Aristotle. During the Protestant Reformation and the post-Reformation period the debate centred around the claims of the emerging bourgeois and the princes of Europe. Since then, dominant theology has shaped the issues raised in Enlightenment and subsequent Western debates. In brief, liberation theologians argue that the questions of the poor of South America are different. The dehumanised person asks a different set of questions. These are questions which ask: 'How can we believe in God in a society that systematically crushes and destroys us?' 'How can we believe in God as personal when everything in the world conspires to deny our personhood?'[10]

Liberation theology is a theology of the poor. As such, while the leading exponents of liberation theology answer the questions and respond to the critique to which first-world theologians expose it, its primary concern is, properly speaking, with questions which are of concern to the poor. Indeed, the liberation theology which we read is already removed from this primary concern. It is written at an intellectual level, in response to the questions of the dominant theological tradition — a process which comes right at the end of the theological exercise engaged in by liberation theologians. Liberation theology first emerges, however, as the popular theology of the poor themselves, who engage in the struggle for life itself, in the light of their faith. The second level is that of the pastors who are engaged in ministering among the poor and who seek to deepen the faith of their congregations as they struggle together for justice and life. Only then does the professional theologian, working within the context of the seminary or university, seeking to promote the interests of the poor at another level, write the books of liberation theology that we read.

It is precisely this 'distance' from the poor that has prompted liberation theologians themselves to reflect critically on the problem. Some suggest that it is the task of 'organic intellectuals' to give expression to a theology *of* the poor, rather than to speak on behalf of the poor. As such, theologians are required to empty themselves in the service of the poor, which sometimes involves a surrender of their own concerns to allow the poor to be heard. It involves working against one's own self-interests or committing 'class suicide' in the service of the poor. The challenge is immense, but perhaps not impossible. The writing of the *Kairos Document* in South Africa is a case in point. It would be naïve to suggest that the writers of the document were themselves the actual poor. Through dialogue and solidarity with the poor and by allowing the participating poor to determine the message of the *Kairos Document*, it did, however, articulate the meaning of the gospel from their perspective to the wider church. The challenge of liberation theology is for theologians to commit themselves consciously to this task, a challenge which can only assist in the process of correcting the bias in favour of the dominant classes that characterises dominant theology.

*Theology as a Critical Reflection on Praxis*

Gustavo Gutiérrez makes the point clearly that liberation theology is 'a critical reflection on Christian praxis in the light of the Word'.[11] The implication is that theology is by definition what has been called a 'second act'.[12] To understand what is meant by this assertion, it is necessary to outline a series of interrelated steps or acts in the theological project as understood by liberation theologians.

The 'first act' is the praxis of the believing community acting in obedience to the gospel. In making this point, liberation theologians emphasise the importance of distinguishing between practice and praxis. The former refers to the application of already worked out principles, while the latter refers to the process of action and reflection of a person engaged in the struggle for justice and liberation.

How does the specific *theological* exercise (the 'second step') relate to this process? It is the response of the faith community to what is happening in society. It is part of the reflection process involved in praxis, a process involving three related mediations.[13] The first is the socio-analytical mediation. Here use is made of social scientific tools to understand and uncover the root causes of the poverty and oppression of the poor, which the community of faith is required to overcome by way of reflection—action (praxis). In so doing, liberation theology has made use of marxist and neo-marxist social analytical tools, for which some have criticised it. While different liberation theologians have employed marxism in different ways, it is enough to indicate that few (if any) have used it in a doctrinaire manner. The argument advanced by the Boffs would enjoy the support of most liberation theologians: 'Marx . . . can be a companion on the way but he can never be the guide, because "You have only one teacher, the Christ" (Matthew 23:10).'[14]

Having engaged in a rigorous attempt to understand why things are the way they are — more specifically why the poor become poorer while the rich become richer — the second mediation involves a conscious turning to the Bible. This involves what Juan Luis Segundo has described as the hermeneutical circle. Segundo describes the circle as containing four steps.[15] The first involves a 'new way of experiencing reality'. Having immersed themselves in the world of the poor and having analysed the structures of oppression from the perspective of the poor, with the help of the social analytical tools to which reference has already been made, liberation theologians realise that society (as well as reality) is often seen in different ways by different people. They recognise that the dominant understanding of reality gives expression to the views of the dominant classes — and that this is not the *only* way of viewing reality. It is also not an objective (value-free) understanding of reality.

The second step in the hermeneutical circle is to apply this 'ideological suspicion' not only to the existing order but to all dominant ideas in society, including religious and theological ideas. Here, too, it was discovered that religious and theological teachings inevitably reflect the values and social perceptions of the dominant classes, primarily because they emerge out of the thinking of scholars who are more or less comfortable with the existing order. The third step in the hermeneutical circle involves 'exegetical suspicion', the suspicion that the dominant interpretation of the Bible has excluded certain important insights into the biblical text (those of the poor) which challenge the position of the dominant classes in society. Fourthly, liberation theologians have developed a new way of understanding the Bible, making use of what they have learned by means of this hermeneutical circle or process. They have discovered major themes of justice and liberation within the Bible that tend to be ignored by traditional theology.[16]

The third mediation is the practical mediation. Having grappled with the socio-economic reality and the biblical record, liberation theologians now return to the issue of practical action (praxis) in the pursuit of justice. As we have said, the aim of liberation theology is not to produce a new and interesting theology but to motivate and empower the church to engage in the struggle for justice. Here the theologian does not sit back in the academy, but returns to the streets to work out practical strategies for the pursuit of liberation, justice and peace.

This process has often been described as the See—Judge—Act process.[17] Once we have sought to understand the existing order at a level of depth and analytical understanding, the situation is assessed or judged in relation to the biblical tradition. Strategies of action are then planned to change the existing order of things. This new way of doing theology is grounded in an inclusive concept of 'knowing', a concept rooted in the Bible rather than in the Western philosophical tradition. Knowing God, in this context, involves more than intellectual theorising. It is a life of active involvement with God, in God's world, as a participant in God's salvific purposes.

The liberation theological understanding of theological knowledge, akin to the biblical notion of doing the truth, constitutes an understanding of theology quite different from the more cerebral first-world theologies that have hitherto dominated theological debate. It represents a challenge which no brand of theology can afford to ignore, locating ethics, Christian witness and pastoral care at the centre of theological discussion.

## Some Key Themes in Liberation Theology

A number of important themes follow from this theological approach. We turn to a brief consideration of some of them.

### Liberation as Integral to Salvation

The doctrine of salvation lies at the heart of the Christian faith and must therefore be central to any reconception of theology. As such, it stands central to liberation theology, which places its concern for the liberation of the oppressed at the centre of this doctrine.

Gutiérrez provides an inclusive understanding of salvation which is axiomatic to liberation theology.[18] He defines it, firstly, in relation to the concrete and immediate desires and aspirations of oppressed people for freedom from all forms of domination and oppression. At a second and deeper level, he sees salvation as operative at the level of empowering (or saving) people to take responsibility for themselves in history, in pursuit of the creation of a new humanity and a new kind of society. At its deepest level, liberation is liberation from sin, which is at the root of all oppression, injustice and domination.

These different levels of liberation are seen to be integrally related to each other. Salvation and liberation cannot be reduced to any one level. God's promise is of a new heaven and a new earth, liberation for captives, freedom for the oppressed, and salvation from our sins. To exclude any of these dimensions is to reduce the dominion and lordship of Christ to a level that denies the essence of biblical teaching.

An important aspect of this understanding of salvation is the perception of sin as both personal and structural. Sin is not to be confined to people's relationship with God or even relationships with their neighbours. It is seen also to be embedded in the structures of society itself. Oppressive and unjust social, economic or political structures are a manifestation of social or structural sin, and salvation includes liberation from such structures. This, of course, has direct implications for the witness of the church regarding political, economic and other social evils. A direct consequence is the realisation that the engagement of the church in such matters is not an optional extension of what it means to be a Christian, but lies at the heart of its evangelical and salvific mission.

Differently stated, Gutiérrez argues that the church must move away from a 'quantitative' understanding of salvation, which sees salvation in terms of the number of people to be saved, to a 'qualitative' understanding which sees salvation in terms of the transformation of all levels of human existence. He suggests that this understanding of salvation is a direct consequence of the teaching of Vatican II, which declared that all human beings can receive God's grace and be in communion with God through active engagement in this transforming activity, even if they do not explicitly confess Jesus Christ as Lord. God's grace is, in other words, seen as a turning away from selfishness towards a love for humanity.[19] God is encountered through loving service of humanity in general and the poor in particular. We encounter God through the poor as we pursue justice and liberation.[20]

For liberation theology, the biblical concept of salvation entails far more than a narrow spiritual relationship with God. It involves the eschatological promise of God's reign, which will remove sin and all its consequences, establishing a new creation of justice, righteousness and peace.

This focus on what is sometimes referred to as 'this-worldly' salvation – to the perceived neglect of future (heavenly) salvation – has suggested to some that liberation theology stands in danger of providing uncritical theological legitimation of political action. Some have gone so far as to suggest it runs the danger of repeating the mistakes of other political theologies, including apartheid theology! While some liberation theologians may well be less dialectic in their understanding of salvation than others, certainly theologians such as Gustavo Gutiérrez and José Miguez Bonino are not unaware of the danger. This becomes clear in Miguez Bonino's reference to what he calls the radical monism of liberation theology. He sees this as occurring when the love of God is collapsed without remainder into love for one's neighbour, when it becomes increasingly difficult to differentiate between liberation and salvation, or when – to use Bonino's words – 'reference to the history of divine revelation is secondary, merely exemplary, or even dispensable'. 'If we carry that tendency', he continues, 'to its ultimate conclusion, we will end up wittingly or unwittingly deifying history or humanity itself. There can be no doubt that contemporary Latin American theology has no such intention. But we must ask ourselves whether the formulations we have worked out so far do enough to rule out that possibility.'[21]

In a similar vein Gutiérrez warns that the gospel continually challenges any attempt to embody it. It militates, he argues, against the 'absolutising of revolution'.[22] While it is recognised that no human society will totally reflect God's eschatological reign, to the extent this is possible liberation theology recognises that salvation is present within history. It includes social, economic and political redemption and transformation.

### Jesus and Liberation

Liberation theologians have written a number of major studies on Christology. The distinctive emphases of these studies are mentioned in only the broadest outline.[23]

The first theme is that Christology needs to be reconceived 'from below'. That is, while liberation theologians are as concerned to give expression to the divinity of Christ as are other theologians, their point of Christological departure is the human Jesus. They view Jesus from within the socio-political context of first-century Palestine as the one who identified with the poor and marginalised members of society. Much like the New Testament community, liberation theologians seek to explain in what way this human Jesus, with whom they can so readily identify, can also be seen to be divine. The answer has partly to do with the affirmation of a Hebraic integration of the spiritual and the material, the divine and human, the spiritual and the secular.

A second theme identifies Jesus as the proclaimer of the kingdom or reign of God. Central to a liberation perspective on Jesus' ministry and the proclamation of God's reign on earth is a demand for the radical reordering of life and society. While not suggesting that Jesus was actively engaged in political revolution, liberation theologians see Jesus' message as a direct challenge to the ruling classes – the Herodians, the Sadducees, the Pharisees and the High Priests. Jesus' rejection of the Zealot option is, in turn, seen by liberation theologians as a rejection not necessarily of armed struggle on behalf of the poor, but of their narrow nationalism. An important emphasis in liberation Christology is the recognition that Jesus' message of liberation transcended the boundaries of Jewish nationalism. It was a message for *all* poor people.

Thirdly, Christologies within the framework of liberation theology see Jesus' death as an inevitable consequence of his message and of his identification with suffering humanity. They further argue that it is not only the human Jesus who suffers on the Cross. In Christ, God identifies with suffering humanity, entering into their pain and death. The resurrection is consequently God's vindication of Jesus and his message of God's reign. It represents also the inauguration of the hope of a future liberation.

### The Church and Its Mission

Liberation theology's ecclesiology follows directly from its Christological focus. Liberation theology calls the church to identify itself with the poor in order to make itself available to God for the realisation of God's liberatory purposes in history.

A direct consequence of this commitment is seen in the emergence of base Christian communities (BCCs) in a number Latin American countries. It is to this development that attention is given in what follows, drawing on an interview which I conducted with Jether Ramaldo, a participant in the BCC movement in Brazil for the past two decades. He spoke of the different phases of struggle through which the BCCs have moved.[24]

*The encounter between laity and priests.* 'This first phase', Ramaldo observes, 'was essentially ecclesial and theological. It involved establishing a new relationship between the clergy and the people. The laity wanted more say in the affairs of the church. BCCs constituted a process of the people themselves becoming the church — taking responsibility for the Christian community and its mission in society. It was a stage of self-empowerment, not as an end in itself but as a means of transforming the larger society.'

*The relationship between the oppressed and the oppressors.* 'The second phase of the BCCs was the level of social and economic analysis. This involved class struggle between the rich and the poor. As a basis for this we sought to understand the political and economic structures that made for this exploitation. This became a basis for our strategic participation in the struggle for transformed political and economic structures.'

*The encounter between the church and popular organisations.* 'This had to do with a realisation by Christians that they did not control the political struggle. It was a phase when members of the BCCs related to the broader struggle through the various civic organisations, learning how to translate theological ideas into political strategies and action. In the process we learned of our vulnerability as church. We were buffeted by various political forces, but resisted absorption by any political party. We at the same time underwent a shift away from "pastoral" ministry to direct "political" engagement. . .'

With the first democratic elections in Brazil behind them, the BCCs are now faced with yet a further challenge. Ramaldo explains:

> This new phase has to do with religion and culture and the grappling with contemporary problems, such as sexuality, gender questions, leisure, unemployment and so forth. We are seeking to work out a practical theological way of enabling people to realise their full God-given potential. We are at the same time seeking to understand what it means to give expression to the Christian faith in different cultural forms. . . By addressing these issues we believe we are freeing people to stand up, to be themselves and to participate more vigorously in the creation of a compassionate society. The real struggle for renewal in Brazil has only just started. All that democracy does is give people an opportunity to share in the creation of their future. People need to be empowered to do so. That is the task of the church.

## A Spirituality for Liberation

The spirituality of struggle follows directly from Ramaldo's concern for empowering people to take responsibility for their own lives. Leonardo and Clodovis Boff state: 'it is in prayer and contemplation, and intimate and communitarian contact with God, that the motivations for a faith-inspired commitment to the oppressed and all humankind spring.'[25] Anyone who visits Latin America is immediately struck by the depth of spirituality which inspires liberation theologians and grassroots Christians participating in the liberation movements.

The spirituality of liberation is opposed to individualistic and privatised tendencies often associated with traditional forms of spirituality. Gutiérrez's book *We Drink from Our Own Wells* describes a spirituality born in the midst of the struggles of the Latin American poor.[26] It is a spirituality which arises out of an encounter with God within the community of the poor. It is also communal rather than individualistic in character, emerging within the communal struggle for justice. Thirdly, it is always a response to God's gracious activity within the world. Fourthly, this response takes the form of a conversion to a life of obedience to Jesus. This new lifestyle integrates those areas of life normally associated with spirituality, such as prayer and meditation, with those which are traditionally excluded from spirituality, such as politics. Fifthly, this spirituality gives rise to hope in the midst of suffering — a hope grounded in the resurrection, which carries the promise of liberation.

Finally, this spirituality can only be experienced in solidarity with the poor. Donal Dorr's *Integral Spirituality* provides a most useful description of an all-embracing, holistic spirituality which embraces all that has been outlined in this chapter.[27] It is a spirituality which empowers people to deal with the challenges of all aspects of life. In brief, this is a spirituality which undergirds the mission of the church to transform society.

## A Black and Feminist Critique

Liberation theology has in some circles been a controversial development, meeting with the opposition of powerful forces within the ecclesiastical, theological and political establishments. Its call to radical engagement in the struggle of the poor and oppressed has brought it into sharp conflict with those who benefit from the *status quo*. Others, notably the poor themselves, have seen within this theology the articulation of the message of the poor man of Nazareth. Christian theology must ultimately be judged in relation to the message of this man whom the poor heard gladly, while the rich turned sorrowfully away.

In closing, it is important to note certain important questions posed by women and Black theologians about Latin American liberation theology, which suggest that there is insufficient clarity on certain issues amongst liberation theologians.

The major challenge presented by women and Black theologians is that oppression is a more complex phenomenon than Latin American theologians would have it. In brief, the Black and feminist critique is that race and gender cannot be reduced to socio-economic factors. Women and blacks, it is argued, are discriminated against, whether they are poor or middle class, capitalists or socialists. The failure of Latin American theologians to deal explicitly with these issues, the argument continues, serves to reinforce the marginalisation of these groups.

In Brazil, for example, with a population of over four million black people (the world's second largest black population), the overwhelming majority of whom are poor, Latin American liberation theology has failed to investigate adequately the link between poverty and colour. The dominant debate, especially between North American Black and Latin American liberation theologians, can be traced back to the first Theology in the Americas Conference held in Detroit in 1975.[28]

Martin Garate sums up the divide between the two approaches to theology: 'Black Theologians are suspicious that liberation theology is a white theology; in the same way theologians in Latin America are suspicious that black theology is more American than black.'[29] Progress has been made in the debate since the late 1970s, but the essential emphases of the two theologies have not changed.

The issue of discrimination against women has not only been raised by North American feminists but, more important (from the point of view of Latin American liberation theology), increasingly from the women involved in the BCCs and the broader struggle for liberation within Latin America. The majority of Latin American church members are women, yet they have been systematically excluded from positions of leadership within the church. Patriarchal ideas and practices, entrenched within the church since its early history, have not been sufficiently challenged by mainstream Latin American liberation theologians. Christian theology and the biblical documents have been shaped by the patriarchal culture in which the Judaeo—Christian tradition emerged. Women theologians are therefore calling for a feminist critique of Christian theology.[30] The chapter on feminist theology included in this volume should be consulted.

These challenges have not gone unheard. Latin American liberation theologians have recognised the need to develop a more sophisticated understanding of oppression that addresses classism, racism and sexism. The dialogue between the various oppressed groups has broadened, and the concept of liberation as originally defined by some Latin American theologians in the 1960s and 1970s is today regarded by most liberation theologians as in need of deeper and broader analysis.

[1] See Zolani Ngwane 'Ethics in Liberation Theology' in the second volume of *Theology and Praxis* (Cape Town: David Philip, 1994).

[2] See, for example, Enrique Dussel, *A History of the Church in Latin America* (Grand Rapids: Eerdmans, 1981), p. 139; Donal Dorr, *Option for the Poor: A Hundred Years of Vatican Social Teaching* (Maryknoll: Orbis Books, 1983).

[3] See M. E. Marty and D. G. Peerman (eds.), *New Theology No. 6* (New York: Macmillan, 1972), pp. 243–54.

[4] Ibid., p. 243.

[5] Dussel, *A History of the Church in Latin America*, pp. 140–44.

[6] See Dorr, *Option for the Poor*, pp. 139–176.

[7] Gustavo Gutiérrez, *A Theology of Liberation* (Maryknoll: Orbis Books, 1973), p. 134.

[8] L. Boff and C. Boff, *Introducing Liberation Theology* (Tunbridge Wells: Burns and Oates, 1987), p. 8.

[9] José Miguez Bonino, *Towards a Christian Political Ethics* (Philadelphia: Fortress Press, 1983), p. 42.

[10] Ibid., p. 43.

[11] R. M. Brown, *Theology in a New Key–Responding to Liberation Themes* (Philadelphia: Westminster, 1978), p. 64.

[12] Gutiérrez *A Theology of Liberation*, p. 13.

[13] See Albert Nolan and Richard Broderick, *To Nourish Our Faith* (Hilton: Cornerstone, 1987), pp. 25f.

[14] Boff and Boff, *Introducing Liberation Theology*, pp. 24–42.

[15] Ibid., p. 28.

[16] J. L. Segundo *The Liberation of Theology* (Maryknoll: Orbis, 1976), p. 9.

[17] See, for example, J. Severino Croatto, *Exodus: A Hermeneutics of Freedom* (Maryknoll: Orbis Books, 1981); I. J. Mosala, *Biblical Hermeneutics and Black Theology in South Africa* (Grand Rapids: Eerdmans, 1989).

[18] This method has been successfully used by Young Catholic Workers (YCW) and Young Catholic Students (YCS) organisations and liberation theologians in many different contexts. See John XXlll in *Mater et Magistra*, 237.

[19] Gutiérrez, *A Theology of Liberation*, pp. 36–7.

[20] Ibid., pp. 150–152.

[21] Ibid., pp. 189–203.

[22] José Miguez Bonino, 'Historical Praxis and Christian Identity', in Rosino Gibellini, *Frontiers of Theology in Latin America* (Maryknoll: Orbis Books, 1979), p. 263.

[23] Gutiérrez, *A Theology of Liberation*, p. 238.

[24] These include L. Boff, *Jesus Christ Liberator: A Critical Christology for Our Time* (Maryknoll: Orbis, 1978); J. Sobrino, *Christology at the Crossroads: A Latin American Approach* (Maryknoll: Orbis, 1976); and J. L. Segundo, *The Historical Jesus of the Synoptics* (Maryknoll: Orbis, 1985).

[25] A interview conducted at CEDI (the Ecumenical Centre for Documentation and Information) in Rio de Janeiro in January 1993. See a fuller account of the interview in *Challenge* 16 (June/July 1993).

[26] Boff and Boff, *Introducing Liberation Theology*, p. 64.

[27] See G. Gutiérrez, *We Drink from Our Own Wells: The Spiritual Journey of a People* (London: SCM, 1984) and *Theology of Liberation*, pp. 203–208.

[28] Donal Dorr, *Integral Spirituality* (Maryknoll: Orbis, 1990), p. 1.

[29] See S. Torres and J. Eagleson (eds.), *Theology in the Americas* (Maryknoll: Orbis, 1976).

[30] Quoted ibid., p. 356.

[31] See E. Tamez, *Against Machismo* (Oak Park: Meyer Stone, 1987); *Through Her Eyes: Women's Theology from Latin America* (Maryknoll: Orbis, 1989); Letty M. Russell, *Human Liberation in a Feminist Perspective: A Theology* (Philadelphia: Westminster, 1974); and Rosemary Radford Ruether, *Sexism and God-Talk: Toward a Feminist Theology* (Boston: Beacon, 1983).

## Select Bibliography

Boff, L. and C. Boff. *Introducing Liberation Theology*. Tunbridge Wells: Burns and Oates, 1987

Dussel, E. *A History of the Church in Latin America: Colonialism to Liberation 1492–1979*. Grand Rapids: Eerdmans, 1981

Ellis, M. and O. Maduro. *The Future of Liberation: Essays in Honour of Gustavo Gutiérrez*. Maryknoll: Orbis, 1989

Fierro, A. *The Militant Gospel: An Analysis of Contemporary Political Theologies*. London: SCM, 1977

Gutiérrez, G. *A Theology of Liberation: History, Politics and Salvation*. London: SCM, 1974

Nolan, A. *God in South Africa*. Cape Town: David Philip, 1988

Miguez Bonino, J. *Doing Theology in a Revolutionary Situation*. Philadelphia: Fortress, 1975

Nolan, A. and R. Broderick. *To Nourish Our Faith*. Hilton: Cornerstone, 1987

Segundo, J. L. *The Liberation of Theology*. Maryknoll: Orbis, 1976

# 17

# Faith and Feminism: Women Doing Theology[1]

## DENISE M. ACKERMANN

### Women, Feminism and Theology

Years ago, as part of the collect in a eucharistic service, I was asked to pray that I 'might grow to my full manhood'. This simple request jarred me into a new consciousness. What was happening? The prayers were led by male priests; God was addressed almost exclusively as 'Father'; in the hymns we sang lustily about 'sons' or 'men' of God; and the sermon was preached by a man who relied for his interpretation of Scripture on men's experience of the world around us.

There have been changes. However, nearly two thousand years of a male-dominated church, backed by theology that is derived from male scholarship and experience, cannot be dealt with simply by ordaining women or a commitment to inclusive language, important as such steps may be. Profound changes are required. Feminist theology is one of the vehicles through which women express a critique of existing theology and religious practices, and contribute creatively towards the unfinished dimension of theology.

### Choices

When doing feminist theology, as in all theology, certain choices have to be made. This chapter reflects a particular feminist theological stance. In the first place, its approach comes from within Christian history and tradition. Certain kinds of feminist theology are done by women who have left the Christian tradition because they have found it profoundly patriarchal.[2] Feminist theology is also done by women in world religions such as Judaism, Islam and Hinduism.[3]

Secondly, this chapter opts for a feminist practical theological stance in which the dialogue between our theological theories and our practices is central. This requires the ongoing examination of the relationship between our theological theories and our faith practices in order to move to healing and liberation. In the belief that we 'cannot know or speak of God at all outside the concrete and daily praxis of who we are and what we do',[4] feminist theologians choose to work in praxis-oriented theology.

Thirdly, the interpretative key for feminist theology begins with an attitude of suspicion towards existing doctrines and interpretations of the Scriptures. Centuries of male scholarship, which has quite naturally seen the world through men's eyes and experiences, cannot be accepted unquestioningly as normative for women. Different feminist theologians work with different hermeneutic keys. The underlying principle for the hermeneutic used here is that women are fully human and are to be valued as such.[5] Any interpretation or understanding, action or practice which discriminates against women or oppresses them is not considered normative.

Feminist theologians believe that *how* we do theology is as important as what kind of theology we do. Feminist theology arises out of communities of women seeking wholeness. This means a commitment to being accountable to the particular community of women one comes from. All theology reflects on the story of human beings' relationship with God. Thus *women's* stories, *our* context and *our* experience give our theology its particularity.

The feminist theological process begins with a critique of existing interpretations. It then goes through a time of struggle and risk as memories, traditions and our source-book dialogue with the present context. Finally, the process moves on to the creative doing of a theology which promotes and affirms women's humanity and is consonant with the values of the reign of God, like justice, love, freedom, equality, wholeness and peace.

*Inherent Tensions*

Certain tensions which become apparent in doing feminist theology must be acknowledged. In the first place, there is an inherent tension in a feminist stance that values the liberation of all people and yet needs to address women's oppression very specifically. This tension between the universal and the particular is also found in the imperative for human dignity, justice and love as universal values, and the very specific need for actions which embody these values in the South African context. Overemphasising the universal aspects of these values can result in an abstract formulation of a utopian dream which avoids direct confrontation with the very specific threats to these values in our context. Focusing on the specific nature of our context can lead to myopia, which sees racism as *the* evil to be eradicated, without paying attention to issues of gender and class and their interrelatedness with race. Feminism attempts to analyse systems of oppression comprehensively in order to hold out a holistic vision for change; yet its particularity is found in its attention to women's oppression. Herein lies the tension.

A further source of strain is the problem of keeping one's faith in a religious tradition which has oppressed one, while simultaneously maintaining one's integrity. One way of coping is to re-image the concepts, metaphors and symbols that are loaded with patriarchal meaning. Language is viewed as both the initiator and expression of human consciousness, and is central to this endeavour.

Lastly, there is a tension inherent in writing as a white woman who has lived on the privileges granted her in an apartheid society. I can only do theology authentically by acknowledging the particularities of my context and its inherent ambiguities, while at the same time holding onto the inclusive, holistic and liberating impulse of feminist theology. Feminist theology emerges from a critical consciousness which entails acknowledging the social contradictions that shape both our personal lives and our collective existence.

## Feminism

Contemporary feminism has its philosophical and political roots in the intellectual traditions of the Enlightenment. As a socio-political movement it has had different political orientations, ranging from bourgeois and liberal to socialist and marxist.[6] It has also, like many such movements, had a morally ambiguous history, at times espousing deeply radical and moral causes and at other times being blind to its own racist and classist assumptions.[7]

Not surprisingly, the term 'feminist' is still viewed by many women with suspicion, if not aversion. In dealing with derisory views of feminism, Rhoda Bertelsmann-Kadalie observes that 'to dismiss feminism as a "bourgeois concept" is to lose sight of its complexity and diversity'.[8]

The statement of a feminist perspective is both a political and a theological act. It is derived from the experience of male dominance in the family, educational institutions, society and the church. It carries with it a history of gender discrimination and spells out a commitment to women's struggles against oppression. Feminism can be defined as the reflection on and commitment to the praxis of liberation for women from all that oppresses us. Feminism does not benefit any specific group, race or class of women, nor does it promote privilege for women over men. It is about a different consciousness, a radically transformed perspective which questions our social, cultural, political and religious traditions and calls for structural change in all these spheres.

## Feminist Theology

When the private and corporate pain of sexist oppression is reflected on critically and systematically by women seeking to make sense of the life of faith, feminist theology is born. It is thus far wider than the academic discourse, and women reflecting on their faith remain an important source and challenge to academic feminist theologians. Feminist theology aims at the liberation of all women and all men and the transforming of religious structures. This means that male hierarchies are no longer held to be normative in determining people's worth. It means that women and men together will be able to contribute to naming and shaping their realities in such a way that all people's humanity is affirmed in just, loving, liberating and healing praxis.

## The Diversity of Feminist Theology[9]

In surveying the field of feminist theology, we should be careful not to appear to be 'splitting' the field into convenient labels, for feminist theologians, although differing radically in their approaches, see themselves as working in constant exchange and communication with each other. Feminist theologians are not a homogeneous group; they represent a variety of voices with different approaches.

These approaches are not necessarily mutually exclusive and remain in dialogue with one another.[10]

First, there is the post-Christian way. This is exemplified in the United States of America by the work of Mary Daly who, in 1968, published her pioneering work on *The Church and the Second Sex*,[11] which represents one of the most important critiques of sexism in the Christian tradition. In a later work, *Beyond God the Father*,[12] Daly's perspective is radicalised and she perceives the women's movement as itself an 'intrinsically religious phenomenon'.[13]

A second approach is found in the work of those feminist theologians who choose to remain within the parameters of the Christian faith. In this category, the works of Rosemary Radford Ruether, Letty Russell, Beverly Wildung Harrison, Carter Heyward, Elisabeth Schüssler Fiorenza, Anne Carr, Sharon Welch and Susan Thistlethwaite are found among a burgeoning group of feminist theologians in the USA.[14] These theologians critique the interstructuring of oppressions and see themselves as involved in the struggle for justice and liberation.

A third route in North America is that taken by black women such as Katie Cannon,[15] Dolores Williams[16] and Jacquelyn Grant.[17] They have chosen to refer to themselves as 'womanist' theologians in order to distinguish themselves from white middle-class feminists.[18]

In Europe, one of the earliest books on feminist theology was published in 1980 by Catharina Halkes who was subsequently appointed to the first chair in Europe in 'Feminisme en Christendom' at Nijmegen University in 1983.[19] Recently, German feminist theologian Elisabeth Moltmann-Wendel published her introduction to feminist theology.[20] Ursula King has done likewise in England.[21]

African women have chosen to take a different route. The Ecumenical Association of Third World Theologians (EATWOT), a major vehicle for dialogue between third world liberation theologies, has, after an initial resistance to feminism as a 'white women's issue', placed women's theology on its agenda.[22] The result has been the creation within EATWOT of a Women's Commission. The formation of the Circle for Concerned African Women Theologians has also given rise to a number of publications. In this regard, the work of Mercy Amba Oduyoye and Musimbi Kanyoro is of importance to anyone doing theology on the African continent.[23]

Feminist theology is by no means restricted to North America, Western Europe or Africa. It is as global as feminism itself. A recently published directory of resources, entitled *Women in the Third World*,[24] illustrates this global dimension of new and creative perspectives on crucial issues concerning women. A corresponding interest in feminist theology is expressed in a series of recent publications.[25]

Despite its relatively recent appearance, feminist theology encompasses more than the women's movement itself, for it not only deals with women in their present contexts, but seeks to reflect on women's experience as a key to understanding women's spirituality. It endeavours to critique all manifestations of male dominance in past and current theologies, and it makes a contribution by reforming and reconstructing our faith concepts, symbols, images and praxis from a feminist perspective. As such, it has a formidable task.

*Feminist Theology in the South African Context*

Judging from the paucity of publications, feminist theology in South Africa is still in its infancy. Few women are working in this field. Examples of contributions in this area include, among others, publications by Felicity Edwards,[26] Marie-Henry Keane,[27] Christina Landman,[28] Megan Walker,[29] Phoebe Swart-Russell,[30] Louise Kretzschmar[31] and myself.[32] More recently, the book *Women Hold Up Half the Sky*, edited by Jonathan Draper, Emma Mashinini and myself, has been a first effort to publish collected writings by black and white women and a handful of men on the theme of women in the church in Southern Africa.

Feminist theology is struggling to emerge in the South African context. A number of reasons have contributed to this situation. We are hamstrung by years of isolation from our African, North American, European and third world counterparts, an isolation which is exacerbated by the fact that our society and our churches are profoundly patriarchal. For so long, the battle against apartheid has understandably prioritised racial oppression as the primary evil; in this process, however, the instructured mechanisms of race, gender and class in the oppression of people have not been adequately understood. Women are separated from birth by class, location and economic status. When this separation has been legislated and enforced over many years of oppressive white rule, our particularities isolate us from one another, instead of serving as a basis for dialogue.

A further compelling reason for the present struggle of feminist theology to emerge in our context is related to its place in the academy. As a theological discipline it is relatively young, but its academic under-representation in our places of learning, in contrast to the representation of other recent theologies, raises questions about priorities, about commitment to non-sexism, about the content of curricula and methods of teaching. In fact, the absence of women's voices raises profound questions about the nature of knowledge and the method whereby knowledge is in fact transmitted.[33] This situation needs to have priority on the research agenda of feminist theologians.

*Toward an Agenda*

The different traditions, cultures and places of women in South Africa will dictate different agendas for our theologies. Women should, therefore, take experience and context as our starting point. It is only in grappling with the dynamics which are particular to specific contexts within communities of accountability that authentic theology can be done. The hope is that the honest statement of particular experiences and views will ultimately lead to dialogue and the identification of commonalities.

*Context and Experience as Point of Departure*

The use of experience as a primary source in theology is open to criticism if it does not specifically address the range of human experience within particular social locations of race, class and gender divisions. For white women in South Africa this means that we explore the question of difference in terms of our place, our history,[34] and our society. Social analysis is a recognised source for understanding our world.[35] A critical analysis of white women's place in our society reveals that our experience is one of being both oppressors and oppressed. The tension between these opposing experiences impacts on how we see ourselves, how we do theology, our relationship with the church, with one another and with women of different racial groups, and also informs our search for transformation.

Black women analysing their context and experience reveal the multi-dimensional nature of their oppression, which incorporates race, class, gender and religious elements.[36] The origins of the alienation between white and black women lie in the history of colonialism, cultural and class divides and, above all, in the policy of apartheid with all its ramifications. Undeniably, white women have been advantaged in every sense at the expense of black people. The unhappy history of white women's oppression of black women adds yet a further dimension to this alienation.[37]

Doing theology as women seeking healing and liberation will therefore start with an analysis of our particular places in the history and present context of our society. This is a process which, for white women, will require vulnerability and will involve pain. Its goal is to state our particularities unambiguously and openly. The starting point for doing feminist theology is the life stories of women in particular contexts. The goal is liberation and wholeness.

*Liberating Praxis*

Feminist theology may never be an 'armchair' occupation. As women doing theology, feminist theologians are always involved 'on the ground' with women struggling against discrimination, violence and oppression. They are involved in praxis which is liberating.

This liberating praxis is the ongoing struggle against oppressive structures that exploit people and rob them of their full humanity. As part of the method of doing feminist theology, it begins with our own lives by naming our experiences, acknowledging that our experiences and our knowledge are relational and relative and therefore partial; it is not simply an individualistic exercise but a desire for the liberation of all who suffer oppression; it works 'on behalf of our own well-being in relation'[38] to our communities of accountability; it takes place in as diverse cultural situations as possible, respecting difference as well as having the freedom to challenge across differences; it is a collaborative effort which requires a shared commitment; it needs creative strategies and is action-oriented; and it has justice, healing and wholeness as its goal, as compellingly material to the South African context.

*Defining Our Humanity*

Why do women need to define our own humanity? The answer is simple: because it has always been done for us. Women's humanity, our experience, perceptions, thoughts and beliefs, have by and large been defined for us by men. This is particularly true in the Christian tradition where women have been subjected to a 'doctrine of man' (known as theological anthropology) which has tended to swing to extremes: we have been categorised as either the sinful Eve or the virtuous Virgin Mary. This kind of stereotyping has made scant allowance for us to define our own humanity.[39]

From a woman's perspective, Christian teaching on what it means to be human is an exercise in contradictions. On the one hand, all of humanity is understood as sharing in the image of God. On the other hand, women have been discriminated against in the Christian church on grounds of their gender, implying that our humanity is not as valued as that of men and that men in some way or other are more acceptable bearers of the divine image.

Against this background, feminist theologians have devoted themselves to finding a more inclusive view of humanity which affirms women's value and integrity.[40] In this search, *relationality* has emerged as a key description for an inclusive view of humanity. Relationality, the opposite of alienation, apathy and exclusion, is understood as the practice of love and justice between people.[41] The theological norm which informs this notion of relationality is Jesus Christ's injunction that 'you shall love the Lord your God with all you heart, and with all your soul, and with all your mind, and with all your strength... You shall love your neighbour as yourself'. (Mark 12:30–31) Active loving is living in relationship with oneself, with one's neighbour, with God and with creation. It endeavours to put into practice our belief that the humanity of all people is inviolable and to be nurtured, a praxis which is not only consonant with our beliefs, but which is sorely needed in our context, where racism and sexism thrive on warped views about humanity. Being in relation with one's neighbour induces liberating praxis.

The origins of relationality lie in our God who is a God-in-relation: God the Parent/Creator, God the Son/Redeemer, God the Holy Spirit/Sustainer. Our trinitarian understanding of the Holy One in Three is a relational understanding. God-in-relation with Godself extends relationality to all creation. We have a God who, from the beginning, sought to be in relation with created humanity. Sin is understood as that which mars, distorts or destroys relationality. Jesus' life is the example of a life lived in relation. 'Relational theology is incarnational.'[42]

## Women and the Church

The history of Christianity is a history of continual tension between conflicting models of church. This conflict between what Rosemary Ruether calls the 'church as spirit-filled community and the church as historical institution'[43] has played a major role in women's experience of alienation in the church. Women seeking relationality and actions which are liberating often encounter the very opposite. The question becomes, 'How can an aware woman survive in a sexist church?'

Women have responded to this question in diverse ways. For a growing number of believing feminists, a meaningful relationship with their churches as their only community of faith has become well-nigh impossible. Some have found solace in small communities of faith while others have invested time and energy in the concept and activities of 'women-church'.

Women-church represents the first time that women collectively have claimed to be church and have claimed the tradition of the exodus community as a community of liberation from patriarchy. This means that patriarchy is rejected as God's will. The need for a period of withdrawal from men and communication with each other is essential for the formation of the feminist community, because women, more than any other marginalised group, have lacked a critical culture of their own.[44] Women involved in women-church are not necessarily in a separatist movement, and many still remain members of their respective churches.

Those conscientised women who have stayed active members of the institutionalised church experience alienation or dissonance in a number of ways when denied participation at every level. Unfortunately, the church all too often merely reflects the patriarchal societal structures and customs within which it functions. Hierarchies of power, a separation of the laity from the clergy, and preaching and teaching based on men's experience and insights of the world, all give rise to a male clericalism which makes it difficult for the church to live out its prophetic calling. Feminist theology suggests that new models for church and ministry are required which, while acknowledging differences, are inclusive and sensitive to patterns of injustice and discrimination.[45]

Any metaphors or images used to depict the church can only be approximations, for the very nature of the church defies precise definition. However, the church understood as the Body of Christ[46] illuminates aspects of the nature of the church which offer possibilities to those who experience alienation. This image portrays the community of believers as being bonded together in union through the graces and gifts of the Holy Spirit used in mutual ministry for the good of the whole body. As all baptised believers are recipients of at least one gift freely given by the Holy Spirit, and as there is no hierarchy of gifts, this model for church can lead to a non-authoritarian, non-hierarchical believing community. In the giving of gifts, the Spirit does not discriminate against women, the poor, the uneducated, the disabled, offering everyone an opportunity to play her or his role in the building up of the Body. Such an inclusive community of believers can be a powerful agent for social renewal in our country. It is the expression of a community in relationship with itself.

*Language Matters*

The search for an inclusivity or 'visibility'[47] which affirms the worth of all people cannot be valid or successful unless the manner in which we speak about it reflects our beliefs. 'To separate language from action is false. Language change is an essential part of action.'[48] When I cease using sexist or racist language, I will not end sexism or racism, but I will have committed myself to the public acknowledgement that gender and race issues are issues of justice to which I am endeavouring to respond in an honourable and caring manner.

I will also be opening myself to an inner conversion, for language is intimately related to thought and experience. Language shapes our consciousness far more profoundly than it expresses it, and the continual use of exclusive discriminatory language will only hamper the search for inclusivity, visibility and justice. King writes: 'The power of naming is one of the most decisive human activities constituting the world as experienced. That power has been an almost exclusive male prerogative throughout most of human history.'[49] To become a truly liberated community of faith, the language used in teaching, preaching, hymns, prayers and ritual will have to genuinely reflect inclusivity. The use of 'man' or 'sons' as generic terms for all humanity is simply not acceptable.

Few topics are likely to arouse such passionate feelings as the discussion of sexism in our God-talk. If, however, language does shape our consciousness, it is a topic which we cannot avoid. Brian Wren writes: 'If our naming of God is distorted, our knowledge of God will be also... Naming God truthfully is important, since to name God untruthfully is to delude ourselves and worship an idol.'[50] Rosemary Ruether, in discussing the proscription of idolatry, contends that it should be extended to verbal pictures. She writes: 'When the word *Father* is taken literally to mean that God is male and not female, represented by males and not females, then this word becomes idolatrous.'[51]

For Christian people, the following three factors play a role in our speech about God: our experience, our community of reference and our interpretative tradition.[52] Unfortunately, our discourse about these factors has been imprisoned in a descriptive vocabulary composed by men who believe that they are speaking on behalf of all humanity.

A further complicating factor is the paradoxical situation we find ourselves in as people of faith. On the one hand, we need to name God and to speak about God. On the other hand, no language can claim to be descriptive of God, who cannot be named, except in tropes and figures.[53] From a feminist perspective, exclusive use of male images for God reflects a God who is captive to patriarchal norms and who is simply too small. Great humility, sensitivity and openness are required when seeking to describe the One whose only name is 'I AM WHO I AM'.

*Women and Sexual Violence*

The goal of a feminist theological agenda is to address those areas in which women seek healing and wholeness. 'The depth of human experience is the data of practical theology...'[54] An appalling and too often unacknowledged side of the endemic violence in our society is the sexual violence inflicted on women and children. Even when this fact is acknowledged, it is often not understood that sexual violence is essentially an evil abuse of power. As such, it is a theological problem.

Racism and sexism are structures of domination which create conditions for the abuse of power, a truth all too evident in South African society. A number of churches and certain church leaders have been justly vocal in their condemnation of apartheid. Few, if any, have spoken out against sexism. The deafening silence of the church on issues of sexual violence, though lamentable, is therefore hardly surprising. This raises questions. Why is the church silent? What is the silence of the church communicating? What taboos are being upheld? Who benefits and who suffers from this silence? What can be done to break the silence in order to start the process of healing for both victims and perpetrators?

In a recent empirical investigation I asked 86 people if they had ever heard a sermon on rape. Only one responded positively. Yet, judging from reports in newspapers, rape is a daily occurrence. In Berlin, delegates to the ninth International Conference on AIDS were told that in South Africa at least one woman is raped every 83 seconds, and 95 per cent of rape victims are black.[55] Researchers estimate that only one in twenty rapes is reported. More than 13 000[2] rape cases involving children under the age of 14 were reported between 1989 and 1993 to the South African Child Protection Unit.[56] In 1993, the United Nations observer Ms Angela Masithela requested that the National Peace Secretariat and the Goldstone Commission should investigate violence against women as critical to the peace process.[57] That same year, the Minister of Justice announced the creation of a special court aimed at dealing promptly with rape, incest and wife battering. Again women ask: Why is the church silent?

The task of feminist theologians is to theologically interpret the unheard voices of violated women and children so that our practices in ministry can be transformed continually to reflect love and justice as values of the reign of God.[58] According to James Poling, theological reflections on issues of sexual violence against women and children give rise to theological questions on human nature, the nature of community and of God.[59]

As feminist theologians do not stop at interpretation but are committed to communities of accountability, we become involved in creating the kind of space which will, to paraphrase Nelle Morton's immortal phrase, allow the victims to be 'heard into speech'.[60] This is both a theological and a critical pastoral issue. Not only is the welfare of women and children concerned, but the values which shape our society and the church's role in shaping these values are at stake. Issues which are central to a feminist theological perspective, like human relationships, the work of justice, caring for your neighbour and liberating praxis, are all directly drawn into this work of healing.

## Feminist Spirituality

The word 'spirituality', rather like the word 'feminism', elicits different reactions and has a variety of meanings. Moreover, the plurality of feminist spiritualities[61] which exist today can be baffling to someone seeking to understand what feminist spirituality is. Spirituality is, however, a core element of our feminist theological agenda as we attempt to tease out how our particular history and context have affected the attributes and distinctiveness of our spiritual journeys.

Sandra Schneiders, grappling with the relationship between theology and spirituality, makes the distinction between spirituality as lived experience and spirituality as the academic discipline that studies such experience.[62] As the material for the academic study of spirituality comes from the lived experience of people, theology and spirituality are indeed difficult to view as quite separate entities and are better understood as being in partnership with one another.

What should characterise the spirituality of feminists in South Africa? In any attempt to answer this question it is helpful to see how other feminists, who work within the Christian tradition, describe spirituality. Sandra Schneiders speaks of spirituality as the 'experience of integrating self-transcendence within the horizon of ultimacy'.[63] Joann Conn points out that spirituality includes every dimension of human life and cannot be exclusively associated with the development of prayer and virtue. As such, she finds it problematic for women in three aspects. In the first place, the possibilities for maturity in human and spiritual development are restricted when women are socialised into conformity and passivity, instead of autonomy and self-reliance. Secondly, much Christian teaching and practice has contributed towards such restriction. Lastly, a growing number of women have decided that spiritual maturity can only be accomplished by rejecting biblical tradition, while others have opted for creatively challenging and reconstructing male-dominated Christian tradition.[64]

Clearly, different nuances exist in feminist spirituality. Certainly, it is different from other spiritualities in that it arises from the experience of feminist consciousness. According to Anne Carr, it is 'that mode of relating to God, and everyone and everything in relation to God, exhibited by those who are deeply aware of the historical and cultural restriction of women to a narrowly defined "place" within the wider human (male) "world." '[65]

Despite its diversity, certain common themes, like mutuality, reciprocity, interdependence, relationality and the desire for wholeness, appear in the majority of Christian feminists' writings on spirituality. A sensitivity to the various dimensions of human oppressions, especially in racism, classism, sexism and elitism, and an affirmation of the inviolable humanity of all people and the liberation of all oppressed groups, are also found.

Feminists in South Africa, faced with the difficult task of redefining our place and our praxis in our society, as well as forging relationships across entrenched barriers, seek to articulate a spirituality which is relevant to our context. For this task we will require a communal vision which is based on a profound desire for justice, healing and wholeness. Implementing this vision will require not only individual awareness and growth, but also being open to the spiritual journeys of others who envisage justice and wholeness through interdependence. As such, it is a risky endeavour.

I want to suggest that a contextual feminist spirituality is most effectively described as 'a spirituality of risk'. Why risk? Because the energy and commitment required to deal with the deeply entrenched power of patriarchy make formidable demands, without the promise of lasting and convincing victories; because a feminist spirituality has to struggle to weave together times of active involvement with the work of justice in liberating praxis, and times of withdrawal, silence and prayer, often a politically unpopular activity; because there is an ambiguity in making allowance for mystery away from the certainties of life; because we know that maturity needs growth, truth demands change, and freedom entails making choices; because there is no guarantee of healing for or critical interdependence between people in our ravaged land; because a feminist spirituality which is a 'lived' spirituality entails making oneself vulnerable in every aspect of one's life.

Understandably women fight shy of vulnerability. Since the beginning we have been socialised into a kind of vulnerability that has suited the cause of patriarchy. Nonetheless, healing and wholeness are not possible until those of us who are white women are prepared to acknowledge our complicity in the oppression of black people. We also become vulnerable when we realise how we have co-operated in maintaining patriarchy in our society. We have to examine critically the damage suffered by internalising oppressive images of ourselves, as well as the damage we have inflicted on others. This critical reflection, which is more productive than guilt, comes from our desire to love ourselves, our neighbour and God. Self-critique can also open us to learning from different perspectives and from others' histories. We risk telling our stories, and in so doing we acknowledge that our views are only partial and that, as whites, our own identities are complex, derived from a mixture of origins and cultures. We risk bringing to consciousness what Johann Baptist Metz called 'dangerous memories' and what Sharon Welch describes as 'stories of defeat and of victory, casting of the past in terms of a present of joy, hope, and struggle'.[66]

Justice is at the core of a spirituality of risk. The work of healing and the search for wholeness begin with the search for justice, itself a risky enterprise. But the conviction, in Alice Walker's words, that 'only justice can stop a curse' does not allow us to draw back.[67]

The greatest risk is that we dare to hope. Sharon Welch writes from the American experience of an 'ideology of cultured despair', which she describes as having two distinct features: '(1) the despair is cultured in the sense of its erudite awareness of the extent and complexity of many forms of injustice; and (2) the knowledge of the extent of injustice is accompanied by despair, in the sense of being unable to act in defiance of that injustice.'[68] 'Cultured despair' is an apt description of the attitudes found in sections of the white community in South Africa.

To hope is to refuse to accept despair or defeat. It is our response to the dilemma of being both oppressors and oppressed. Hope is resistance. It actively avoids the void of hopelessness by wrestling with all that seeks to deprive us of hope and disempower us. It risks active daily engagement in liberating praxis. It risks the ambiguity of hoping for relationality while starting from particularity.

Faith and feminism, theology and spirituality, theory and praxis, all come together when aware and committed women become involved in the work of justice and healing. We can choose to claim our power and our capacity to effect good in our society by being willing to risk tension, paradox, uncertainty and even ridicule. To choose to live relationally is to choose to undo evil. As feminist theologians, this is our passion.

[1] See Wilma Jakobsen, 'Ethics in Feminist Theology' in the second volume of *Theology and Praxis* (Cape Town: David Philip, 1994).

[2] Women such as Mary Daly, Carol Christ, Christine Downing and Daphne Hampson come to mind.

[3] See Arvind Sharma (ed.), *Women in the World Religions* (New York: State University of New York Press, 1987).

[4] Katie Cannon *et al.* (The Mud Flower Collective), *God's Fierce Whimsy* (New York: The Pilgrim Press, 1985), p. 94.

[5] See the work of Elisabeth Schüssler Fiorenza in this regard, in particular her *Bread Not Stone* (Boston: Beacon Press, 1984) and *But She Said* (Boston: Beacon Press, 1992). See also Denise Ackermann, 'Liberating the Word: Some Thoughts on Feminist Hermeneutics', *Scriptura*, 44, pp. 1–17.

[6] See Caroline Ramazanoglu, *Feminism and the Contradictions of Oppression* (London: Routlege, 1989) and Cass Sunstein, *Feminism and Political Theory* (Chicago: University of Chicago Press, 1990).

[7] Cannon *et al.*, *God's Fierce Whimsy*, p. 10.

[8] 'The Importance of Feminism for the Women's Movement', *JTSA*, 66, p. 48.

[9] The bibliographical references appearing after authors mentioned in this section merely indicate important works by the specific theologian in her chosen field. For a more detailed account, see Denise Ackermann, 'Pre-empting Patriarchy: A Brief Background Perspective on Feminist Theology', *Apologia*, 2: 6, pp. 7–20.

[10] For a discussion on the different feminist liberation movements, see Rosemary R Ruether, *Sexism and God-Talk: Toward a Feminist Theology* (Boston: Beacon Press, 1983), pp. 216–232.

[11] (Boston: Beacon Press, 1968).

[12] (Boston: Beacon Press, 1973).

[13] Cannon *et al.*, *God's Fierce Whimsy*, p. 138.

[14] See bibliography below.

[15] *Black Womanist Ethics* (Atlanta: Scholars Press, 1988).

[16] 'Womanist Theology,' in J. Plaskow and C. Christ (eds.), *Weaving the Visions: New Patterns in Feminist Spirituality* (San Francisco: Harper and Row, 1989), pp. 179–186.

[17] *White Women's Christ, Black Women's Jesus: Feminist Christology and Womanist Response* (Atlanta: Scholars Press, 1989).

[18] The term is derived from Alice Walker's work *In Search of Our Mothers' Gardens* (New York: Harcourt Brace Jovanovich, 1983), pp. xi–xii. Womanist theologians are deeply connected to the work of black women writers, such as novelists Zora Neale Hurston, Pauli Murray, Toni Morrison, Audre Lorde and Alice Walker, and feminist theorist Bell Hooks.

[19] *Met Mirjam Is Het Begonnen* (Kampen: Kok, 1980). By the same author see also *Zoekend Naar Wat Verloren Ging* (Ten Have: Baarn, 1984) and *New Creation: Christian Feminism and the Renewal of the Earth* (London: SPCK, 1991).

[20] *A Land Flowing with Milk and Honey: Perspectives on Feminist Theology* (Philadelphia: Fortress Press, 1986).

[21] *Women and Spirituality: Voices of Protest and Promise* (London: Macmillan, 1989).

[22] Virginia Fabella and Mercy Oduyoye (eds.), *With Passion and Compassion: Third World Women Doing Theology* (Maryknoll: Orbis, 1988), p. x.

[23] Mercy Oduyoye, *Hearing and Knowing: Theological Reflections on Christianity in Africa* (Maryknoll: Orbis, 1986), and Mercy Oduyoye and M. Kanyoro (eds.), *The Will to Arise: Women, Tradition and the Church in Africa* (Maryknoll: Orbis, 1992).

[24] Thomas Fenton and Mary Heffron, *Women in the Third World* (Maryknoll: Orbis, 1987).

[25] See Letty Russell, Kwok Pui-lan, Ada Maria Isasi-Diaz and Katie Cannon (eds.), *Inheriting Our Mothers' Gardens: Feminist Theology in a Third World Perspective* (Louisville: Westminster Press, 1988); Elsa Tamez, *Through Her Eyes: Women's Theology from Latin America* (Maryknoll: Orbis 1989); Ivone Gebara and Maria Bingemer, *Mary Mother of God, Mother of the Poor* (Maryknoll: Orbis Books, 1987); H. Kyung Chung, *Struggle to be the Sun Again: Introducing Asian Women's Theology* (Maryknoll: Orbis Books, 1990).

[26] 'Neo-Feminist Spirituality: An Evolutionary Perspective', *JTSA*, 66, pp. 53–61.

[27] 'Woman in the Theological Anthropology of the Early Fathers', *JTSA*, 62, pp. 3–13.

[28] *Europe's Role in a South African Methodology: A Sideline and Female Perspective* (Frankfurt: Peter Lang, 1991).

[29] 'The Challenge of Feminism to the Christian Concept of God', *JTSA*, 66, pp. 4–20.

[30] 'The Ordination of Women: A Contribution to the Debate Within the CPSA', *JTSA*, 66, pp. 34–47.

210 Theologies in South Africa

31 'The Relevance of Feminist Theology Within the South African Context' in Denise
Ackermann, Jonathan Draper and Emma Mashinini (eds.), *Women Hold Up Half the Sky: Women
in the Church in Southern Africa* (Pietermaritzburg: Cluster Publications, 1991), pp. 106–121.

32 'Feminist Liberation Theology: A Contextual Option', *JTSA*, 62, pp. 14–28; 'Women,
Human Rights and Religion', *Journal for the Study of Religion*, 5: 2, pp. 65–82; 'Critical Theory,
Communicative Actions and Liberating Praxis: Views of a Feminist Practical Theologian',
*JTSA*, 82, pp 21–36; 'Meaning and Power: Some Key Terms in Feminist Liberation
Theology', *Scriptura*, 44, pp. 18–32.

33 See Mary F. Belenky, Blythe M. Clinchy, Nancy R. Goldberger and Jill M. Tarule,
*Women's Ways of Knowing: The Development of Self, Voice and Mind* (New York: Basic Books,
1986). See also Kathleen Weiler, *Women Teaching for Change: Gender, Class and Power* (South
Hadley: Bergin and Garvey, 1988) and 'Freire and a Feminist Pedagogy of Difference', *Harvard
Educational Review*, 61: 4, pp. 449–474.

34 See the forthcoming work of Christina Landman, *The Piety of Afrikaans Women*
(Pietermaritzburg: Cluster Publications).

35 See Joe Holland and Peter Henriot, *Social Analysis: Linking Faith and Justice* (Maryknoll:
Orbis, 1984).

36 See the contributions of Roxanne Jordaan, Nangula Kathindi, Emma Mashinini, Bernard
Mncube, Brigalia Bam and Thoko Mpumlwana, in Ackermann, Draper and Mashinini, *Women
Hold Up Half the Sky*. See also Bernadette Mosala, 'Black Theology and the Struggle of the
Black Woman in Southern Africa', pp. 129–134, and Bonita Bennett, 'A Critique on the Role
of Women in the Church', pp. 169–174, in Itumeleng Mosala and Buti Tlhagale (eds.), *The
Unquestionable Right to be Free: Essays in Black Theology* (Braamfontein: Skotaville Publishers,
1986).

37 See Jacklyn Cock, *Maids and Madams: A Study in the Politics of Exploitation* (Johannesburg:
Ravan Press, 1980).

38 Cannon *et al.*, *God's Fierce Whimsy*, p. 23.

39 Denise Ackermann, 'Being Woman, Being Human', in Ackermann, Draper and
Mashinini, *Women Hold Up Half the Sky*, pp. 93–105.

40 See Carter Heyward, *The Redemption of God: A Theology of Mutual Relation* (Lanham:
University Press of America, 1982) and Ruether, *Sexism and God-Talk*, pp. 93–115.

41 Denise Ackermann, 'Defining Our Humanity: Thoughts on a Feminist Anthropology',
*JTSA*, 79, pp. 13–23.

42 Heyward, *The Redemption of God*, p. 31.

43 Rosemary R. Ruether, *Women–Church: Theology and Practice* (San Francisco: Harper and
Row, 1985), p. 10.

44 Ibid., pp. 57, 59.

45 See Ruether, *Sexism and God-Talk*, pp. 193–213; L. Russell, *Household of Freedom:
Authority in Feminist Theology* (Philadelphia: Westminster Press, 1987); Susan B. Thistlethwaite,
*Metaphors for the Contemporary Church* (New York: Pilgrim Press, 1983).

46 1 Cor. 12.

47 Susan Thistlethwaite argues that 'linguistic visibility/invisibility' is a more accurate
indicator of what is at stake than the common terminology of 'inclusive' and 'exclusive'. See
Brian Wren, *What Language Shall I Borrow? God-Talk in Worship: A Male Reponse to Feminist
Theology* (London: SCM Press, 1989), p. 241.

48 Ibid., p. 82.

49 King, *Women and Spirituality*, p. 44.

50 Wren, *What Language Shall I Borrow?*, pp. 3, 61.

51 Ruether, *Sexism and God-Talk*, p. 66.

52 Ibid., p. 149.

53 Janet M. Soskice, *Metaphor and Religious Language* (Oxford: Clarendon Press, 1985), p. ix.

[54] Ibid., p. 187.

[55] *Cape Times*, 9 June 1993.

[56] *Argus*, 6 May 1993.

[57] *Cape Times*, 8 March 1993.

[58] James Poling, *The Abuse of Power: A Theological Problem* (Nashville: Abingdon Press, 1991), pp. 186–189.

[59] Ibid., pp. 13–14.

[60] Nelle Morton, *The Journey is Home* (Boston: Beacon Press, 1985), p. 202.

[61] Apart from feminist spiritualities found in different world religions, there are, among others, the spiritualities of the Wicca tradition (Starhawk and Z. Budapest), the Goddess religions (C. Spretnak, C. Christ and N. Goldenberg), eco-feminism (J. Plant) and Mary Daly's 'elemental feminism'.

[62] 'Theology and Spirituality: Strangers, Rivals or Partners', *Horizons*, 2: 13, pp. 253–274.

[63] Ibid., p. 267.

[64] Joann W. Conn, 'Restriction and Reconstruction' in Joann W. Conn (ed.), *Women's Spirituality: Resources for Christian Development* (New York: Paulist Press, 1986), pp. 10–17.

[65] 'On Feminist Spirituality' in *ibid.*, p. 53.

[66] Sharon D. Welch, *A Feminist Ethic of Risk* (Minneapolis: Fortress Press, 1990), p. 155.

[67] Alice Walker, *In Search of Our Mothers' Gardens: Womanist Prose* (San Diego: Harcourt Brace Jovanovich, 1984), pp. 338–342.

[68] Welch, *A Feminist Ethic of Risk*, p. 104.

## Select Bibliography

Ackermann, D., J. Draper and E. Mashinini (eds.) *Women Hold Up Half the Sky: Women in the Church in Southern Africa*. Pietermaritzburg: Cluster Publications, 1991

Daly, Mary. *Beyond God the Father: Toward a Philosophy of Women's Liberation*. Boston: Beacon Press, 1973

Daly, Mary. *The Church and the Second Sex*. Boston: Beacon Press, 1985

Fabella, Virginia and Mercy A. Oduyoye (eds.) *With Passion and Compassion: Third World Women Doing Theology*. Maryknoll: Orbis Books, 1988

Fiorenza, Elisabeth S. *In Memory of Her: A Feminist Theological Reconstruction of Christian Origins*. New York: Crossroad, 1984

Harrison, Beverly W. *Making the Connections: Essays in Feminist Social Ethics*. Boston: Beacon Press, 1985

King, Ursula. *Women and Spirituality: Voices of Protest and Promise*. London: Macmillan, 1989

Plaskow, Judith and Carol P. Christ (eds.) *Weaving the Visions: New Patterns in Feminist Spirituality*. San Francisco: Harper and Row, 1989

Oduyoye, Mercy A. and M. R. A. Kanyoro (eds.) *The Will to Arise: Women, Tradition and the Church in Africa*. Maryknoll: Orbis Books, 1992

Ruether, Rosemary R. *Sexism and God-Talk: Toward a Feminist Theology*. Boston: Beacon Press, 1983

Russell, Letty M. *Household of Freedom: Authority in Feminist Theology*. Philadelphia: Westminster Press, 1987

Tamez, Elsa (ed.) *Through Her Eyes: Women's Theology from Latin America*. Maryknoll: Orbis Books, 1989

Thistlethwaite, Susan B. *Sex, Race, and God: Christian Feminism in Black and White*. New York: Crossroad, 1989

Trible, Phyllis. *Texts of Terror: Literary–Feminist Readings of Biblical Narratives*. Philadelphia: Fortress Press, 1984

# 18

# Kairos Theology

## ALBERT NOLAN

Kairos theology is the name we give to the type of theology which was first committed to writing in a well-known document signed by more than 150 church persons and published in South Africa on 25 September 1985. It was entitled *The Kairos Document: Challenge to the Churches. A Theological Comment on the Political Crisis in South Africa*. Very seldom, if ever, in the history of South Africa had a theological statement made such an impact upon the country – its churches, its politicians and its people. Never before had so many people in South Africa been caught up in a theological controversy, for the document was thought of as indeed very controversial.

Nor was the impact of the *Kairos Document* limited to South Africa. It was read and discussed in many parts of the world and gave rise to Kairos groups in several countries, as well as other Kairos documents (for example, in Central America) and a seven-nation document known as *The Road to Damascus: Kairos and Conversion*.

While the idea of a Kairos theology originated in South Africa and while articles on this kind of theology can be found in numerous journals, the only book that explores the different expressions of Kairos theology was edited in Nicaragua and published in Spanish, *El Kairos en Centroamerica*. It has not been translated into English.

Our study of Kairos theology in this chapter will be based almost exclusively upon the original South African document of September 1985.

### The Story Behind the Document

The *Kairos Document* was an initiative of the Institute for Contextual Theology (ICT) in Johannesburg. However, it was not planned or even foreseen by the staff of ICT. It simply happened as a result of ICT's method of doing theology.

The Institute does not teach theology; it simply enables people to do their own theological reflection upon their own praxis and experience. The staff of ICT are active in bringing Christians together, facilitating discussion and action, recording what people say, and doing whatever research may be required to support the reflections, arguments and actions of the people.

It was in pursuance of this method that two staff members brought together a group of about ten interested parties in Soweto one Saturday morning in July 1985 to reflect upon South Africa's latest crisis, the recently declared State of Emergency. As usual, it was thought that this meeting might lead to a plan of action which might involve some more Christians. Nobody was thinking about a theological document or anything like that.

The meeting was more animated and fruitful than usual. More meetings were held. More and more people were involved. The staff were given assignments to do, like biblical research into the meaning of Chapter 13 of the letter to the Romans and historical research into the Christian tradition on violence and tyranny. Minutes were taken at these meetings, and the insights of the participants and the research done by the staff and others were collated into a document. This was amended again and again with a view to the publication of a pamphlet, until someone suggested that it should become a document or a statement signed by all the participants, as well as others from around the country, as a challenge to the churches *from below.*

And that indeed is what it became: theology from below. The seriousness of the crisis, together with the anger and frustration of the people, motivated the participants to speak about what they believed and what they did not believe. The Institute as a facilitating rather than an authoritative body recorded what the participants said without any censorship or amendment. All the participants became what we later called 'the Kairos theologians'.

## A Contextual Theology

Contextual theology is the kind of theology which reflects, explicitly and consciously, upon its context in the light of the gospel of Jesus Christ. In other words, it deals with the problems, the issues and the questions that arise for a Christian in any particular context and especially in a context of oppression and suffering.

The *Kairos Document* was vividly and dramatically contextual; it came straight out of the flames of the townships in 1985. Those who had no experience of the oppression, the repression, the sufferings and the struggles of the people in the townships at that time were not able to understand the faith questions that were being tackled here, let alone the answers. What were these questions or concerns?

The first question or concern was about the intolerable suffering of the people at the time. In their meetings and discussions the theologians, priests, ministers and other church workers who came to be known as the Kairos theologians related one horror story after another about what the police and the army were doing to the people in the townships. Most of these Kairos theologians were quite ordinary pastors, and many of them had never been involved in anything that might be called 'political'. They were simply horrified by what they had seen with their own eyes, and they came to the meetings with the smell of teargas still in their nostrils. They came with very serious and urgent faith questions. Where was God in all of this? What did God want his ministers to do in this crisis? What could they do or say to stop the violence, the violence of the aggressor?

It is ironical that the *Kairos Document* should subsequently have been accused of promoting violence and even murder. Or perhaps this is just another indication of the very different perceptions of what was happening in the townships and of who was responsible for the violence.

The second concern was that all of this was being done in the name of Christianity. The Bible (especially Romans 13) was being used to justify the actions of the State. This gave rise to urgent questions about the 'Christianity' of the State and about the way in which it used the Bible. As ministers of the Word of God, the Kairos theologians felt that they simply had to contradict this 'State Theology' — as strongly and as unequivocally as possible. People had to know that this was not Christianity but, in fact, the very opposite of all that we mean by Christianity.

A third concern was the ineffectiveness of the official church response to apartheid and, even more so, to the crisis created by the State of Emergency. Official church statements were not only too mild and too vague but they were simply not bringing the full power and challenge of the gospel of Jesus Christ to bear upon the actual situation. There was no wish to be disloyal to the churches or to embarrass church leaders. The question that arose out of the realities of this socio-historical context was: How can we enable the gospel to come across powerfully and effectively to all the people in these times?

Closely linked to this was the concern about the dangerous temptation of neutrality or sitting on the fence. We had all seen or experienced the temptation to remain on the sidelines and to argue that the problems were political and therefore none of our business or, at least, that the church must never take sides but offer the people some kind of 'third way'. The very serious concern of the Kairos theologians was that we might be tempted to betray the gospel and to betray the suffering people of the townships by our neutrality. Was it not our neutrality, among other things, that had enabled this oppressive system to continue for so long and to reach the brutality and fierceness of the repression of the 1980s? How could we possibly not take sides against such evil, injustice and cruelty? And what does reconciliation and forgiveness mean in such circumstances? These were serious theological questions.

Another concern that gave rise to some real searching questions was the crisis in the church itself. The church itself was divided. There was now a white church and a black church even within the same denominations. The two no longer understood the implications of their Christian faith in the same way. Both the oppressor and the oppressed had allegiance to the same Christ, the same beliefs and the same church. That was a really serious crisis for Christianity. Some of the participants were asking whether in such circumstances Christianity had not become so ambiguous that it no longer had any meaning at all.

One of the greatest concerns of the Kairos theologians was that the church had not been the bearer of hope in our society. It had criticised, it had blamed, it had been cautious and careful but it had not preached the bold and prophetic Christian message of hope. It was felt that the Christian message of hope was being neglected and overlooked precisely at a time when almost everyone in South Africa was desperately in need of hope for the future. But just how does one preach hope in such circumstances?

Last but not least, it was strongly felt that the time for talking was over. What was needed and what the people were crying out for was action. The church was being accused of discussing, debating, preaching and making statements but not acting. This gave rise to the very important question: What action must the church, as church, take in these circumstances?

We see, then, how this particular socio-historical context of oppression in 1985 gave rise to numerous theological questions. We can also see that although the questions have some similarity to the questions asked by people in other contexts of oppression, these were decidedly the questions arising out of the context of South Africa in 1985.

## A Theology of Liberation

Kairos theology has much in common with liberation theology. In fact it might well be described as a species or type of liberation theology. Like other theologies of liberation, it makes use of social analysis and is driven by Christian faith to struggle for the liberation of the oppressed.

Social analysis permeates every page of the *Kairos Document*. One section of the document is entitled 'Social Analysis', but the process of analysis and references to social analysis and its importance can be found throughout the document.

The social analysis of the *Kairos Document* was simply the commonly held analysis of black people in South Africa, namely that our society was racially divided into white and black and that structurally the whites were oppressors and blacks were the oppressed. This was not a matter of accusing all whites or excusing all blacks. Some whites might be on the side of the oppressed and some blacks might be themselves oppressors, as in the homelands. But a social analysis of the structure of our society reveals a power relationship of oppressor and oppressed — just as it does in Latin America and many other countries.

Kairos theology, like all other theologies of liberation, has no difficulty with this analysis of society into oppressor and oppressed because it is exactly the same as the analysis we find throughout the Bible. The *Kairos Document* is at pains to point out what the Bible says about the oppressor and about the oppressed — and therefore about the liberation of the oppressed. But the analysis of the *Kairos Document* goes one step further. The South African government is not only oppressive, it is also illegitimate, and at that moment (1985) it had become tyrannical. According to the Kairos theologians, a tyrannical regime has no moral legitimacy and has become the enemy of God.

One sees here how closely related social analysis and theological reflection are. And yet theology must go one step further in order to qualify as a genuine Kairos theology. It must analyse and reflect upon a particular *kairos* or critical moment of history.

Kairos theology does not only do social analysis of the general situation, it does conjunctural analysis, or analysis of the particular crisis at that point in time because of the conjuncture, or meeting, of opposing forces. The crisis in 1985 was brought about by, on the one side, tyrannical repression (detentions, trials, killings, torture, bannings, propaganda, states of emergency) and, on the other side, all-out resistance (boycotts, strikes, uprisings, burnings and armed struggle). This was the *kairos* at that time.

## A Prophetic Theology

A prophetic theology is one that begins by reading the signs of the times. This is done not only by means of a social analysis of the times, but also by interpreting the times from God's point of view. Thus a particular point in time can be seen as a visitation from God, a warning, an opportunity, a promise, a punishment, a reward or a call to conversion. Theological interpretation here means discerning what kind of time we are living in and what God is saying to us at this particular moment of time.

Prophecy or prophetic theology always includes, implicitly or explicitly, a call to conversion, or *metanoia*. And this call is generally preceded by a warning about what terrible consequences or punishments will ensue if there is no repentance and conversion. On the other hand there is also the prophetic promise of rewards and blessings in the future if there is a change of heart, or *metanoia*.

Kairos theology is really just another name for prophetic theology. The *Kairos Document* describes what it is trying to do as prophetic theology. In other words, the Kairos theology of the *Kairos Document* was simply the explicit revival of doing theology in a prophetic mode with a strong emphasis upon the reading of the signs of the times at a very particular time, or *kairos*, in the history of church and society in South Africa.

*Kairos* is a Greek word which is used in the Bible to refer to 'a moment of truth', 'a crisis that is shaking the foundations', 'a moment of grace and opportunity, a favourable time in which God issues a challenge to decisive action'. This is how the *Kairos Document* interpreted the crisis of 1985 in South Africa. It goes on to say: 'It is a dangerous time because, if this opportunity is missed, and allowed to pass by, the loss for the church, for the gospel and for all the people of South Africa will be immeasurable.'

One recognises the prophetic warning here, which is then underlined in the document by the quotation from Luke 19:44, where the word *kairos* is actually used in the Greek text. The reference to this time as 'a moment of grace and opportunity' constitutes the prophetic promise that this *kairos* holds out for the future of South Africa — for church and society. The statement that God is issuing 'a challenge to decisive action' is of course the call to conversion and action.

The essence of Kairos theology is the act of interpreting a particular crisis as a *kairos* in the biblical sense of an encounter with God, who is speaking to us now with warnings, promises and a call to action. It is an act of reading the signs of the times. It is a reflection upon a faith experience rather than an intellectual conclusion drawn from biblical texts and principles.

Still more important is the recognition that when we read the signs of the times or interpret our *kairos* we are saying something about the future. Prophetic theology is concerned not only about the present but also about the future. In fact prophetic theology can see the future, or various possible futures, in the present crisis. It can predict future catastrophes if nothing is done now, and it can promise great blessing if the present opportunity is taken seriously.

In the Greek words of our theological tradition, the present moment of truth and decision is our *kairos* and the future catastrophe or blessing is our *eschaton*. In practice, what this means is that prophetic theology, and therefore Kairos theology, should always be, in the final analysis, a theology of hope.

The *Kairos Document* is in the end a message of hope, and the section on hope (4.6) should be noted and emphasised. The hopefulness of this kind of theology is sometimes overlooked because of the powerfully critical stance that the document takes towards the *status quo* of church and government. The theology of the government and dominant white minority, the theology of the oppressor, is called State Theology and is condemned in no uncertain terms. It is associated with the devil and the Antichrist.

Not only that, even the usual unprophetic theology of the church is criticised. The Kairos theologians were unanimous in their criticism of church statements and abstract generalisations. They began to label this as 'Church Theology'.

Like all prophets, the Kairos theologians were critical of the present and hopeful about the future. Like all prophets, they were also very emotional about the evils of the present. Feelings of anger and frustration, and condemnations in terms of clear-cut distinctions between good and evil, God and the devil, are characteristic of the *Kairos Document*. One of the criticisms of the document at the time was that it was too emotional.

When you think about it, this is an accusation that could have been levelled against any of the great biblical prophets. They were all very emotional, but that was their strength. One of the things that made the *Kairos Document* so powerful (and so controversial) was the feelings that pervaded its message. There is, of course, no other way of doing prophetic theology.

Perhaps there is one difference between Kairos theology and what is generally thought of as prophetic theology. Kairos theology is a community theology. It is not the theology of an individual but the reflections and feelings of groups of Christians at a particular time in particular circumstances. Prophetic theology is generally associated with an individual prophet or an individual writer. In producing a document signed by 153 Christians, Kairos theology initiated the process of democratising theology itself.

## Assessment

Despite its obvious value and importance, Kairos theology has its limitations. Theology and theological reflection must cover a far larger area of issues and concerns than only social and political crises. There are matters of permanent concern like sin, values, God, creation, Jesus Christ, salvation, the environment and so forth. And there are more personal concerns like relationships, prayer and death that any comprehensive theology would have to deal with. Kairos theology could never claim to be a complete and comprehensive theology.

There are also very serious limitations with regard to the practice of Kairos theology. Very few people today are *doing* Kairos theology, and nothing much is being written in this prophetic mode. South Africa faces even more serious crises today than it did in 1985, but there is very little theological reflection upon our present *kairos* as our moment of truth. A few years ago, ICT published a pamphlet about 'the violence'. They called it the new *kairos*. But this line of thought has not generated much interest.

In 1989 Christians from seven third-world countries co-operated in a venture that has been called the international Kairos. A document entitled *The Road to Damascus: Kairos and Conversion* was signed by hundreds of Christians in South Africa, Namibia, South Korea, the Philippines, El Salvador, Nicaragua and Guatemala. The document issued a prophetic call to conversion addressed to all Christians who are associated with the oppression of the poor and the indigenous people of the third world. It caused a stir at the time, but the initiative was not followed up, and it is difficult to assess how much this kind of Kairos theology still influences the thinking and the actions of Christians in the world today. Perhaps that in itself is part of our present crisis.

## Select Bibliography

Brown, Robert M. (ed.) *Kairos: Three Prophetic Challenges to the Church*. Grand Rapids: Eerdmans, 1990. This book contains the texts of the *Kairos Document, The Road to Damascus,* and *Kairos Central America.*

*Kairos in Africa* (workshop proceedings). Harare: EDICESA, 1989

*El Kairos en Centroamerica*, coordinator Jose Maria Vigil. Managua: Ediciones Nicarao, 1990

*Challenge to the Church: The Kairos Document and Commentaries.* Geneva: World Council of Churches, 1985

'The *Kairos* Debate: A Dutch Reformed Response', *JTSA*, 57 (December 1986)

Suggit, J. 'The *Kairos* Debate: Words or the Word?', *JTSA*, 60 (September 1987)

Albert Nolan, 'The Eschatology of the *Kairos Document*', *Missionalia*, 15:2 (August 1987)

# 19

# Theological and Religious Pluralism

## ROBIN PETERSEN

The preceding chapters have outlined some of the models current in South African theology today. In light of the variety of these' options, the question of theological pluralism emerges with extreme urgency. Clearly, these different models represent different understandings and interpretations not only of the Bible and the Christian tradition, but also of theological method and analyses of the social and political context. There is, therefore, a *de facto* pluralism of theological models. The question that this poses, however, is how one is to assess the nature and status of this pluralism. Is it something to be celebrated or to be overcome? On what grounds can one, or should one, make a choice between options? Do the models make competing claims, or are they complementary to each other? If competing, then by what norms could one possibly assess these competing claims? What of those models excluded in this analysis? Are there limits to pluralism? And what of the claims made by other religious traditions in our religiously pluralistic society?[1]

Only some of these questions will be tentatively answered in this chapter. All, however, need to be kept in mind. And they are not the only ones, for the issue of pluralism goes far deeper than this theological or even religious context. As David Tracy has argued, pluralism is the basic context of our post-modern life.[2] It is not simply that we have different theological options available to us; these different options are signs of a far more fundamental realisation that life is inherently plural, made up of irreducible differences.

This pluralism is seen in wide variety of contexts. In our political life it is reflected in the recognition that we do not all think alike, and that even in the liberation movements there are significant and irreducible differences in analyses of the situation and in visions of a new society. This political pluralism is in turn expressed in the felt need for political tolerance and multi-party democracy as necessary components of a democratic social and political life. In our cultural life, the compelling arguments – advanced by feminists and by theorists of race and identity – that politics is about respecting difference, not seeking to overcome it and reducing everything to the same, are further signs of this radical pluralism. So too is the conflict of interpretations over significant events, texts, rituals and symbols that occupies much of our political, social and cultural debate.

Finally, pluralism is seen to be the defining feature of post-modern philosophy. If modernity was premissed on the idea that all reality could ultimately be subsumed by reason (Kant), or by the movement of the World Spirit (Hegel), or by a rigorous quest for its essence (Husserl), post-modern thought vigorously resists this 'totalising', all-encompassing quest. For it is precisely this quest, in the opinion of Levinas,[3] that expresses and contributes to the repressive, imperialist and ultimately destructive impulse of modern Western thought and politics. Resistance to this universalising and imperialist tendency, therefore, means an assertion of the radically, irreducibly plural nature of human existence. It implies a fundamental respect for the Other, one that does not and will not attempt to reduce the Other to the Same. Life, according to Levinas, is basically dialogical, like a good conversation. It is a relation that retains its distance; it is a face-to-face engagement that respects the 'otherness of the other'; it is a commitment to hearing the voice of the other.

To summarise: Pluralism is a given fact of political, cultural, theological and religious life. It is not merely a surface phenomenon that can somehow be subsumed under a grand account of the whole. It is radical and irreducible. It calls for great sensitivity, for putting aside preconceived notions of the Other and of oneself. It means that easy reductions of otherness to our own comfortable categories must be resisted as imperialistic and authoritarian. It implies the ethical response of dialogue and conversation, themes that will be explored below.

## Theological Pluralism

Theological pluralism is nothing new. It begins within the biblical text itself: in the conflicts between Paul and Peter, between Paul and James, and, even more crucially, between the four gospel presentations of Jesus. It has become increasingly clear to modern scholarship that attempts to harmonise these accounts does them a fundamental disservice, and that it is precisely their theological and interpretative pluralism which is their strength.

In terms of the development of the Christian tradition, the fact of pluralism is a constant threat and challenge to theology. Indeed, most surveys and analyses of the history and development of Christian thought are structured in terms of this fact. It seems that each generation produces its defining conflicts of interpretation: Augustine and Pelagius over the nature of salvation and grace; the Antiochenes and Alexandrians over the correct understanding of the nature and person of Christ; the split between West and East over the relation of the Spirit to Christ in the Trinity (the *filioque* controversy); Abelard and Anselm and their confrontation over the meaning of the atonement and salvation; Thomas and Bonaventure and their conflict over the nature of theology and its relation to philosophy; the understanding of the spiritual life and the 'soul's return to God' in the radical mysticism of Meister Eckhart and in the love mysticism of Bernard of Clairvaux.

All these 'inner-Catholic' conflicts were radicalised by the Protestant

Reformation, which in turn had very soon to face conflicts within its own ranks between Lutherans, Calvinists and Zwinglians, and between all three of these and the Anabaptists. In later centuries, conflicts emerged within these respective traditions themselves between the orthodox, the pietists and the emerging theological liberalism. In our century, one of the major inner-Protestant conflicts has been between the neo-orthodoxy of Barth and the theology of culture and history of Tillich. More recently there is the conflict between evangelicals and ecumenicals, between charismatics and liberation theologians, between feminists and marxists, and so on *ad infinitum* (and sometimes *ad nauseam*).

Different strategies have been adopted in different periods to deal with this pluralism. Generally speaking, a distinction has been made between those differences that are seen to be unessential (*adiaphora*) and those that are considered essential to the faith. This strategy partly explains why even at its narrowest, a fairly wide range of theological options has been tolerated in the tradition. It also explains why, at certain crucial moments, this tolerance has been restricted and positions have been condemned as heretical.

This distinction between tolerated difference and heresy is, quite clearly, not a fixed one. Even a cursory reading of the traditions will show that positions once considered orthodox often become defined as heretical. (Unfortunately, the reverse process does not usually occur, except by default.)

Defining something as heretical is no trite matter. The church, therefore, has traditionally attempted to safeguard the procedure by linking it to the authority of the apostolic councils. These councils (the most famous of which were Nicaea where the trinitarian formulations were settled, and Chalcedon, where the Christological settlement was reached) adjudicated between competing positions, and often developed compromises that reflected the central concerns of both parties. However, the authority of the councils was always fairly tenuous, a fact seen in the reversals of decisions of previous councils, and made particularly visible after the split between East and West, and the refusal of the Eastern Church to recognise any of the councils that took place subsequent to that split.

But the most crucial crisis for the authority of the councils emerged with the Protestant Reformation. With their appeal to *sola Scriptura*, the Reformers sought to locate a new source of authority that would allow them to justify their own theological position over against Catholic tradition as it had developed down through the centuries.[4] This appeal to Scripture alone provided them with a powerful weapon against what they saw as the departures of the Catholic Church from the gospel. However, the conflicts that emerged between them at a very early stage — especially over the nature of the eucharist — showed that this principle did not, in fact, establish a more secure position from which to decide between theological models and options. Rather, it led to an increasing inability for these churches to use this standard to resolve their fundamental disputes with each other and, even more critically, with the Anabaptists, who used the Reformers' own critique against them.

This breakdown in authority — or, at very least, its radical dispersal — meant that the reality of theological pluralism established itself as a major feature of the Christian landscape. The consequences of this pluralism were not always happy —

different traditions, denominations, and defenders of theological positions literally went to war over these differences. Far from being a source of celebration, theological difference became for many a source of terror.

In some crucial ways, the eighteenth-century Enlightenment was a reaction to this religious and theological intolerance. The hope of the philosophers of modernity was that the exercise of reason would enable a peaceful resolution of these disputes, or at least show that they were not worth fighting about. In its early confidence, it was hoped that pluralism itself could be overcome by the exercise of reason (Kant) or the progress of reason through history (Hegel). This optimism was, of course, not to last, although it set the stage for almost a century of theological toleration and exploration, at least within the Protestant West.

The traumas of the twentieth century shattered this easy confidence, and in that crisis of confidence the voices of a new generation of theologians, led by Karl Barth, radically challenged this liberal pluralism by a restatement of the great Reformed theme of *sola Scriptura, sola fide*. Barth insisted once more that all theological construction be premissed on the centrality of Jesus as God's Word witnessed to by Scripture. In the struggle of the German Confessing Church against Hitler, Barth and others reintroduced in the Barmen Declaration the language of 'confession' as a normative statement of faith in a given situation.[5]

In our own South African context, the trajectory established by Barmen has been pursued in the struggle against apartheid. The history of this development has led from the Cottesloe Conference of 1960 to *The Message to the People of South Africa* issued by the South African Council of Churches in 1968; from the Ottawa Declaration of the World Alliance of Reformed Churches that apartheid is a heresy, to the Belhar Confession that the heresy of apartheid constitutes a *status confessionis* (in other words, that this confession is central to the faith and cannot be left to individual conscience); and finally from the *Kairos Document*, with its strong prophetic denunciation of the 'god of apartheid' as the Antichrist, to the Lusaka Declaration that the church is called to side with the oppressed in the liberation struggle.[6]

These developments have brought to the fore the question of the limits to pluralism. Despite recognition of difference, tolerance of other positions and hesitation to assert that any one position is capable of expressing the whole, the debates on apartheid and its theological justification have indicated that the need to be able to say no at critical moments remains an important dimension of theological practice. But it is also clear from this trajectory from Barmen to Lusaka that the terms of the discussion have changed fundamentally. For the debates around heresy, confession and declaration are now couched far more in terms of ethical praxis than strictly inner-theological ones. So although the relevance of heresy and confession has seemingly been reinstated, this has taken place within the context of a fundamental shift to a basically pluralist theological position. Thus, for instance, the old confessional, denominational and even religious dividing lines are subordinated to a greater unity against ethico-theological threats to the understanding and interpretation of the gospel and Christian faith.

## Theological Pluralism and the Ambiguity of All Traditions

It is important to bring together these two insights: that theological pluralism is rooted in Scripture, tradition and in the nature of human reality, and the fact that it still remains necessary to be able to say no at crucial times and in crucial instances. One way is to suggest that pluralism is something to be celebrated at the same time as stressing the fundamental ambiguity of all traditions and interpretations. This means that all traditions and interpretations need continually to be tested, not only by fidelity to Scripture, or to the tradition in which they stand, or even by the mutually enriching perspective of other traditions with which they are in dialogue, but also by a continual assessment of the ethical and political consequences of their position.

The claim of past South African constitutions that this is a 'Christian country' is contradicted not only by the travesty of Christianity which this claim implies, but by the facts of religious pluralism themselves. As David Chidester has pointed out, South Africa has always been a place of religious pluralism, with significant minority populations of Muslims, Hindus, Jews, as well as Buddhists, Confucians and Parsees.[7] Despite this, the fact of religious pluralism has not had a significant impact on theological thinking in South Africa until fairly recently. It is really only with the growing involvement of people of different religious faiths in the struggle against apartheid that the reality of religious pluralism has begun to have an impact on theological production.

One of the footnotes to the second edition of the *Kairos Document* stated: 'What is said here of Christianity and the Church could be applied, *mutatis mutandis*, to other faiths and other religions in South Africa; but this document is addressed to "all who bear the name Christian." '[8] This brief concession to the fact of religious pluralism was a somewhat unsatisfactory answer to a challenge levelled by a prominent Muslim theologian, Moulana Faried Esack. He had written:

> The Kairos theologians have not understood the universal nature of what they have produced and so they offer it only to Christians. Their inability to do so does not stem from a 'Christian humility' or a fear that adherents of other faiths may reject it. It comes from a deep-rooted Christian (European) arrogance that leads to ignorance of other faiths and indifference to the possible contribution of their adherents to the creation of a just society.[9]

Clearly, the challenge of pluralism must go beyond the easy dismissal of the critique in the *Kairos Document*.

What, then, is the status of Esack's challenge? It is this. As Christians and Muslims have discovered in their united struggles against apartheid, there is more that unites them than divides them. Furthermore, the continual production of theology, even progressive liberation theology, that takes place outside of the context of the inter-religious, inter-faith dialogue, continues to perpetuate another form of exclusion and domination of a minority. Inter-religious dialogue and solidarity is therefore a profound ethical and theological challenge. In fact, as theological reflection in South Africa turns from resistance to reconstruction,[10] its challenge will become intensified. At that point it is possible that David Tracy's claim that 'there is no more difficult or more pressing question on the theological horizon than that of inter-religious dialogue'[11] will become a reality in our situation.

Tracy also illuminates a challenge thus far all but ignored in the limited inter-religious dialogue that has occurred in South Africa, and that is the way in which all three monotheistic religions unite against the 'archaic Other' of 'traditional'[12] African religion.[13] The paradigm of African theology has perhaps more than any other insisted on the importance of these religions and practices for a reconstructed Christian theology,[14] but this has nevertheless still been done from the perspective of Christian faith and not dialogue. Perhaps the site of this dialogue is located outside the so-called mainstream, as members and leaders of the African indigenous churches think through their faith in dialogue with these religious and cultural practices. Whatever the case, the challenge of this dialogue becomes ever more clear.

## Confrontation, Co-optation or Dialogue?

The foregoing discussion has already slipped from religious pluralism to the notion of dialogue as the response to this fact.[15] But it is by no means uncontested that dialogue is the best response, and so we need to step back somewhat and reflect on different responses to the phenomenon of religious pluralism.

### Confrontation

For many centuries the fact of other religions was dealt with by means of confrontation. This took two forms: conquest or conversion. It may seem, at first glance, somewhat unfair to lump these two strategies together. After all, there is a significant difference between seeking to eradicate one's Other and seeking to convert them. But the differences notwithstanding, both positions operate with two common assumptions that often feed into each other: that Christian faith is the one true religion, and that all other religions will therefore gradually disappear through its spread.

That this advancement sometimes took the form of conquest and coercion, and other times took the form of evangelisation and persuasion, often seems more the product of historical circumstance than theological rationale. Even the most well-intended of missionaries caused such radical and disruptive changes in the cultures, customs, religions and social structures of pre-colonial African life, for instance, that their evangelistic 'success' can in no small part be attributed to the effectiveness of this disruption. In other words, even seemingly non-coercive conversions were often the result of a long process of uprooting and disrupting the social and cultural life of a people, thus 'making them ripe' for conversion.[16]

Despite the recognition that other religions are not simply going to disappear in the triumphal march of Christian history, and despite the realisation that conversions to Christianity from the other major historical religions remain extremely few, significant sectors of the Christian church continue to believe in the superiority of Christianity for all people and the necessity to convert adherents of other religions, who, in this understanding, are outside of salvation.

This position cannot, of course, acknowledge pluralism, except as a challenge to greater evangelism. It certainly will not subscribe to a commitment to dialogue as the appropriate response to the question. Within this position, however, there are differences in emphasis and understanding that need to be acknowledged. Perhaps the most nuanced and the most influential of theological positions in this mould is that of Karl Barth.

It is often believed that Barth maintained that all religions, except Christianity, were in fact an expression of unbelief, the attempt by human beings to grasp God rather than be grasped by God. This is not an accurate picture of his position. True, he does claim this of all religions, but he does not exclude Christianity *seen as a religion* from this critique.[17] To the idolatry of religion, Barth counterposes faith as the obedient response to revelation. Faith is thus the critical principle that cuts across all religions.

Thus far, Barth's position could be construed as a prophetic critique of all religion by means of faith. As such, it provides a rhetorically useful polemic against the very real ambiguity of religion, and a powerful response to critiques of religion as mere projection. In terms of dialogue between the religions, it is a timely warning of this danger. But Barth does not stop there. He goes on to exempt Christianity from this general critique by means of an argument that God in Christ is revealed to the church, and thus this *one* religion has been justified and made true by God.[18] Thus once more, the possibility of inter-religious dialogue is closed off.

## Co-optation

The recognition that the other world religions were not simply going to 'go away', and the growing understanding that they have something significant to offer Christian faith, generated many new attempts at a theological understanding of them that did not give up on the claim of the centrality of Jesus for salvation. The most famous of these attempts was the notion of the 'anonymous Christian' developed by Karl Rahner, the most influential Catholic theologian of the twentieth century. This important notion argued that the other faiths provide authentic understandings of God and ways of salvation that are ultimately the ways of Jesus Christ. Other believers, therefore, are not strangers to the faith, but are in fact anonymous Christians. This, Rahner hoped, would promote a sensitive and fruitful dialogue, where the Other is not treated as a complete stranger.

Critics of his position point out that to enter a dialogue with people of other faiths with the presupposition that they are, in fact, already like us, but they just don't know it, undermines the fundamental respect necessary for dialogue to continue. To be fair to Rahner, his intent with the doctrine was an 'inner Christian' one; that is, the doctrine was meant for Christians and not as the starting point for conversation with others. However, one cannot so easily separate the two, and dialogue partners of other faiths were justifiably annoyed at being claimed as Christians, and anonymous ones at that.

## Dialogue

Separating dialogue from confrontation and co-optation, as is done here, is not meant to imply that these other strategies do not also talk of the need for serious dialogue. The problem, however, is that in 'confrontation' dialogue is reduced to another, less overt form of evangelism, and in 'co-optation' it is compromised by the starting assumption that Christ is normative for all religions, whether they accept him or not. It has been argued that these qualifications fundamentally undermine the grounds of true dialogue.[19] What then are those grounds, and how do Christian theologians come to terms with the universalistic claims associated with their faith and theology?

### 'Theocentric Moves'

In this move, what is proposed is a 'paradigm shift from a Christianity-centred or Jesus-centred to a God-centred model of the universe of faiths'.[20] Likewise, Raimundo Pannikar of India calls for a theocentric model which stresses that the Ultimate Reality is precisely the many names and understandings of God in the different religions. What this means for dialogue is that all religions, including Christianity, must give up the claim to be universal. All religions are limited embodiments of the many-sided Ultimate Reality. In dialogue, therefore, each religion in its specificity is enriched by the insights of the other.

What of the universal claims of the Christ? Pannikar argues for a notion of the universal Christ as mediator between God and humans, and the necessity for this universal Christ to take on historical and particular form. But he goes on to argue that no one historical embodiment of the universal Christ is possible, including Jesus. Jesus is the embodiment of the reality of the universal Christ, but he is not the only one. As this embodiment, he is able to save, but he is not the only saviour. For Christians, however, the claim that Jesus is the Christ means that for them 'this Lord [Christ] whose Lordship can appear in innumerable forms has taken for me an ultimate form which is indissolubly connected with Jesus of Nazareth'.[21]

## The Uniqueness of Christ and the Inter-Religious Dialogue

The move to a theocentric model raises the question of the place and role of Jesus for Christians. Does true dialogue involve the necessity of moving away from a Christocentric model to a God-centred model?

Knitter helpfully outlines the various ways in which the role of Christ is formulated by various theologies.[22] Evangelicals hold to an *exclusive uniqueness* in which true revelation and salvation are found in Jesus alone; Catholics hold to an *inclusive uniqueness* where God's salvation in Jesus includes other religions (the anonymous Christian); and the theocentric model, which he proposes, argues for a *relational uniqueness*, which affirms that Jesus is unique but not exclusive or normative.

David Tracy has questioned this move, as it seems for him to merely 'postpone the question'. In other words, he argues, as Christians it is only through Christ that we know God as pure, unbounded love. Moving to a theocentric model thus simply raises the question of how we come to know the God of Jesus outside the revelation of that God in Jesus Christ.[23] It is thus *as Christians* that we enter the dialogue, with our specific claims and faith experience, but at the same time ready to risk all in a true confrontation with the otherness of the Other. Three things are crucial for dialogue, according to Tracy: self-respect and respect for one's own tradition; self-exposure to the Other as Other; and a 'willingness to risk all in the questioning and inquiry that constitutes the dialogue itself'.[24]

Knitter's argument, however, seems to have much in common with Tracy's, for he too states that for true dialogue to occur, three basic attitudes must exist: it must be based on personal religious experience and firm truth-claims (there must, in other words, be the willingness not only to affirm another but also to challenge another); it must be based on the recognition of the possible truth in all religions; and finally, it must be based on openness to the possibility of genuine change and conversion.[25]

## Conclusion

This chapter raises far more questions than it answers. But this is precisely the nature of theological reflection in the context of theological and religious pluralism. As was argued at the beginning of the chapter, the nature of our pluralistic world means the end of any totalising narratives of truth, knowledge or even religion. What confronts us is the ethical, epistemological and practical challenge of 'dialogue with the Other', a dialogue which takes our self and the Other seriously, and which binds us together in the solidarity of a mutual struggle for human freedom, dignity and understanding.

[1] David Chidester's book *Religions of South Africa* (London: Routledge, 1992) provides a good background for the understanding of the histories and realities of our religiously pluralistic context.

[2] *Plurality and Ambiguity: Hermeneutics, Religion, Hope* (San Francisco: Harper and Row, 1987).

[3] E. Levinas, *Totality and Infinity: An Essay on Exteriority* (Pittsburgh: Duquesne University Press, 1969).

[4] Neither Calvin nor Luther, however, rejected the authority of the Councils completely; they simply applied the same standard of *sola Scriptura* to them as well.

[5] For a good discussion of the importance of the Barmen Declaration, its relevance for South Africa, and a revised translation of the document itself, see the *Journal of Theology for Southern Africa*, 47, June 1984.

[6] A good historical account of the earlier developments is found in John de Gruchy, *The Church Struggle in South Africa* (Cape Town: David Philip; Grand Rapids: Eerdmans, 1979); of the Ottawa Declaration and the Belhar Confession in J. de Gruchy and C. Villa-Vicencio (eds.), *Apartheid Is a Heresy* (Cape Town: David Philip; Grand Rapids: Eerdmans, 1983); and of the *Kairos Document* and the Lusaka Declaration in C. Villa-Vicencio, *Trapped in Apartheid* (Cape Town: David Philip; New York: Orbis, 1989).

[7] *Religions of South Africa*, p. 148.

[8] *The Kairos Document: Challenge to the Church*, revised second edition (Johannesburg: Skotaville; Grand Rapids: Eerdmans, 1986), p. 33.

[9] F. Esack, 'A Muslim Perspective on the Kairos Document', *Newsletter of the World Conference on Religion and Peace, South African Chapter*, 3.1 (1986), p. 2.

[10] See C. Villa-Vicencio, *A Theology of Reconstruction* (Cambridge: Cambridge University Press, 1992).

[11] *Dialogue with the Other: The Inter-Religious Dialogue* (Grand Rapids: Eerdmans, 1991). p. 27.

[12] 'Traditional' understood in the sense argued for by David Chidester, *Religions of South Africa*, p. 1, 'not as something handed down, but as something taken up, as an open set of

cultural resources and strategies that can be mobilized in working out the meaning and power of a human world'.

[13] 'All three of the radically monotheistic religions have produced a projected Other to their prophetic faith in the God of the covenant: they have named this 'Other' the 'pagans'.

[14] See G. Setiloane, *Towards an African Theology* (Johannesburg: Skotaville, 1989).

[15] One of the best books on the subject of inter-religious dialogue is that of Paul Knitter, *No Other Name? A Critical Survey of Christian Attitudes Toward the World Religions* (Maryknoll, New York: Orbis Books, 1985).

[16] See J. and J. Comaroff, *Of Revelation and Revolution: Christianity, Colonialism and Consciousness in Southern Africa,* Vol. 1 (Chicago: University of Chicago Press, 1991).

[17] It has been convincingly argued by G. Marquard — in G. Hunsinger (ed.), *Karl Barth and Radical Politics* (Philadelphia: Westminster Press, 1976) — that the basis of this critique comes from Barth's acceptance of Feuerbach's and Marx's critique of religion.

[18] *Church Dogmatics* I:2 (Edinburgh: T. and T. Clark, 1956), pp. 295–307.

[19] Knitter, *No Other Name?*

[20] John Hick, *God and the Universe* (New York: St. Martin's Press, 1973), p. 131, as cited in Knitter, *No Other Name?*, p. 147.

[21] R. Pannikar, *The Unknown Christ of Hinduism* (Maryknoll, N.Y.: Orbis, 1981), p. 7, as cited in Knitter, *No Other Name?*, p. 156.

[22] *No Other Name?*, p. 171.

[23] *Dialogue With the Other*, p. 97.

[24] Ibid., p. 73.

[25] *No Other Name?*, pp. 208–11.

# Index

*Abba* (Father) 48, 49
Abelard, Peter 118–19, 220
Adam: and Eve 113, 160; before the fall 102; defeated by devil 117; his sin 95
adoptionism 57
African: chiefs 156: indigenous churches 155; religion 44, 224; theology 152–60, 224
All Africa Conference of Churches (AACC) 153, 158
Almighty, the (*pantokrator*) 49
Anabaptists 221
*anakephalaiosis, see* recapitulation
Anselm, archbishop of Canterbury 5, 117, 220
apartheid 86, 87, 164, 177, 201, 205, 222; and identity 104; and orthodoxy 132; as heresy 11; complicity in 169; heresy of 163; ideology 108, 156; legislation 170; theology 22, 24
Apocalyptic eschatology 147
Apollinarianism 58, 62
Apologists: and Stoic ideas 79; Christian 7–8
Apostles' Creed 48, 162
Aquinas, Thomas: and medieval theology 95; and natural theology 7; and Trinity 82; his *Summa Theologiae* 7, 9; reason and revelation 8
Arian heresy 57, 58, 62

Aristotle 187; and metaphysics 8; and Thomas Aquinas 7; his *Nichomachean Ethics* 121–2
Ascension 64–5, 66
Asian Christians 159
Athanasian Creed (*Quicumque*) 78
Athanasius, bishop of Alexandria 58, 78, 118
Augustine of Hippo 47, 152; and salvation 220; and self-love 110; his *Civitas Dei* 120; his psychological models 79, 80
AZAPO 180
baptism 120, 128, 134–7; Jesus' 84
*Baptism, Eucharist and Ministry* (WCC document) 136
Barmen Declaration 44, 164, 167, 222
Barth, Karl 5–6, 102–3, 110, 128, 162, 163, 176, 225
base Christian communities (BCCs) 192, 195
Basil of Caesarea 80
Belhar Confession of Faith 166, 167, 222
Bible: and ordinary people 16–17; and theology 15–25; as people's book 16; Hebrew 77; in African theology 158; in historical context 23; in literary context 23; in sociological context 23; in South African context 18–19; in symbolic context 23; in

thematic context 23; reading criti-
cally 21–23; reading in community
19; reading the 16–18; study process
18
Biko, Steve 156, 166, 179
Black Consciousness Movement
(South Africa) 155, 173, 174, 177
Black Messiah 175
Black Panthers 173
Black Power (USA) 173, 174, 177
Black theology 26, 73, 132, 146; future
of 180–2; sources 175–80
Bloch, Ernst 146
Body of Christ 127
Boesak, Allan 166, 174, 176, 177–8,
180
Boff, Clodovis 187, 193
Boff, Leonardo 73, 186, 187, 193
Bonaventure 220
Bonhoeffer, Dietrich 12, 51, 62, 163,
164, 166, 167, 169; his Cost of
Discipleship 12; relationship to God
33; secret discipline 129
Bosch, David 133–4
Breath of the Risen Lord (Greek
pneuma) 75
bride of Christ 127
Buddhists 223
Bultmann, Rudolf 62, 176; and de-
mythologisation 10; grace and law
145
Buthelezi, Bishop Manas 157, 176, 179
Cabral, Amilcar 180
Calvin, John 6, 121; penal substitution
theory 118; his Institutes of the
Christian Religion 6
Cartesianism 96, 97
celibacy 155
Chalcedon, Council of 56, 58, 62, 221
Chalcedonian definition 60, 61, 62
charismatics 221
Christian anthropology 176
Christian community 125–37
Christology 55, 176, 192; negative to
positive 61–2

church: and its mission 192; and reign
of God 129–31; dogmatics 6; images
of 125; of the Lord 126, 129; of the
poor 132; theology 217
Church Theology 166, 188
Circle for Concerned African Women
Theologians 200
Clement of Alexandria 152; and
divinity of Christ 58
colonialism 174
communal theology 36–7
community: African ubuntu-botho 156;
and the Bible 17, 18; diachronic 33,
35; divine–human 84, 85, 87; Greek
koinonia 127; of faith 189; of Father,
Son and Spirit 85; synchronic 33, 35;
the Christian 120
Cone, Dr James H. 173, 175, 176, 177;
and Black theology 26
Confessing Church 44, 164, 166;
German 222
confessing: Christ against apartheid
164–6; guilt 169; theology 11,
162–71
Confucians 223
contextual theology 44, 34–5, 180
conversion, or metanoia 216
Copernicus 96
correlation, method of 28, 37
cosmic Christ 94
Cottesloe Conference 222
Council: of Chalcedon 56; of Ephesus
61; of Nicea 59
covenant partner 102, 103–5
covenants 103
creation 90–100
Creator–Spirit 71
Cross 45; God and the 51
crucifixion 63–4, 66, 142, 169
culture 8; and Africanness 157; and
Black theology 179–80; patriarchal
44
Cyprian of Carthage 120, 152
dangerous memory 22–3, 33
Darwin, Charles 96

death, the last enemy 111; ultimate evil 149

deism 98

demythologisation 10

denominations 162

Descartes, René 96, 145

dialectical theology 144

dialogue 225—6

discipleship 65

Divinity of Christ 58; denial of 57—8

Docetic heresy 58—9

doctrine: of creation 91, 92—4, 102; of hell 87; of Jesus Christ, *see* Christology; of man 202—3; of predestination 118; of providence 93; of salvation 190; of sin 102, 110; of the Holy Spirit 69; of the Trinity 94

doing theology 2—4; a new way of 186—7; discipline of 11—12; in context 9—11; tradition in 7; with ordinary people 17—18; women 192—208

Dorr, Donal 185, 194

doubt and faith 28—9

dualism 94—7

Dutch Reformed Church (NGK) 165, 166

Dutch Reformed Mission Church (NG Sendingkerk) 166

Eastern Orthodox Church 56, 60, 221

Ebionite heresy 57

ecclesiology: a false 170; Protestant 130; task of 129

Eckhart, Meister 220

ecological crisis 90

ecology and understanding creation 97—100

economic Trinity 83, 84, 87

Ecumenical Association of Third World Theologians (EATWOT) 180, 200

ecumenism 48, 132

Enlightenment 6, 8, 144, 179, 187, 222

Ephesus, Council of 61

Esack, Moulana Faried 223

eschatology 139, 146; Apocalyptic 147; for today 147—49; modern facets of 144

ethical praxis 222

ethics, Christian 11, 56

eucharist 123, 128, 134—7, 221

Eusebius, bishop of Caesarea 58

evangelicals 221

evangelism 225, 226

evolution 147

exegetical suspicion 189

existential theologians 146

existentialism 145; and Martin Heidegger 8

faith 7, 23, 225; and doubt 28—9; and feminism 192—208; and knowing God 53; and liberation 27; and order 48; and praxis 26; and theology 26—38; in resurrection 149; justification by 9; rule of 162

faithful praxis (orthopraxis) 132

false church 131

false gospel 165

fascism 170

female wisdom (*sophia*) 72

feminist liberation theology 178

feminist spirituality 206

feminist theologians 72

feminist theology 26, 44, 49, 132, 146, 168, 181; diversity of 179—201; in South African context 201; issue of praxis in faith 26

Feuerbach, Ludwig 12

*filioque*: controversy 220; meaning 81, 83

Fiorenza, Elisabeth Schüssler 72, 200

First World War 144

foundational theology 36, 37

Frankfurt School of Critical Theory 26

Freud, Sigmund 12

Galilei, Galileo 96

General Conference of the Latin American Episcopacy (CELAM) 185

generation: the Spirit's 'spiration' 82; *see also* Son's procession, the

German Confessing Church 222
Gnosticism 94
'God of the gaps' theory 97
God the Father and early Christians 49–51
Goldstone Commission 206
Graeco–Roman culture 153
Greek: philosophers 4; philosophical thought 43; philosophy 61, 62
Gregory of Nazianzus 59, 69
Gregory of Nyssa 117
Gutiérrez, Gustavo 11, 122, 185, 188, 190, 191, 194; and liberation theology 26; his *Theology of Liberation* 11; his *We Drink from Our Own Wells* 194
Hebrew Bible 77
Heidegger, Martin 8
hell: doctrine of 87; eternal damnation 111
Hellenistic culture 7; philosophy 58, 58–9; world 10
heresy 56, 61, 221; Apollinarian 58, 62; Arian 57, 58, 62; Docetic 58–9; Ebionite 57; Monophysite 60, 62; Nestorian 60, 62
hermeneutical circle 189
hermeneutics 131; of suspicion 12; problem of 5; theology as 10
Hinduism 28, 197, 223
Hitler, Adolf 164, 222
Holocaust 168
Holy Roman Emperors 56
hope 147–8; and the church 214; is resistance 208
human image of God, broken 102–11; situation 113–14; solidarity (*ubuntu-botho*), see also community 156
humanity: defining our 202–3; of Christ, denial of 58–9; of Jesus Christ 57
idolatry 205
immanent Trinity 83
immortal soul 144
incarnation 63, 66; denied 55

Institute for Contextual Theology (ICT) 16–17, 155, 181, 212
inter-faith dialogue 44
inter-religious dialogue 225, 226–7
Interdenominational Theological Center (Atlanta) 177
Irenaeus, bishop of Lyons 79, 94–5, 117
Islam 28, 197
Jesus: and liberation 192; as Lord 162–3, 167, 171, 164, 168, 170; is Lord 169; of history 168; the Christ 55–66; the Jew 169
Jewish: background 57; law and Gentile Christians 9; Passover ceremony 136; Torah 145
Jewish–Christian relations 168
Jews 169, 223; and Messiah, Jesus as Lord 105; persecution of 164
John XXIII, pope 186
Judaeo–Christian tradition 106, 195
Judaism 10, 28, 192, 197; first-century 9
judgement, last 144
justification by faith 9, 116; Luther's use of 10
*kairos* 121, 165; issue of praxis in faith 26; meaning the crucial time 145; theology 212–18
*Kairos Document* 132, 166, 188, 213, 217, 222
kingdom of God 64
*koinonia*, see community
Küng, Hans 128, 130
language and feminist theology 204–5
Latin American liberation theology 28–9, 186, 194
liberation: and Black theology 177–8; as integral to salvation 190; Christology 192; theologians 11, 146; theology 26, 132, 166, 184–95, 215; struggle for 18
life-giving breath (Hebrew *ruach*) 74, 75
local theologies 27, 35–7

*logos*: expressed 79; immanent 79
*logos–anthropos* doctrine 59; formula 60
*logos–sarx* doctrine 59; formula of Apollinaris 60
Lordship, language use of 168
love: and creation 92; divine capacity to 81; God is 102; gratuitous 81; indebted 81
Lusaka Declaration 222
Luther, Martin 10, 47, 121; and creation 95–6, 99; penance 135
Lutheran theology 176
Lutheran World Federation 166
Maimela, Simon 181
Mariology: Christotypical 30; ecclesiotypical 30; new contextual 32
Martyr, Justin and divinity of Christ 58
martyrdom 75, 163
Marx, Karl 12
marxism 168, 189
marxists 221; and Jesus 55
Mary: and women of Mpophomeni 29–30; filled with Holy Spirit 73
'mask of God' and Luther 95
Mbiti, John 156, 179
Medellin Conference 185
*Message to the People of South Africa, The* (SACC) 165, 222
*metanoia, see* conversion
metaphysics 96; Aristotle's 8
method of correlation 8, 28, 37
Metz, Johann Baptist 146; and dangerous memories 33, 208
Middle Ages 6, 95, 121, 128; and methodology of theology 4; and theology as scientific study 5
Miguez Bonino, José 187, 191
ministry 134–7
Minjung theology 26
*missio Dei*, church participation in 133–4
missiological theology 36, 37
mission 135
missionary enterprise 155; theologies 153
Moffat, Robert 160

Moltmann, Jürgen 146; and creation 91–2; and ecological awareness 98; and political theology 26; unity of church 133
monism 94–7
Monophysite heresy 60, 61, 62
monotheism 57, 58
Moore, Dr Basil 173, 181
Mosala, Itumeleng 157, 176, 179, 180
Mother of God (*Theotokos*) 61
Muslims 223; and Jesus 55
National Committee of Negro Churchmen 173
National Peace Secretariat 206
nationalism 87
natural theology 44; and Thomas Aquinas 7
Naudé, Beyers 165
Nazism 44, 132, 163–4, 169, 170
neo-Nazism 170
neo-orthodox theology 164
Neoplatonic concept and image of God 107
Neoplatonism 8, 80
Nestorian heresy 60, 62
New Age sects and Jesus 55
Newton, Isaac 96
Newtonianism 97
NG Mission Church 166
Nicene Creed 59, 162, 221; and divinity of Christ 58
Nicene–Constantinopolitan Creed 48, 49
Nietzsche, Friedrich 12
Ntsikana, Xhosa prophet 154
Ntwasa, Sabelo 73, 173
nuclear disarmament 168
Nxele, Xhosa prophet 154
oppression 11, 16; and emancipatory theologies 27; and the Bible in SA 16
ordination of women 55
Origen 152; and divinity of Christ 58; and Trinity 79–80
Orthodox churches 48; tradition 221
orthodoxy 37–8, 56, 61, 170

orthopraxis 170; see also faithful praxis
Palestine 57
panentheism 99
Pannenberg, Wolfhart 9, 72, 146
pantheism 99
pantokrator 49
paradosis 7
parousia 65, 66
patriarchal culture 44
Paul VI, pope 185, 186
Pelagius 220
penal substitution theory 118
penance as sacrament 135
Pentecost 70-1, 72, 78, 84, 126
People of God 126
perichoresis 82, 85
Person of Jesus Christ 62, 66
Pietism 145, 221
Plato 187
Platonic concept and image of God
   107; thought 58
pluralism: political 219; theological and
   religious 219–27
pneuma, see Breath of the Risen Lord
pneumatology 72; see also doctrine of
   the Holy Spirit
political ethics 170
political theology, issue of praxis in
   faith 26
poor, option for 63
popular religion 26–30
positive Christology: content of 61–2;
   style of 62
poverty and oppression 11
praxis 3, 130, 131, 169, 187, 188, 189;
   and creation 97; in faith 26
praxis-oriented theologies 26, 192
prayer 99, 134; and knowing God
   52–3; and Trinity 86
preaching of the Word 135
predestination doctrine 118
procession 82
Programme to Combat Racism 165
prophetic theology 132, 216
prosopon, see Person of Jesus Christ

Protestant Church 56, 162, 167;
   ecclesiology 130; in Germany 164;
   Reformation 187, 220; Reformers
   131, 135
providence, doctrine of 71, 93
racism 170, 174, 205
Rahner, Karl 128, 225; and Thomism
   8; and Trinity 83
reason and Kant 220, 222; and Thomas
   Aquinas 7; God's capacity for 79
recapitulation (anakephalaiosis) 95
redemption 113–23; and nature 97
Reformation 135, 145, 162; and
   revelation 44
Reformed: theology 95, 118
reign of God, the church and the
   129–31
relationality 203
resurrection 44–6, 49, 50, 64, 66, 111,
   169; of the dead 142
revelation 225; in Jesus Christ 43–4;
   not yet complete 46–7; story-
   shaped 44–6
Richard of St Victor, his family model
   of Trinity 81
Road to Damascus: Kairos and Conversion
   212, 218
Roman Catholic Church 44, 56, 131,
   184; and Martin Luther 10; theology
   8; 160
Romanticism 144
Ruether, Rosemary Radford 200, 203,
   205; and feminist theology 26; and
   the church and Mary 30
rule: of faith 162; over the world,
   God's 64–5
sabbath 88, 92
sacraments 134, 135
salvation 65, 66; and creation 94; and
   Trinity 85; Christian view of 56; its
   implications 56
Schleiermacher, Friedrich 3–4; and
   liberal theology 10
Schweitzer, Albert 62
science, theology as 4–9

Second Coming 65, 136
Second Vatican Council 184, 185
Second World War 164, 167
See—Judge—Act process 190
Segundo, Juan Luis 11, 189
self-disclosure of God 42–53; according to Christians 42–4; content of 47–9; God, experience of 51–3
Septuagint 126
Setiloane, Gabriel 153, 156, 160
sexism 205
sexual violence, women and 205
Sharpeville massacre 165
sin: consequence of 110; doctrine of 102, 110; the broken image 109–11
situational theology 174
slave trade 174
social transformation 24
Soelle, Dorothee 178
*sola Scriptura* 221
Son's procession, the 82
*sophia* (Wisdom of God); *see also* female wisdom 72
soteriology, a false 170; *see* salvation
soul 80; immortal 144
South African Council of Churches 165
Spirit: as Life-giver 71; as Liberator 73–4; as Life-sustainer 71; as Mother 72; forgetting the 69; of Life 68–76; life breath of 74–5
spirituality: for liberation 193–4; theology as 4–9
State Theology 214, 217
*status confessionis* 164, 165, 171, 222
Stoic ideas 79
Student Non-Violent Co-ordinating Committee 173
syncretism 154
systematic theology 42; and Martin Heidegger 8; and Wolfhart Pannenberg 9
Tertullian 8, 152; and divinity of Christ 58; and Trinity 78, 79
theologians, feminist 72

theological and religious pluralism 219–27
theological anthropology, *see* doctrine of man 202–3
theologies: contextual 44; emancipatory 26–7; feminist 44, 49; incipient 34–5; local 27; praxis-oriented 26
theology: and faith 26–38; as hermeneutics 10; as science 6; as spirituality 8; Black 26, 73, 132, 146; Catholic 95, 128; communal 36–7; contextual 34–5, 213–15; dialectical 144; feminism 132; feminist 26, 146; foundational 36, 37; from below 213; Kairos 26; liberal 26; liberation 132; local 35–7; meaning of the word 4; medieval 95; Minjung 26; missiological 36, 37; natural 44; nature, necessity and task of 2–12; of creation 90, 93; of culture and history (Tillich) 221; political 26; practical 4; prophetic 132; Reformed 95, 118; systematic 8, 42; traditional 44; Trinitarian 79, 83; Western European 9; without the Bible 16
Theophilus of Antioch 78
*Theotokos*, *see* Mother of God
third-world church 184
Thomism 8
Tillich, Paul 26, 28, 37; and method of correlation 8
Torah, Jewish 145
tradition 7; and religion 32–8
traditional African religions 44
traditional theology 44
transformation, personal and social 24
trinitarian framework 48; models 85; theology 79, 83; classic Western 79
Trinity 58, 220; and creation 92; as divine–human reality 83–8; doctrine of 77–88
Tutu, Desmond 157, 176
*ubuntu-botho*, meaning human solidarity 156; *see also* community

United Nations 87, 206
universalism 154
University Christian Movement
  (UCM) 173
Vatican II 30, 186, 191
violence 217
Virgin Mary 58
Wisdom of God, Hebrew understanding of 58
womanist theologians 159—60, 200
womanist theology 181
women: and sexual violence 205;
  doing theology 192—208

women, ordination of 55
Word of God 5, 58, 116, 164, 176
workers and the Bible 16—17
World Alliance of Reformed Churches
  (WARC) 166
World Council of Churches 48, 165;
  its document *Baptism, Eucharist and
  Ministry* 135
worship in knowledge of God 52
Xhosa people 156; prophets 154
YHWH (Yahweh) 116, 126, 140, 141
Zwinglians 221